The Economics of the Euro Area

The Economics of the Euro Area

Macroeconomic Policy and Institutions

Edited by

Peter A.G. van Bergeijk
Ron J. Berndsen
W. Jos Jansen

Monetary and Economic Policy Department,
De Nederlandsche Bank, Amsterdam

Edward Elgar
Cheltenham, UK • Northampton, MA, USA

332.494
E192

Published by
Edward Elgar Publishing Limited
Glensanda House
Montpellier Parade
Cheltenham
Glos GL50 1UA
UK

Edward Elgar Publishing, Inc.
136 West Street
Suite 202
Northampton
Massachusetts 01060
USA

A catalogue record for this book
is available from the British Library

Library of Congress Cataloguing in Publication Data

The economics of the euro area : macroeconomic policy and institutions / edited by Peter A.G. van Bergeijk, Ron J. Berndsen, W. Jos Jansen.
   Includes bibliographical references and index.
   1. Economic and Monetary Union. 2. Monetary unions—Europe. 3. Europe—Economic integration. 4. Monetary policy—Europe. I. Bergeijk, Peter A.G. van, 1959– II. Berndsen, Ron J. III. Jansen, W.J.

HG3942.E254 2000
332.4'94—dc21

99–049366

ISBN 1 84064 166 5

Printed and bound in Great Britain by Bookcraft (Bath) Ltd.

Contents

Figures, Tables and Boxes

Figures

Tables

Boxes

Contributors

Ronald Albers
Carel van den Berg
Peter van Bergeijk
Jan Marc Berk
Ron Berndsen
Martin Bijsterbosch
Hans Brits
Paul Cavelaars
Reinder van Dijk
Gerrit van den Dool
Irene de Greef
Willem Heeringa
David Hofman
Aerdt Houben
Henk Huisman
Jos Jansen
Jan Kakes
Jacob Meesters
Niek Nahuis
Cindy van Oorschot
Renske Oort
Cees Ullersma
Focco Vijselaar
Coen Voormeulen
Marc de Vor
Broos van der Werff
Carlo Winder

Monetary and Economic Policy Department
De Nederlandsche Bank, Amsterdam

Preface

The start of Economic and Monetary Union (EMU) may be considered the most remarkable step in the post-war monetary history of Europe. On 1 January 1999, 11 currencies were irrevocably linked and a new currency, the euro, was born. The Governing Council of the European Central Bank (ECB) assumed sole responsibility for monetary policy in the euro area. This voluntary transfer of monetary sovereignty of 11 nations to a supranational body is unprecedented in history.

At the same time, there is also continuity, of course. Although at the moment of writing, the ECB is only 16 months old, it is well teamed up with 11 national central banks which exhibit a long track record: on average they were established 130 years ago. Furthermore, the introduction of the euro itself did not change the parities of the currencies of the participating countries. It fixed indefinitely the parities among the strong ERM currencies that have prevailed since 1987.

EMU implies the creation of a new economic area. The euro area is neither a simple aggregate of the constituent countries nor an average of only the largest countries. It needs to be analysed as an independent entity. In addition, EMU has had its implications for the economic analysis and policy preparation of De Nederlandsche Bank. The switch in the frame of reference was quite dramatic: from a small open economy with a fixed exchange rate regime to a large relatively closed economy with a flexible exchange rate regime. This book takes stock of the work undertaken at the Monetary and Economic Policy Department of De Nederlandsche Bank aimed at coping with that regime change. As such, it is the first comprehensive analysis of the new euro area economy, its institutions and its macroeconomic policies. No doubt in the coming years the literature on euro area economics will grow. I hope that this book may serve as a useful stepping stone towards a better understanding of the euro area economy.

Nout Wellink
President of De Nederlandsche Bank

F33 F36 F42

1. At the Birth of the Euro Area

Peter van Bergeijk, Ron Berndsen and Jos Jansen

This book is about the emergence of a truly European economy, with a focus on monetary integration. This increasingly economically integrated area has long shared a number of institutions, such as a common trade policy and competition policy, culminating in the completion of the internal market – at least from an institutional point of view – in 1992. Since then the set of shared institutions has continued to grow. A major extension was the establishment of the European Monetary Institute (EMI) marking the start of the Second Stage of Economic and Monetary Union (EMU) in 1994. A second major step was a number of agreements on fiscal policy leading to the Pact for Stability and Growth in 1997. Finally, in 1998 the common monetary framework was created with the establishment of the European Central Bank (ECB), the successor to the EMI, followed by the introduction of the euro on 1 January 1999 in Austria, Belgium, Finland, France, Germany, Ireland, Italy, Luxembourg, the Netherlands, Portugal and Spain.[1]

Throughout the book, the analysis focuses on euro area aggregates, although references to individual European countries are given where appropriate. After all, the European nation states have been the unit of observation for a very long time. Our perspective is sharpened by the fact that we have all been involved in applied policy analysis regarding the introduction of the euro and the further shaping and strengthening of the institutions of the Economic and Monetary Union. Reflecting our fields of expertise, the next ten chapters concentrate on macroeconomic policies, that is monetary policy, fiscal policy and exchange rate policy, and the economic analysis underlying the conduct of these policies.

The rest of this introductory chapter is organized as follows. In Section 1 we present some key features of the new economic area. We then discuss two issues that will be decisive in shaping the future environment in which macroeconomic policy is formulated and implemented. These are the continuing process of European integration (Section 2) and structural reforms in product and labour markets in the euro area (Section 3). The two issues are linked in several ways. First, structural reforms are necessary to ensure that EMU will work smoothly. Second, there is an ongoing debate on the desirability of structural policies being centralized, harmonized or coordinated at the EU level. Section 4 contains brief introductions to the ten chapters that make up the body of the book.

1. INTRODUCING THE EURO AREA

We refer to the above group of 11 countries as the 'euro area' rather than the 'euro zone'. Defying the *Académie française*, which prefers 'zone' to 'area',[2] we note that in economic terms the 'euro zone' would refer to the larger group of countries where the euro plays a major role in the monetary framework. Some non-EU countries may use the euro as an anchor currency or a reserve currency. In some cases the money circulation may even consist of euros, for example where the French franc or Portuguese escudo performed this role in former colonies. As our investigation of the process of economic integration focuses on the 11 European countries that introduced the euro, the choice of 'euro area' is both logical and consistent with the terminology of the economics profession.[3] For reasons of convenience we will also refer to this group of countries as the euro area when we deal with developments before 1999, although it would perhaps have been more appropriate to use the label 'pre-euro area' in this case.

Key characteristics of the euro area

As a first introduction to this new economic area we present in Table 1.1 some broad characteristics of the euro area. To put them into perspective we also give the corresponding numbers for the US economy. The table shows that the euro area is smaller in size but more densely populated than the US. Despite its smaller population, the US has a larger GDP. GDP per capita is 37 per cent higher in the US than in the euro area. Both economies are services-based, with services accounting for 72 and 67 per cent of total output in the US and the euro area respectively. The bigger share of the services sector in the US may reflect higher demand for services on account of its higher per capita income.

As to openness, the euro area is more open to trade in goods and services. Merchandise imports and exports average 11.4 per cent of GDP for the euro area against 9.4 per cent for the US. The US has larger net inflows of foreign direct investment, which can partly be explained by the fact that the US runs a current account deficit, while the euro area has a current account surplus.

Table 1.1 Key features of the euro area, 1998

	Euro area	US
Surface area (1000 km^2)	2400	9400
Population (million)	290	270
GDP (bn. euro)	5800	7300
Production structure (% GDP)		
agriculture	2	2
industry	31	26
services	67	72
Openness (% GDP)		
foreign trade	11.4	9.4
foreign direct investment	0.9	2.5
current account balance	1.4	-2.7
Financial landscape (bn. euro)		
domestic bank credit	7100	5900
domestic debt securities	5000	11400
stock market capitalization	3200	9700
Government (% GDP)		
budget balance	-2.3	1.4
gross debt	73.8	59.3
size (level of expenditure)	48.7	30.9
Labour market		
unemployment (% labour force)	11.0	4.5
labour force participation (%)	65.1	77.8

Sources: OECD, Eurostat, ECB.

Measured in terms of foreign direct investment flows, the euro area invested in the period 1995–97 more in the US than vice versa.

From a financial perspective, the euro area economy relies more on credit financing by the banking sector and less on marketable debt securities. Stock market capitalization in the US is triple in size relative to the euro area, while the outstanding amount of domestic debt securities is more than twice as large.

The state of government finances seems more favourable in the US than in the euro area. The US recorded a fiscal surplus in 1998 compared to a fiscal deficit in the euro area, and gross debt is lower as well. In addition, the US government is much smaller in size.

The main difference between the euro area and the US lies in the labour market. The euro area economy as a whole generates far too few jobs, as indicated by the high unemployment rate and the low labour force participation rate. Unemployment in the euro area is more than twice as large as in the US, while its participation rate is 11 percentage points lower. The creation of jobs clearly is the most urgent policy challenge in Europe.

2. EUROPEAN INTEGRATION: TOO MUCH OR TOO LITTLE?

The introduction of the euro on 1 January 1999 marks an obvious moment in time that many observers may want to use as a starting point for the political-economic history of the European monetary union. Indeed, the changeover weekend is both easily identified and correct *de jure*. However, the euro area was *de facto* created in the weekend of 2–3 May 1998, when the decision was made which countries were to participate in the Third Stage of EMU. Moreover, the creation of the single European market for goods, services, labour and capital, which took place in several stages over a span of decades, can be seen as an ancestor of EMU. The abolition of capital controls in particular made the move to monetary union practically unavoidable (Wyplosz, 1997). This is a direct implication of the 'eternal triangle' which is discussed in Chapter 11 (see Figure 11.1). This triangle illustrates that only two of the following three structural features are mutually compatible: full capital mobility, fixed exchange rates and independence of monetary policy.

Clearly, whereas the birthday of the euro area can be identified exactly, understanding the seeds and its conception requires a much longer time perspective. Many economic and political developments have promoted stronger integration and greater interdependence of the European economies. These are processes worth studying, as they are relevant to the understanding of the prevailing arrangements in Europe. Hence our investigation into the foundations of the euro area must begin well before the introduction of the euro.

Taking a longer view, the birth of the euro area is a process that started with the conception of European economic integration in the early 1950s. Although it started as a free trade area, the process of integration has always had an important political component. The preamble to the Treaty of Rome (1957) stated the ambition 'to lay the foundations of an ever closer union among the peoples of Europe . . . to preserve and strengthen peace and liberty'. European integration has proceeded in two modes: a deep supranational mode and a shallow intergovernmental mode (CEPR, 1995). Under the supranational mode the European countries have created common institutions and policies, while under the intergovernmental mode they have coordinated policies, which remained largely determined by national policy makers and implemented by national institutions. The logic behind supranationalism is the wish to create a political union, while the logic behind intergovernmentalism is the wish to preserve the nation state as a politically independent entity. Deeper integration is characterized by decisions based on (qualified) majority rule rather than unanimity and by reliance on common institutions to implement Community laws and policies.

The trade-off between scope and depth of integration has been at the heart of the European integration process in the past decades. Proponents of deep integration assumed that deep integration in one specific policy area, for example free trade in goods, would over time demonstrate the desirability of deeper integration in other policy areas. The idea was that economic union would ultimately lead to political union, as supranational institutions are needed to support economic integration. Due to this opportunistic approach the pace of the integration process has been uneven. Periods of rapid advancement were followed by periods of stagnation. Economic interdependence among EU member states has deepened as measured by the greater importance of intra-European trade. The share of intra-EU trade as a percentage of total foreign trade rose from 40 per cent in the early 1960s to 63 per cent in the early 1990s (European Commission, 1996). The EU has also created a number of truly European institutions, like the European Commission, the Council of Ministers, the European Parliament, the European Court of Justice and the European Central Bank.

How far has integration gone?

Table 1.2 presents a list of policy responsibilities that have been transferred to central EU institutions. It also indicates the extent of EU involvement for each policy area (extensive, shared with national governments and limited). The table shows that European institutions have acquired responsibilities in a host of policy areas, including some that have little to do with fostering intra-EU trade or economic integration. Of course, in many of these policy areas, such as education, welfare and cultural issues, the nation states have a (much) greater say than the EU. On other issues, such as monetary policy and international trade policy, the supranational level has exclusive competence. Table 1.2 shows that the EU has become much more than an area of free trade and loose policy coordination, although it still falls short of a political federation by a large margin. Given the extent and scope of the transfers of policy prerogatives and the *ad hoc* way the integration process has advanced,

Table 1.2 Policy responsibilities of the EU and their extent

	Extensive	Shared	Limited
Economic and social areas			
Competition		x	
Cultural policy			x
Regional policy		x	
Employment and social policy		x	
Enterprise policy		x	
Equal opportunities		x	
Industrial policy		x	
Public health			x
Solidarity/welfare			x
Consumer policy		x	
Monetary policy	x		
Education, training and youth			x
Environment		x	
Internal market	x		
Research and technology		x	
Trans-European networks/mobility			x
Sectoral policies			
Agriculture	x		
Fisheries	x		
Transportation		x	
Information and telecommunications		x	
Audivisual policy			x
Energy		x	
External policies			
Common foreign and security policy			x
Development policy		x	
Humanitarian aid		x	
Common trade policy	x		
Justice and home affairs			
Asylum, external borders, immigration		x	
Judicial and police cooperation		x	
Drugs		x	

Source: Alesina and Wacziarg (1999).

the question naturally arises about the extent to which these transfers are optimal. Which policy decisions should be centralized, and which should be left to the member states or even regions? To tackle that question the Treaty of Maastricht (1992) introduced the principle of subsidiarity according to which 'the Community shall take action, . . . only if and in so far as the objectives of the proposed action cannot be sufficiently achieved by the Member States' (Article 3b).[4] CEPR (1993) provides a wide-ranging discussion of the subsidiarity principle and how it might be applied (see also Sinn, 1993).

A framework for applying subsidiarity

Until now the principle of subsidiarity has remained vague and largely devoid of operational content. We use the analytical framework in Alesina and Wacziarg (1999) to discuss the distribution of policy responsibilities between different levels of government. Their framework consists of two elements. First, they point out that the relationship between economic integration and political integration is rather subtle. On the one hand, economic integration introduces the need for supranational institutions (for example, international courts and institutions for international arbitrage). On the other hand, large political units are not needed to enjoy the benefits of large markets in a world of free trade. Every country has access to the same large world market.

The costs of being a large country hinge on the heterogeneity of preferences concerning public goods within the population. When one of the benefits of size is eroded by free trade, the optimal size of a country falls as the provision of public goods can be better tailored to the needs of a smaller, more homogeneous population. Alesina, Spolaore and Wacziarg (1998) show that the expansion of world trade in the post-war period has been accompanied by political disintegration, as reflected in a surge in the number of countries from 74 in 1946 to 192 in 1995. At first glance the European integration process seems to buck this global trend, but here too we observe growing economic integration along with a rise of regionalist movements in several EU countries, like Spain (Catalonia, Basque country), the UK (Scotland), Belgium (Flanders, Wallonia) and Italy (Northern Italy). Moreover, it is unlikely that the EU will ever develop into a fully fledged federal state.

The framework's second element draws on the literature on fiscal federalism, which investigates what level of government should produce which public good. The optimal distribution of policy tasks across the levels of government is driven by the trade-off between the wish to keep policy tailored to the voters' preferences at home and the need to correct externalities which may spill over beyond the boundaries of the political unit. On the one hand, centralization of a policy task increases the likelihood that the final outcome will differ from local preferences. On the other hand, if the externality is ignored certain public goods will be underprovisioned. In the ideal situation, a policy task should be allocated to the level of government that corresponds to the frontier of the externality so that the externality can fully be internalized.

Alesina and Wacziarg (1999) thus end up with the following sensible rule for justifiable centralization. The benefits of internalizing Europe-wide externalities should exceed the costs of imposing a single policy upon heterogeneous populations. In the European context, policies should be delegated to the Community level in case of geographically wide-ranging externalities and free rider problems. Responsibility for policies that involve large cross-country differences in preferences and interests should remain at the national level, or even be transferred to the regional level in order to reap additional benefits of free trade. Based on these criteria, many policy areas on the list in Table 1.2 should be kept national (or regional) responsibilities, because they involve both a high degree of cross-country heterogeneity and no significant Europe-wide externalities. These policy fields include cultural policy, education, social policy, public health, agriculture and development policy. For other policies the case for centralization is much stronger, especially for policies aimed at fostering deep economic integration within Europe, and policies designed to guarantee the adequate functioning of free markets. Examples are common standards, antitrust policy, state aid, and the regulation of certain natural monopolies. Here Europe needs more centralization. All in all, there is much to be said for Alesina and Wacziarg's (1999, p. 3) main conclusion that 'Europe is going too far on many issues that would be better dealt with in a decentralized fashion, while it is not going far enough on policies that guarantee the free operation of markets both across and within the countries of the Union'.

3. THE POLICY AGENDA FOR EUROPE

The future environment in which macroeconomic policy makers, among them the ECB, will operate and the future performance of the euro area economy will to an important degree be determined by the structural policies followed by euro area governments. In this section we argue why structural policies and wage formation processes should be high on the agenda of European policy makers. Essentially two reasons call for the implementation of structural reform measures related to the fields of privatization, deregulation, competition policy and labour market institutions. The first is the lack of economic dynamism in the euro area as reflected in comparatively low growth rates of employment, production and productivity, and a comparatively low level of innovation. The second reason is the need to improve the ability of the euro area economy to adjust to shocks. This has gained significance with the move to monetary union. Adjustment processes in product and labour markets in Europe generally suffer from strong hysteresis.

The euro area's lack of economic dynamism

The lagging performance of the euro area economy is exemplified by its high and persistent unemployment, which is undoubtedly Europe's most pressing economic problem. There is broad agreement that the observed high unemployment is largely of a structural nature.[5] The consensus view considers the current severe unemployment problem to be the result of the interaction of labour market rigidities and a series of adverse shocks since the early 1970s. This implies that the bulk of the unemployment can only be eliminated by adopting structural reform measures related to privatization, deregulation, competition policy and institutional arrangements in the labour market. The IMF (1999) provides an excellent discussion of the causes of and possible solutions to the euro area's persistent unemployment problem.

The proper functioning of European labour markets is hampered by structural rigidities such as job protection legislation, working time regulations and minimum wages. Labour mobility is low, geographically as well as occupationally. In fact, the lack of labour mobility is not a national but a regional phenomenon. The degree of labour mobility between states in the US exceeds the degree of labour mobility within the borders of individual euro area countries, let alone that among euro area countries (Obstfeld and Peri, 1998). Under such conditions, the wage formation process will in general act poorly as an equilibrating mechanism. The studies collected in Van Bergeijk and Haffner (1996) show that the price mechanism in other markets is also characterized by a lack of flexibility, mainly because of excessive regulation, lack of price transparency and lax competition policy. Figure 1.1 compares a sample of industrialized economies with respect to product market inertia (measured as the degree of hysteresis on product markets[6]) and wage rigidity (measured as the elasticity of unemployment with respect to the wage level[7]). Typically, the European economies are in the upper-right hand quadrant of Figure 1.1, whereas the US and Canada are in the lower-left quadrant, signalling substantial room for improvement on both counts for Europe. As to the functioning of the market mechanism, the euro area thus suffers from a double deficit with respect to product market and labour market flexibility.

The Economics of the Euro Area

Figure 1.1   Wage and price rigidity in nine OECD countries

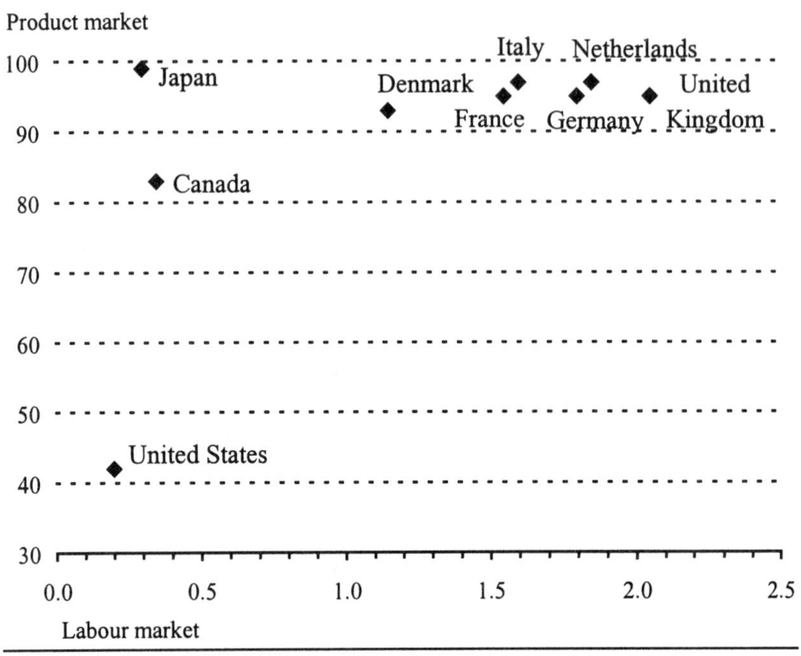

Product market

Sources: Van Bergeijk, Haffner and Waasdorp (1993) and OECD (1989).

This double deficit carries a high cost. The high level of structural unemployment represents a major loss of output. A rough estimate by the IMF (1999, p. 89) indicates that reducing structural unemployment from its current level of 11 per cent to 5 per cent would increase the level of GDP by 4 per cent. The papers in Van Bergeijk, Van Sinderen and Vollaard (1999) review a large number of econometric studies that show that substantial output gains are to be expected if the European economies embark on the road of structural reform. Typically these studies find a potential increase in the annual growth rate of real GDP of about 1 per cent in the medium term. Considerable gains in employment growth are also possible, provided that the synergy between product market reform and labour market reform is reaped. Endogenizing knowledge in macroeconomic models for the Netherlands, Den Butter and Folmer (1997) and Van Bergeijk *et al.* (1997) uncover related gains in terms of technological progress due to structural reforms of product and labour markets. As to the issue of wage moderation the findings are mixed, with questions being raised on the applicability of this policy instrument in large economies (Stokman, 1999).

EMU and the need for flexible markets

Under EMU, the monetary policy stance will be the same for all participating countries. Variations in interest rates or depreciations will no longer be available as natural shock absorbers at the national level. Many economists have pointed out that the euro area is not an optimum currency area, hence imposing a common monetary policy may imply a substantial cost in terms of macroeconomic stabilization (Feldstein, 1997; Obstfeld, 1998). This observation has particular relevance to the euro area, since it lacks a system of transnational fiscal transfers which is typically in place in political unions. At this moment, European countries are simply not prepared to pool resources for macroeconomic insurance purposes. Moreover, De Grauwe (1996a), among others, argues that the stabilizing properties of fiscal policy on the national level are also impaired due to the restrictions imposed by the Stability and Growth Pact. In the present circumstances, adjustment to asymmetric shocks may therefore involve a larger variability of real variables, such as employment and production. Not only may adjustment costs be larger, adjustment processes may also take longer as a consequence of the double deficit on product and labour market flexibility. For example, the average level of cyclical unemployment may rise, and hysteresis in labour markets may even cause an increase in long-term unemployment rates.

Proponents of monetary union argue that it is only natural that the euro area is not an optimal currency area yet. In their view, the only way to become an optimum currency area is to become a currency area first, and then to go from there. The economies and institutions will adapt to the new regime.[8] Ultimately, the criteria for an optimum currency area are endogenous, which is also suggested by the findings of Frankel and Rose (1998). But this endogeneity does not imply a free ride: getting there will require conscious efforts on the part of policy makers. They are responsible for a balanced and sustainable policy mix at the national level. For the smooth operation of EMU it is essential that the euro area economies get better adjustment mechanisms to handle external demand shocks and supply shocks. Failing mechanisms like cross-border labour mobility and transnational fiscal transfers, the only alternative left is to enhance the flexibility of product and labour markets by reducing structural rigidities. In the case of Europe, the road to an optimum currency area appears to go via structural reforms. European policy makers should consider this an asset rather than a liability in economic policy making. The fresh impetus EMU may give to long-needed structural reforms may turn out to be its chief dividend.

Policy coordination versus policy competition

An important issue is how to achieve as efficiently as possible a better structural environment for the euro area economies. In essence, there are two models for the implementation of structural reform measures (Oudshoorn, 1999). The first is policy coordination, which aims at the orchestrated simultaneous implementation of a common set of structural policies in all euro area countries. The second model is policy competition, whereby the introduction of structural reforms in individual countries is driven by their national policy agendas.

Applying the Alesina and Wacziarg framework for optimal devolution of policy prerogatives we argue that it depends on the type of policy whether centralized or decentralized decision making is desirable. Policy coordination is obviously called for in case of the unfinished agenda of the single market. Policies that fall under this heading are the harmonization of standards and regulations that can be strategically used as informal barriers to trade, antitrust policy, the regulation of certain natural monopolies and the rules governing state subsidies. With respect to other structural reforms, and especially labour market reforms, subsidiarity in economic policy making should be taken seriously, because countries differ in their preferences and interests on many issues. Countries should thus be able to decide freely on the sequence, timing, pace and intensity of their structural reform measures.

Heterogeneity of preferences is not the only reason why decentralized decision making in general seems to be more appropriate, however. In many cases there is uncertainty as to what policies will work best. Decentralized structural policy making will stimulate local policy 'experiments', because reform measures can be implemented relatively quickly and experimentation is less costly. Policy experiments that turn out to be a fiasco will *ceteris paribus* involve lower costs as (i) they are implemented on a smaller scale and (ii) other countries may in the meantime have developed promising alternatives, which could be copied and adapted to local circumstances. Decentralized policy making will over time generate a set of best practices, enabling euro area policy makers to learn from each other and allowing them to review and change policy stances more quickly and efficiently. By exploiting the scope for learning, decentralized policy making may in a sense become a comparative advantage for European policy makers.

The advantages of policy competition are the disadvantages of centralization. As policy coordination requires consensus and compromise it may ultimately result in less ambitious and less coherent policies

(Oudshoorn, 1999). Since the policy agenda is the outcome of negotiations, any pressure group that is strong enough to develop an influential platform in one country may block or slow down progress in the euro area as a whole. Moreover, a process that aims at consensus among 11 countries that have substantial differences in preferences on a host of issues will not only be very time consuming but may also increase the scope for conflict. Pushing too hard for common policies on such issues may lead to polarization within Europe, which in turn may undermine cooperation in those areas where centralized decision making is efficient, such as policies that foster 'deep' integration of the euro area economies. Indeed, people across Europe seem to become increasingly critical of the European integration process. This could be viewed as resistance, on the part of heterogeneous constituencies, to attempts to impose excessively uniform policies in an increasing number of areas (Alesina and Wacziarg, 1999).

4. READING GUIDE TO THE BOOK

The structure of the book is presented in Figure 1.2. Depending on the background and the field of interest of the reader, four different routes of reading through the book are envisaged. The historian should read at least Chapters 2, 3 and 8, to know how EMU came about. The pure economist should read at least Chapters 4 through 7 to know how the economy of the euro area works. The policy maker should read at least Chapters 8 through 11 in order to assess where the euro area is heading. Finally, there is the good old-fashioned way of reading the book from cover to cover to get the intended full picture.

In Part One of the book ('The Road to EMU') the historical perspective is dominant. In Chapter 2 Paul Cavelaars and Gerrit van den Dool provide an in-depth discussion of post-war European monetary cooperation in order to sketch the historical background of the Economic and Monetary Union that has just been created. It will become apparent that the European integration process has had its ups and downs. The authors conclude by listing some of the challenges awaiting the European Union in the next century.

In the next chapter entitled 'Qualifying for Stage Three of EMU', Ron Berndsen, Willem Heeringa and Cees Ullersma take a closer look at the political decisions reached in the first weekend of May 1998 when the 11 countries constituting the first wave of entrants were selected. EU countries had to meet the so-called convergence criteria in order to be admitted to the Third Stage. As a check on the robustness of the outcome of the selection procedure the authors also investigate whether the same 11 countries would have joined EMU had the decision been made a year later (in May 1999

Figure 1.2 Reading guide

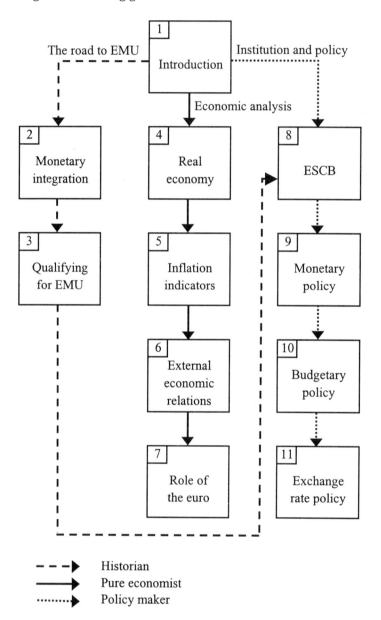

instead of May 1998). Finally, they look ahead and discuss how candidates for EMU membership should be judged in the future.

Part Two of the book ('Analysis of the Euro Area') looks at the euro area from a purely macroeconomic point of view. In Chapter 4 Ronald Albers, Martin Bijsterbosch and Focco Vijselaar examine the degree of real (as opposed to nominal) convergence among the countries of the euro area. They show that inflation rates have to a large extent converged to a low level and that business cycle fluctuations display a substantial degree of synchronicity. By contrast, the euro area labour market is still fragmented witness the large differences in labour market performance within Europe.

In Chapter 5 Niek Nahuis and Carlo Winder set out on the search for the European central bankers' 'holy grail': indicators for future inflation in the euro area. Reflecting their belief that there is no single best all-purpose model or methodology, they use both VAR methodologies and a NAIRU-like concept of capacity utilization to tackle this issue. They find that credit growth is a leading indicator of longer-term inflationary prospects. Nominal effective exchange rate changes are useful for medium-term purposes, while producer price changes are appropriate as a short-term indicator of future inflation. Another finding is that the deviation of capacity utilization from the NAIRCU – that is the level of capacity utilization consistent with a stable inflation rate – appears to be a useful indicator of inflationary pressures originating from the demand side of the economy.

The next two chapters provide an outward look. In Chapter 6 Irene de Greef, David Hofman and Niek Nahuis explore the euro area's external economic relations. They first assess the degree of openness to trade in goods and services and to foreign direct investment. Next they go into the short-run and long-run determinants of the euro area's current account. They conclude their contribution by estimating empirical models of the current account for the euro area, the US and Japan. Government finances and demographic factors appear to be important long-run determinants of the current account. Current accounts adjust gradually to changes in desired foreign assets holdings. The authors also find evidence of J-curve effects.

Chapter 7, written by Henk Huisman, Jacob Meesters and Renske Oort, investigates the process of deepening of the euro area's financial markets and its implications for the international role of the euro. They argue that although the longer-term perspective for the euro seems rather bright, history teaches that becoming a top currency will not happen overnight, but will take many years even in the best of circumstances.

Part Three ('Policy and Institutions') consists of an in-depth discussion of the institutions and macroeconomic policies of the euro area. In Chapter 8 Carel van den Berg, Reinder van Dijk and Broos van der Werff focus on the organizational structure and internal procedures of the European System of

Central Banks (ESCB). An understanding of these arrangements is a prerequisite for appreciating some of the finer points the way in which policies of the euro area are designed and implemented. Furthermore, to put things in perspective, they compare the ESCB with the US Federal Reserve System from an institutional point of view. Lastly, they briefly touch upon possible future developments of the ESCB.

Chapter 9 is devoted to the Eurosystem's single monetary policy strategy. Jan Marc Berk, Aerdt Houben and Jan Kakes extensively explain this strategy, which consists of three elements: (i) a precise definition of price stability as primary objective, (ii) a reference value for broad money growth, which serves as a privileged indicator, and (iii) a broad array of other indicators of future inflation. They compare this strategy to past and present strategies of other central banks. In addition, they address the issue – hotly debated time and again – whether there is room for other objectives besides price stability in the Eurosystem's monetary policy strategy.

The topic of Chapter 10, written by Hans Brits and Marc de Vor, is fiscal policy and the central role of the 'contract' between the euro area governments on this matter, called the Stability and Growth Pact. They illuminate the economic rationale behind the Pact and evaluate its first-time implementation in 1999. Moreover, the authors argue that a thorough interpretation of the key requirement of the Pact goes beyond the current interpretation by the European Commission.

In the final chapter, Cindy van Oorschot, Focco Vijselaar and Coen Voormeulen analyse exchange rate policy issues for the euro area, distinguishing three geographical levels. In this chapter the distinction between euro area and euro zone is particularly relevant. First, they look into the desirability and feasibility of target zones *vis-à-vis* the other major currencies of the world, the dollar and the yen. Second, the relation between the euro and currencies of neighbouring regions like Central and Eastern Europe and North Africa is explored. Third, they describe the features of the successor to the European exchange rate mechanism (ERM). Although it is seemingly aptly termed ERM-II, its character and purpose are quite different from that of the original ERM.

Because its main subject is so young, this book is to a large extent a stocktaking exercise. It describes the birth and historical background of the euro area and extensively analyses this new economic entity and its policies from different angles. Of course, the euro area will change because European economic integration is an ongoing process. Monitoring this process in the coming years will undoubtedly yield a promising and challenging research agenda. Our hope is that this book may serve anyone who wants to contribute to our knowledge of the economics of the euro area.

NOTES

1. Four EU member states stayed outside the euro area. Denmark and the UK had negotiated opt out clauses, Sweden did not want to join yet, and Greece did not meet the convergence criteria for admission to the Third Stage of EMU. See Chapter 3 of this book for details.
2. *The Financial Times*, 9 January 1999.
3. We owe this point to Vitor Gaspard.
4. The Treaty of Amsterdam (1997) introduced a new numbering of the Articles of the EC Treaty. Throughout this book numbers of EC Treaty Articles refer to the renumbered Articles. The table in Appendix 8.A links the 'old' and 'new' Article numbers.
5. The unemployment also has a cyclical component (about 2 per cent) reflecting the negative output gap in the euro area economy, estimated at -1.2 per cent (OECD, 1999).
6. The degree of hysteresis is defined as the market inertia criterion estimated by Van Bergeijk, Haffner and Waasdorp (1993). A value of zero indicates full price flexibility, while a value of 100 indicates complete hysteresis.
7. The wage rigidity measure is defined as the increase in the unemployment rate needed to reduce wages by 1 per cent. The data were taken from OECD (1989).
8. Calmfors (1998b) shows that the incentives for labour market reform are stronger inside a monetary union than outside. However, Sibert and Sutherland (1997) and Calmfors (1998a) present arguments pointing into the opposite direction.

PART ONE

The Road to EMU

2. European Monetary Cooperation: From Rome to Maastricht

Paul Cavelaars and Gerrit van den Dool

The question of which historical events have been crucial to the emergence of Europe can be answered in many ways. Over the centuries, a great many countries and persons have, after all, contributed to European integration. To begin with, the Greeks could point out that their decisive victory over the Persians in 479 BC drew a boundary between Asia and Europe (the name is said to derive from the Semitic word *ereb* for sunset). But Rome, Aix-la-Chapelle and Paris could lay equal claims, citing the major contributions made by the Roman emperors, Charlemagne and Napoleon. Be that as it may, the road towards Europe as we know it has been long and bumpy. It was only after the Second World War that most barriers were eliminated, and the process towards economic integration consequently accelerated.

West European developments in the past two centuries have been dominated by Germany and France, which were opponents in many political conflicts, culminating in two World Wars. Therefore, it was necessarily the cooperation between Germany and France that played a decisive role in the European integration process after the war. It has taken many years to reach an agreement on the role of monetary and fiscal policy in the pursuit of economic stability and growth. But once all parties agreed on the importance of stability-oriented policies, the way was paved for a unique and historic change, the adoption of a single currency.

This chapter focuses on the political and institutional context of the economic and monetary union, rather than on the economics of the euro area, and thus provides a natural starting point for the remainder of this book. The first section deals with the early post-war years, leading up to the Treaty of Rome which established the European Economic Community. Section 2 discusses the integration process during the 1960s and the so-called Werner Plan of 1970, which went a long way towards monetary and fiscal integration. The third section focuses on the foreign exchange turmoil of the 1970s and the establishment of the European Monetary System (EMS).

Section 4 goes into the turnaround in the history of the EMS in the first half
of the 1980s and the Delors Report of 1989. The fifth section describes the
intergovernmental conferences that worked towards the Treaty of Maastricht.
The final section discusses the last couple of miles on the road towards EMU
and looks ahead.

1. THE TREATY OF ROME

Post-war cooperation in Europe could be said to have started in 1948, when
the first Europe Congress was held in The Hague. It was here that Winston
Churchill exhorted the hundreds of representatives from over 30 countries to
strive for what could be called a United States of Europe. With the war only
just over, that was obviously a dream of the future, but the need for
cooperation, especially on economic matters, was generally acknowledged.
After all, everyone was immersed in the reconstruction effort. The
willingness to cooperate, on a scale stretching even beyond Europe, had
already begun to take shape in 1944, with the introduction of the Bretton
Woods system of fixed exchange rates linked to the US dollar and to gold.

A major impulse came from the Marshall Plan under which the United
States was prepared to give aid to Europe in the years 1949–52 on the
condition that the European countries' reconstruction efforts would be more
closely coordinated. (Here a role was also played by the threat posed by
communism, as evidenced in the blockade of Berlin by the Soviet Union in
1949.) In 1948, the countries receiving Marshall Aid set up the Organisation
for European Economic Cooperation, the precursor of the later OECD, to
facilitate the distribution of aid.

The first transfer of economic powers

Consultations were also being held about more far-reaching forms of
supranational economic cooperation, but on this subject opinion was still
highly divided. So much was clear when, in an attempt to bring about
Franco-German rapprochement, the French Foreign Minister, Robert
Schuman, presented a plan (drawn up by the head of the French Bureau of
Reconstruction, Jean Monnet) to place the heavy (war) industries under a
single authority. In 1950, the Schuman Plan was welcomed only by
Germany, Italy and the Benelux countries, three countries that had been
united in a Customs Union since 1948. In 1952, the six nations concerned set
up the European Coal and Steel Community (ECSC), the first common
market, for a limited number of products, under a 'High Authority' to which
the six participants had delegated a number of national powers. Mutual trust

was growing in Europe, but it was still fragile, witness French resistance to the rearmament of Germany advocated by the Americans in the early 1950s in connection with the Korean War, as well as to a European Defence Community with a European army.

The establishment of the European Economic Community

The sights were consequently set on a less ambitious goal, namely the elimination of trade barriers in various areas. On 27 March 1957, the six ECSC countries signed the Treaty of Rome establishing the European Economic Community. Over a period of 12 years, a common market was to be created, starting with the gradual abolition of customs duties within the Community and the introduction of common tariffs *vis-à-vis* the rest of the world. The second objective was the free movement of capital and persons. In order to realize these aims various institutions with supranational powers were set up, such as the European Commission, which is the EEC's executive body, the Council of Ministers, which decides on European legislation, and the European Parliament, which has mainly advisory and monitoring powers. The EEC set off on 1 January 1958 (Table 2.1).

Greater cooperation in the monetary field as well

An important aspect of the Treaty of Rome was that it also provided the basis for further cooperation in the monetary field. A Monetary Committee was installed to promote the coordination of the Member States' monetary policies and to give advice on the transfer of payments. Although the Treaty of Rome described exchange rate policy as a matter of common concern, each country remained responsible for the development of its own balance of payments and for confidence in its currency, that is its exchange rate against the dollar under the Bretton Woods regime.

Incidentally, in 1958 exchange rate relationships had not yet begun to pose problems. Five out of the six nations had balance-of-payments surpluses. Tensions first arose when the European countries began to catch up with the United States economically and the dollar gradually became overvalued, also as a result of President Kennedy's expansionary policy and the United States' growing balance-of-payments deficits. When the flow of dollars to Europe, and to Germany in particular, surged, exchange rate relationships among the European currencies came under pressure. In 1961, Germany and the Netherlands therefore decided, incidentally without first consulting the other EEC Member States, to revalue their currencies by 5 per cent. This prompted the Monetary Committee and the European Commission to draw up proposals for better policy coordination. In this context, a committee of

Table 2.1 Gradual deepening of economic and monetary cooperation

Year	Monetary Union	Single Market	New Members
1952		European Community for Coal and Steel	
1958		European Economic Community	Belgium France Germany Italy Luxembourg Netherlands
1968		customs union for industrial products	
1972	'snake' agreement		
1973			Denmark Ireland UK
1979	European Monetary System		
1981			Greece
1986			Portugal Spain
1990	EMU Stage One (capital account liberalization)		East-German *Länder*
1993		common market	
1994	EMU Stage Two (economic convergence)	European Economic Area	
1995			Austria Finland Sweden
1999	EMU Stage Three (monetary union)		
20??			New entrants

central bank governors was set up in 1964, with the task of coordinating central bank policies on the banking system, the money market and the foreign exchange market. The Member States agreed that exchange rate parities would be adjusted only after consultation.

Complicated decision making

The successful cooperation among the EEC Member States had a magnetic effect. However, when the United Kingdom, Ireland, Denmark and Norway applied for membership, the negotiations ran aground because France, ambitious to play a leading role within the EEC, feared that the Franco-German axis would be weakened if the United Kingdom joined. There were other issues, such as agricultural policy, on which France did not agree with the other Member States. This was a bad omen. Especially on monetary matters there turned out to be pronounced differences between the Member States. By contrast the establishment of the customs union proceeded successfully, and state subsidies and other preferential treatment of domestic industries were abolished. At the same time, however, deadlocks occurred on an increasing scale. The year 1966 saw the conclusion of the Compromise of Luxembourg, which entailed that Council decisions would no longer be taken by majority voting but, in contravention of the EEC Treaty, unanimously. The French furthermore reserved the right to veto what they saw as matters of vital national importance. It was only after Georges Pompidou succeeded Charles de Gaulle as President in 1969 that the broadening and deepening of the EEC came up for discussion again.

2. THE WERNER PLAN

The resumption of deliberations between the Member States was also prompted by the circumstances, because diverging policies in Europe and the United States had again given rise to tensions in the foreign exchange markets. The resulting parity realignments caused serious problems for the settlement of agricultural subsidies (based as they were on fixed prices in European units of account and on fixed exchange rates).

In this context, a working party, established in 1970 and chaired by Prime Minister Werner of Luxembourg drew up a plan for Economic and Monetary Union. According to the plan the union was to be set up over a period of ten years. To begin with, exchange rate fluctuations would have to be contained (it was proposed that the bandwidth on either side of the central rate against the dollar be reduced from $\pm\frac{3}{4}$ per cent to $\pm\frac{1}{2}$ per cent), and the first steps would be taken towards the coordination of monetary and fiscal policies. Any divergences would have to be reduced further in the course of the second stage. In the last stage, the currencies were to be locked together, and a

monetary and a budgetary authority would determine monetary and economic
policy. Although in 1971 the first stage of the Werner Plan (covering the
period to the end of 1974) was adopted, no agreement had as yet been
reached about how it was to be implemented.

Differing views in Germany and France

France, for instance, believed in monetary cooperation without a transfer of
monetary sovereignty, in the expectation that economic convergence would
automatically ensue. Germany and the Netherlands, on the other hand, held
that a single currency could only be a viable proposition on the basis of
economic stability in all participating countries. Germany and the
Netherlands consequently favoured a speedier abolition of the (remaining)
exchange restrictions and the disciplining impact of liberalized capital
movements. Below the surface, France was becoming increasingly irritated
by the growing dominance of the Deutschmark and would like to get more
influence on the Bundesbank's monetary policy. It also feared for the
exchange rate of the franc if capital restrictions were eased all too abruptly.
In the late 1960s, the process of integration began to slow down as a result of
antagonism between France and Germany. Europe began to suffer from
eurosclerosis. However, when the European foreign exchange markets fell
prey to increasing unrest (see below), it was again realized that common
problems were best faced by a united front.

3. THE 1970s: FOREIGN EXCHANGE TURMOIL

The tensions in the foreign exchange markets were generated by the growing
balance-of-payments deficits of the United States, which was embroiled in
the Vietnam War. Within the Bretton Woods system, only the United States
had the 'privilege' of being allowed to meet its external liabilities by printing
dollars. Dollar-denominated capital flows, destined for Germany in
particular, swelled. But as these dollars could be converted into gold at the
Fed, the US gold stock rapidly shrank and along with it confidence in the
dollar. Germany and the Netherlands revalued their currencies in the spring
of 1971, and then, several months later, abandoned the dollar peg. On 15
August, President Nixon suspended the dollar's convertibility to gold.

At the end of 1971, the countries participating in the Bretton Woods
system agreed on a realignment of their exchange rates and a widening of the
bandwidth on either side of the dollar's central rate from ±1 per cent to ±2¼
per cent. However, this allowed of fluctuations of ±4½ per cent among the
European currencies (and of 9 per cent at different points in time). On 21

March 1972, the EEC Member States therefore decided in Basle to adopt margins of at most ±2¼ per cent among their currencies, and to provide each other with intervention support in each other's currencies and no longer in dollars. This compelled the central banks to cooperate more intensively. The Basle Accord constituted the birth of the 'snake' in the dollar tunnel. In 1973, the European Monetary Cooperation Fund (EMCF) was set up to provide intervention support.

Integration under pressure

However, the unrest in the foreign exchange markets continued unabated, partly because the oil crisis hit one country harder than the next. Currencies were continually leaving the snake, to join again some time later. The snake itself survived, but in 1973 it was uncoupled from the dollar. In the meantime, the problems shared by the European countries only augmented their desire and need for cooperation. The United Kingdom, Denmark and Ireland joined the EEC and also temporarily took part in the snake arrangement.

In addition, it was decided that a 'European Summit' of the heads of state or government, that is the European Council, be held every six months to boost political convergence. During the first summit, the Werner Plan was endorsed: European Union was to be achieved not later than by the end of 1980. Given the circumstances, this again did not seem very realistic, because the Community's reaction to the consequences of the oil crisis, the recession, rising inflation and growing unemployment was anything but coordinated. The lack of convergence of the economic and monetary policies of Germany and France, in particular, gave rise to diverging developments in inflation rates, and thus continued to fuel the tensions in the foreign exchange markets.

The European Monetary System: no panacea

The continuing foreign exchange unrest compelled the Member States to work more intensively towards monetary cooperation. During the Copenhagen summit of 1978, a committee of senior civil servants from Germany, France and the United Kingdom was installed to draw up a concrete plan. After the committee had met five times with no results (owing to the sceptical attitude of the United Kingdom), German Chancellor Helmut Schmidt and French President Valéry Giscard d'Estaing took the initiative to boost cooperation at least on the foreign exchange front. This resulted in the European Monetary System (EMS) which took off on 13 March 1979. It was a new system of fixed but adjustable exchange rates, meant to create a zone of monetary stability. Only the UK did not join as yet.

One of the novelties of the EMS was the introduction of the European currency unit, the ECU (sharing its name with a French coin from the thirteenth century), which served as the unit of account. It consisted of a basket of currencies, each currency's share being based on its country's GNP and external trade. The central rate for each currency against the ECU implied bilateral central rates, *vis-à-vis* which the countries observed fluctuation margins of ±2¼ per cent. For the lira, a ±6 per cent bandwidth was in force. The EMS also came with extended credit mechanisms (the so-termed short-term credit facility and the medium-term monetary assistance), while each country transferred 20 per cent of its gold and foreign exchange holdings to the EMCF in exchange for ECUs.

In contrast with the Werner Plan, the EMS was not intended to be a stepping-stone towards economic and monetary union. Many capital account restrictions remained in force. Neither was there an agreement to eliminate national policy differences. Fiscal policies and inflation rates continued to diverge substantially in the early 1980s. Germany favoured a stability-oriented policy, while France, under President Mitterand, pursued an expansionary policy. As a result, the EMS, like the snake, had to cope with many realignments in its early phase.

4. THE DELORS PLAN: POLICY CONVERGENCE

The year 1983 may be seen as an important turning point in the history of the EMS. France made a U-turn when President Mitterand decided to give priority to a stable exchange rate between the French franc and the Deutschmark and hence to price stability, which was Germany's main policy objective. It consequently began to make sense to reach more detailed agreements on cooperation in the face of currency unrest. This was notably highlighted by the rise of the dollar's exchange rate in the mid-1980s. In 1985 and 1986, the major industrialized countries laid down agreements in the Louvre and Plaza accords. In the European context, the ministers of finance and the central bank governors in 1987 concluded an accord at Nyborg, Denmark. Intramarginal interventions would from then on be permitted at an early stage so as to make it possible to counter speculation more effectively. Interest rate policy would also be adjusted sooner, and the financing possibilities for interventions at the limits of the fluctuation margins were to be expanded.

The time had become ripe for ideas launched earlier by the French Minister, Jacques Delors, who had already advocated greater monetary cooperation in 1981. France had come to favour monetary union and a European central bank. The German Foreign Minister, Hans-Dietrich Genscher, went even further in his plea for a European Union where economic and monetary integration were to run parallel with political cooperation. In 1985, France and Germany presented a joint proposal for greater political cooperation. And during an Intergovernmental Conference in that same year, the Community's ten Member States (Greece had joined in 1981) agreed on the necessary Treaty amendments, to be laid down in the Single European Act. It was of major importance that majority voting would be reinstalled for decisions concerning a wider range of issues. In 1986, Spain and Portugal became EC members.

The White Paper and the Delors Plan

Thus the process of integration moved into a higher gear. That became clear when the European Commission published the White Paper, written by Britain's EC Commissioner Lord Cock, indicating – on the basis of a clear time schedule – which trade barriers (physical, technical and fiscal) still needed to be removed before the single market could be completed by 1991. Another controversial issue, for which a solution was ultimately found, was how to contain the ever-expanding agricultural expenditure. It was furthermore decided to abolish the remaining capital account restrictions in 1990. Now it was time for a more dynamic approach to the completion of Economic and Monetary Union. At the 1988 Hannover summit it was decided that stage one of EMU would set off on 1 July 1990. A committee made up of central bank governors, chaired by Mr Delors, then President of the European Commission, was given a mandate to draw up concrete proposals to that end.

The Delors Report (1989) centred on proposals for irrevocably fixed exchange rates, a single monetary policy, a European system of independent central banks, and a European Central Bank striving for price stability. So far the plan was very much like the 1969 Werner Plan. As to budgetary policies the plan was less far-reaching, however. There was no mention of a fiscal authority, although the level and manner of financing budgetary deficits would be subjected to rules. EMU was to be realised in stages over a period of ten years. In the monetary field, the changes would imply a transfer of national sovereignty. To that end, the Treaty of Rome would have to be modified and this required unanimity. The United Kingdom fiercely opposed the Delors proposals because they entailed the transfer of powers to a supranational institution. But in 1989 a compromise was reached at the Madrid Summit, albeit only on the first stage of EMU. This stage, during which policy convergence was to be attained, would in any case begin on 1

July 1990. Further negotiations were intended to be held as soon as possible about the second stage, during which the Treaty would be amended, and about the third (and final) stage during which the currencies would be locked together.

5. THE MAASTRICHT TREATY

The crumbling of the Berlin Wall on 9 November 1989 marked the beginning of a swift and relatively peaceful end to communism in Central and Eastern Europe. German chancellor Kohl was quick to realize that the opening of the Brandenburg Gate opened up the possibility of German reunification. At the same time, this German desire provided for a powerful driving force towards the creation of a monetary union in Europe. The timing of the reunification was fortunate, in that it gave political momentum to the proposals in the Delors Report that had been published in April 1989. French President Mitterand and German Chancellor Kohl went as far as to propose the transformation of the European Community into a political union by 1993. Their proposal included increasing democratic control, making Community institutions more effective and conducting a common foreign and security policy (Vanthoor, 1999).

Stage One of EMU: towards a common market

Stage One of economic and monetary union aimed at strengthening both monetary and non-monetary cooperation within the existing framework. This stage formally started on 1 July 1990. Any remaining capital account restrictions were abandoned in most Member States. Four member states (Greece, Ireland, Portugal and Spain) were allowed a transitional period until the end of 1992.[1]

In order to achieve an area without borders as of 1 January 1993 it was agreed to adjust value added taxes and excise duties. A year later the European Economic Area (EEA) was created, under which Norway, Sweden, Finland, Iceland and Austria joined the free single market of the European Community (Table 2.1). This construction enabled a free flow of goods and services, capital and people within Europe without altering the *acquis communautair* (the body of legislation) of the European Community. However, practically speaking it took until the end of 1997 before passport controls at intra-EU borders were lifted under the Schengen agreement.

Negotiations about the characteristics of the ultimate objective defined in the Delors Report, economic and monetary union, continued in the course of

1990. A number of proposals were made on the Treaty changes needed to that end.[2]

In support of the preparations for EMU, the governors of the central banks of the Member States drafted a statute for the European System of Central Banks. The draft ESCB statute was then transmitted to the governments of the Member States. Whereas there was a high degree of political consensus about monetary policy, opinions differed about the assignment of responsibilities for exchange rate policy. All Member States agreed that in EMU the political authorities should remain responsible for the choice of the exchange rate regime, acting in close cooperation with the ECB. However, views differed as to whether the political authorities might determine exchange rate policy in the absence of international agreements, given the possible resulting obligations for the ECB which could undermine the pursuit of internal price stability.

With regard to fiscal policy, views still differed on the question as to the extent to which binding limits could be imposed on the size of individual national budget deficits.

Intergovernmental conferences

The intergovernmental conferences on economic and monetary union and European political union had their first meeting in Rome in December 1990. It was decided that both conferences would work in parallel. In the following year, there would be a sequence of some ten intergovernmental conferences on both issues.

Some proposals on political union were rather far-reaching, but relatively little was accomplished in the end. The German and French ministers of foreign affairs put forward the so-called Genscher–Dumas plan, which proposed majority voting on foreign policy issues and which envisaged the West-European Union as a liaison between the European Community and NATO. These proposals were rejected by the Member States which were not members of the West European Union and by the United Kingdom and the Netherlands, which were concerned about relations with the United States. The Netherlands, which then held the presidency of the European Community, published a draft treaty on political union later in 1991, which included the right of the European Parliament to veto decisions of the Council of Ministers by simple majority. The draft was severely criticized by other Member States. Some, including the United Kingdom, considered it too radical. Others, including France, thought that it did not go far enough (Vanthoor, 1999).

As regards EMU, the first conclusion of the intergovernmental conferences was that a single currency requires a common monetary policy, to be conducted by a European Central Bank. The second element was the principle that, in order to be lastingly viable, a monetary union also requires more extensive convergence of economic policies. The third element was that the accomplishment of EMU would be accepted as an obligation upon the Member States when they signed the Treaty.

The concluding conference in Maastricht

The European Council in Maastricht at the end of 1991 concluded the intergovernmental conferences. It agreed on the Maastricht Treaty, which amended the existing EEC Treaty. The Maastricht Treaty envisaged the establishment of a European Union consisting of three pillars (Table 2.2). The first pillar was economic and monetary union. In this area, the European Commission had a substantial role to play and the Council of Ministers could decide on most issues with qualified majority. This, however, was not the case on issues relating to the common foreign and security policy, which formed the second pillar, or for cooperation in the field of domestic and legal affairs, the third pillar. In these areas European institutions received almost no role of importance and veto power for each Member State in the Council of Ministers was maintained.

Table 2.2 The Maastricht Treaty: three pillars

First pillar	Economic and monetary union
Second pillar	Common foreign and security policy
Third pillar	Domestic and legal affairs

In the Maastricht Treaty, the Member States committed themselves to aiming at reducing excessive deficits during Stage Two and making preparations enabling the establishment of a European System of Central Banks. Member States would have to fulfil so-called convergence criteria before adopting a single currency in Stage Three of EMU (see Chapter 3). This requirement was combined with the notion that Stage Three would start in 1999 at the latest with however many Member States satisfied the criteria by that time. The United Kingdom negotiated an opt-out clause to the mandatory transition to Stage Three. Also, at the request of the United Kingdom, the social chapter was left out of the body of the Treaty and was reduced to a protocol that applied to only 11 out of 12 Member States.

The Treaty of Maastricht was officially signed on 7 February 1992 and had then to be ratified by all Member States. In some countries, parliamentary approval was sufficient. In other countries, referendums were required in order to be able to do this. The Danish people, who were the first in a row of European countries to be consulted on the Treaty, turned it down in a referendum in June, after the Danish parliament had approved the Treaty by a large majority only three weeks before.

EMS crises in 1992 and 1993

The second half of 1992 marked the end of a period of more than five years of relative calm within the European Monetary System. The doubts about EMU which arose in the wake of the negative outcome of the Danish referendum and the uncertainties in France about the results of the forthcoming referendum in that country led to a sudden awareness of the fundamental disequilibria which had arisen within the EU. Worsening economic conditions made countries hesitant to raise interest rates in defence of the exchange rate. Market developments forced the authorities to undertake a series of realignments following official statements denying their imminence in September 1992. What resulted was a currency crisis in the run-up to the French referendum. Sterling, which had joined the exchange-rate mechanism (ERM) of the European Monetary System in 1990, was now forced to leave again. One day later, the Italian lira was forced to leave the ERM as well and the Spanish peseta was devalued.

The outcome of the French referendum provided a stabilizing effect: a majority, albeit slim, of the population approved ratification of the Treaty. The German parliament approved ratification of the Treaty too, but conditional upon having the last say on introducing the single currency. A similar qualification was made by the Dutch parliament, which demanded to be consulted again before the final decision was made. The Treaty, which contained an opt-out clause this time, was approved in a second referendum in Denmark in May 1993. Despite this favourable course of events, market doubts about the preparedness and ability of authorities to raise interest rates in defence of exchange rates in cases where such policies might conflict with the requirements of the domestic economy led to new pressures within the ERM. As a result, in August 1993, the finance ministers and central bank governors of the Member States decided to widen the margins within the exchange rate mechanism of the European Monetary System temporarily to 15 per cent, while maintaining the existing central rates. Within this framework, Germany and the Netherlands decided to stick to the narrow bilateral band of ±2¼ per cent between their currencies. The EU Treaty entered into force in November 1993, shortly before the beginning of Stage Two.

6. ECONOMIC AND MONETARY UNION

Three of the European Free Trade Area (EFTA) countries, which had joined the common market via the European Economic Area in 1994, joined the European Union on 1 January 1995. The membership of these countries (Austria, Finland and Sweden) had become politically viable as a result of the demise of the Soviet Union. In Norway, a referendum was held in 1994, but this resulted in a decision against joining the European Union. There was a substantial difference between the new Member States. Whereas Austria joined the exchange rate mechanism several days after becoming an EU member, thus continuing its existing exchange rate policy of closely following the Deutschmark, Sweden created its own opt-out to the Maastricht Treaty by stating that it would only introduce the single currency if its parliament agreed at the time.

Stage Two of EMU: economic convergence

One goal of Stage Two of EMU was to prepare the establishment of the European Central Bank. To that end, the European Monetary Institute (EMI) was established on 1 January 1994, with Frankfurt as its location, after having been temporarily located in Basle.[3] The EMI Council, the EMI's highest decision making body, was made up of all national central bank governors. The so-called *Comité des Gouverneurs,* which had been the meeting platform for European central bank governors since 1964, ceased to exist. Numerous central bank sub-committees and working groups supported the EMI Council in preparing the creation of an organization, which would be able to conduct a single monetary policy for a substantial number of countries in line with the set-up envisaged in the Maastricht Treaty.

Another goal of Stage Two was to achieve economic convergence between the Member States. However, it soon became clear that the required convergence of government finances of the Member States did not occur as quickly as had been hoped. In May 1996, within the framework of the excessive-deficit procedure, almost all Member States were 'convicted' for having government finances that did not meet the criteria, the only two exceptions being Ireland and Luxembourg. In reaction to this, six German research institutions argued in favour of a flexible interpretation of the convergence criteria so as to ensure that high-debt but hard-currency countries like the Netherlands and Belgium would be able to qualify. This suggestion was immediately turned down by German minister Waigel. Unwilling to soften the admission criteria, Bundesbank president Tietmeyer indicated that a postponement of EMU should be considered as an option.

Given the adherence to the criteria, public speculation and political tension mounted in 1996 as to which countries would be able to qualify for EMU. Reacting to public doubts about Italian participation, Spanish prime minister Aznar made it clear that Spain would be among the first entrants to EMU, whether Italy participated or not. Italian prime minister Prodi declared that he was determined to bring Italy into EMU at its start. Realizing that EMU entry required participation in the exchange rate mechanism of the European Monetary System for at least the last two years before the examination, the Finnish markka joined the ERM in October 1996, followed by the Italian lira the next month.

Preparing the Community for Stage Three: Stability Pact and ERM-II

June 1997 brought the conclusion of a round of intergovernmental conferences that started in Turin in March 1996 and which was intended to lead to a breakthrough on institutional issues. A meeting of the European Council in the building of the Nederlandsche Bank in Amsterdam did not result in the far-reaching institutional reform of the Union that was hoped for. However, the resulting Treaty of Amsterdam contained important additions to the institutional framework of EMU. Probably the most important of these was the Pact for Stability and Growth, which provided for a sanction mechanism in order to prevent a weakening of budgetary positions in EMU. German finance minister Waigel had originally called for such a pact in 1994.

The European Council in Amsterdam also decided on a new exchange-rate mechanism between the euro and the currencies of non-participating Member States, the so-called ERM-II, which would replace the ERM at the beginning of Stage Three. Agreement was also reached on a Council Regulation providing for legal certainty for businesses and individuals about the continuity of contracts at the time of the changeover to the euro.

The Treaty of Amsterdam provided several moves towards future expansion of EU membership. For instance, it stipulates that the rules for the composition of the European Commission will be altered when the Union is enlarged with new Member States. This had become practically relevant after the decision made in Copenhagen in 1993 that all applicant countries of Central and Eastern Europe would become Member States of the European Union as soon as they fulfil the membership criteria.

Another important element of the new Treaty was that it made possible a Europe of several speeds, where some Member States can decide to go faster than is commonly agreed. The United Kingdom agreed to the social chapter of the new Treaty, thus submitting itself to the social policy that the other Member States had already agreed upon in Maastricht.

Discussion continued about the possibility of a delay of the start of EMU. Four German professors argued for a postponement of EMU, because Germany and other Member States were using one-off measures and accounting tricks to satisfy the convergence criteria. They finally filed a complaint with the German constitutional court in Karlsruhe in order to ensure that the German government would not be allowed to agree on the start of EMU. However, the judges argued that the Maastricht Treaty had been approved by parliament in 1992, providing for a sound constitutional basis for joining EMU, and dismissed the complaint in April 1998.

By the end of 1997, the Member States agreed on the coordination of the economic policies of the participating countries of EMU. Policy coordination would take place in an informal council, the Euro-11, which was then called 'Euro-x' as the number of EMU participants was still unknown. It was the result of the French desire for a political counterpart to the ECB and the German desire for a platform which would give the finance ministers of the participating countries the opportunity periodically to review the economic and budgetary situation. It was made clear that the competence to take formal decisions remained fully with the EU Council of Ministers.

Decision on the first group of EMU participants

The European Council held a special meeting in Brussels in the first weekend of May 1998 in order to decide which countries could participate. Before this meeting, the European Commission, the European Monetary Institute and several national central banks published their convergence reports, based on the final deficit figures of the EU Member States for 1997. Denmark, Finland and the Netherlands had already been removed from the list of 'convicted' countries based on 1995 and 1996 figures. Eurostat, the statistics bureau of the Community, was confronted with unusual political attention as this agency decided on the accounting treatment of certain transactions that affect government deficit and debt in the reference year 1997. From the convergence reports, it appeared that 11 countries would be able to join EMU. Denmark, Great Britain and Sweden had indicated earlier that they preferred not to participate in the first round. Greece had joined the exchange-rate mechanism in March 1998, but was found not to be economically ready to participate in EMU as of the beginning of 1999 (see Chapter 3 for a more detailed account of the qualification for EMU).

The European Council, after a lengthy meeting, appointed Willem Duisenberg, who had been the president of the EMI since the summer of 1997, as ECB president. The European Council also formally approved the appointment of the other members of the ECB Executive Board, which made it possible to formally establish the ECB on 1 June 1998.

The Council of Ministers and the central bank governors used the opportunity to pre-announce that the ERM central rates would be used to determine the conversion rates of national currencies towards the euro. As a result, some say that the currency union had already started in May 1998. In any case, by reducing uncertainty for market participants, the pre-announcement was probably key to a smooth changeover towards the euro at the turn of the year.

The changeover to Stage Three of EMU

The changeover to the euro went along the lines foreseen in the introduction scenario. This had been decided on by the Madrid European Council at the end of 1995, along the lines of the so-called Green Paper of the European Commission. The exchange rates were irrevocably fixed on the last day of 1998, enabling the monetary union to start on 1 January 1999. The first impressions are that the launch has been very successful from a technical point of view.

New challenges

Even before the dust of the start of Stage Three has settled down the European Union is facing several new challenges. Three of the most important ones are defining the European presence on the international stage; the expansion of the Union towards the East; and coping with diverging ideas on the desirability of a political union.

European integration must not result in a Europe that is more inward-looking. The Union can be expected to be somewhat more self-confident on the international stage. At the same time, it would not be very helpful if this resulted in ongoing conflicts in the area of international trade or in a neglect of euro exchange rate developments. All in all, European politicians seem well aware of this. Often coming from relatively small countries, they have a natural tendency to pay attention to what is going on abroad. This bodes well for a Europe that will participate actively in the international arena.

As to the second challenge, the countries of Central and Eastern Europe that have signed Association Agreements will be allowed to join the European Union as soon as they meet the economic and political conditions for membership. Actual negotiations started with a first group of six applicant countries in November 1998 (Table 2.3). The foreseen EU expansion calls for a number of substantial changes to ensure that the Union will be able to function smoothly with 20 Member States or more.The financing of the Union seems to have been settled for the coming years, but this may not be true for important other issues. For instance, the

Table 2.3 EU Member States and applicant countries

EU Member States		Applicant countries	
EMU	Non-EMU	First group	Second group
Austria	Denmark	Czech Republic	Bulgaria
Belgium	Greece	Cyprus	Latvia
Finland	Sweden	Estonia	Lithuania
France	United Kingdom	Hungary	Malta
Germany		Poland	Romania
Ireland		Slovenia	Slovak Republic
Italy			Turkey
Luxembourg			
Netherlands			
Portugal			
Spain			

Note: Situation as of 1 January 1999.

representation of Member States in European institutions will need to be agreed. In addition, the Common Agricultural Policy and other Community programmes need more than marginal changes. Discussions started some time ago, but have yet to be brought to a conclusion.

Finally, the European Union will need to cope with diverging ideas about the desirability of a political union. Germany has been the most important proponent of a political union in Europe. France, the United Kingdom and several other countries have generally been much more hesitant. If the past 40 years can provide some lessons, the road ahead may be bumpy and full of potholes, but the journey is unlikely to stop now that Europe has a single market and a single currency.

NOTES

1. See Bakker (1996) for an in-depth discussion.
2. For instance, Bundesbank president Pöhl proposed a 'Europe of two speeds', which meant that monetary union would start off with a small group of core countries, whereas other countries would join after they had reached a similar degree of convergence.
3. See Van den Dool and Frankena (1997).

3. Qualifying for Stage Three of EMU

Ron Berndsen, Willem Heeringa and Cees Ullersma

During a historical European summit in Brussels in May 1998 it was decided that 11[1] out of 15 EU Member States qualified for participation in Stage Three of EMU. The May 1998 decisions marked the end of a long political process towards monetary integration. The driving force behind monetary union was the German willingness to give up Deutschmark supremacy – for decades a thorn in the flesh of France – in return for Germany's full political integration in Europe and under the condition of a fully independent European central bank and guarantees for sound economic policies.[2] This was worked out in the Maastricht Treaty. To qualify for participation in EMU, EU Member States had to pass a test on the progress in economic and legal convergence based on the so-called 'convergence criteria' (also known as the Maastricht criteria).

This chapter looks back at the qualification for EMU. With the benefit of hindsight, we review whether the convergence criteria, created for political reasons, facilitated economic convergence. We also assess whether economic convergence has further increased since May 1998 and map out the implications of the convergence process for future participating countries. This chapter is in four parts. First, it discusses the convergence procedures. Second, the chapter offers a re-examination of the May 1998 decisions to assess whether the euro area would consist of the same 11 members if the decision were made in May 1999. If one year later the same countries qualified, this would indeed be a reassuring signal. Remember, only a few years earlier most analysts expected a first wave of only seven or eight participating countries. This part also reviews the *interim period*, that is, the time between the decision on EMU participation in May 1998 and the formal start of monetary union on 1 January 1999. This will shed some light on whether the decision to allow these 11 countries in was sensible. Third, this chapter focuses on the consequences of these decisions for countries wishing to join EMU in the future. Finally, it sums up the conclusions.

1. RATIONALE OF CONVERGENCE PROCEDURES

In May 1998 it had to be decided which EU Member States qualified for
participation in Stage Three of EMU. This follows from the EC Treaty,
which states that Stage Three should start on 1 January 1999 at the latest. The
EC Treaty gives a detailed description of the decision making process
regarding the qualification for EMU membership. In accordance with this
procedure, the EMI, the predecessor of the ECB, published its Convergence
Report on 25 March 1998 (EMI, 1998). This Report records the progress
made by each Member State towards complying with the convergence
criteria. On the same day, the European Commission also published its
Convergence Report and recommended that 11 out of 15 Member States
qualified (European Commission, 1998). Only Greece and Sweden did not
meet the convergence criteria in the view of the Commission. The United
Kingdom and Denmark had negotiated a clause allowing them to remain
outside EMU. The Council of Economics and Finance Ministers (Ecofin)
took the same position as the Commission, and on 2 May the Council
meeting in the composition of the Heads of State and Government confirmed
that the 11 Member States singled out by the European Commission met the
necessary conditions for the adoption of the single currency.[3]

It has always been clear that a successful EMU requires Member States to
have converged economically through the pursuit of sound economic policies
and are able to maintain this convergence in the future. For this reason, the
EC Treaty and subsequent agreements of the European Council provide a
number of important guarantees for a stable EMU. These relate to the
application of the convergence criteria and the Pact for Stability and Growth.
This Pact requires Member States to strengthen budgetary discipline after the
start of EMU (see Chapter 10). Here the focus is on the convergence criteria.

The procedure for joining EMU is not only based on economic criteria but
also includes an examination of legal convergence; in other words, whether
each Member State's national legislation, including its central bank law, is
compatible with the EC Treaty. Legal convergence ensures both that the
national central banks, which together with the ECB form the ESCB, are
ready to function as an integral part of the ESCB before the ESCB is
established and that the national central banks enjoy complete independence
from political influences. Central bank independence is essential for a stable
monetary union. Its independence gives the ESCB a strong position to gear
its policy towards its primary objective, namely the maintenance of price
stability.

The examination of economic convergence was conducted to determine
whether a high degree of sustainable convergence had been achieved, based
on the economic convergence criteria. These relate to a high degree of price

stability, the level of long-term interest rates, the sustainable character of the budgetary position and the observance of the normal fluctuation margins of the Exchange Rate Mechanism of the European Monetary System.

The first economic convergence criterion is the inflation criterion. Sustainable convergence of inflation rates between Member States prior to Stage Three is necessary to ensure that the ESCB is able to pursue an effective policy geared to price stability right from the outset. If inflation rates within EMU differ too much, problems could arise over monetary policy. For countries with a relatively high inflation rate the uniform interest rate level could prove to be too low to control inflation, while growth in the Member States with a satisfactory inflation performance could be slowed down unnecessarily, leading to welfare losses in terms of GDP growth and employment.

The second criterion relates to the convergence of long-term interest rates to a low level. On the one hand, interest rate convergence reflects the financial markets' perception of the likelihood of EMU membership. On the other hand, favourable developments in interest rates indicate the success of individual countries' policy measures.

The third convergence criterion, on the budgetary position, reflects the notion that individual Member States' budgetary policy may have important repercussions for other Member States and the monetary union as a whole (Bovenberg, Kremers and Masson, 1991). First, excessive deficits stimulate inflation and may therefore undermine the ESCB's objective of price stability. Second, excessive deficits may drive up long-term interest rates. Third, a high level of government debt makes government finances more vulnerable to interest rate increases.

The exchange rate criterion is the fourth convergence criterion. Since the introduction of a single currency represents a once-and-for-all fixing of the bilateral exchange rates of the Member States participating in EMU, compliance with the rules of the Exchange Rate Mechanism of the EMS is a logical requirement in the run-up to the introduction of a single currency.

Although the importance of economic convergence for admission to EMU has seldom been contested, in the economic literature doubts have been expressed about the feasibility of testing by use of the Maastricht criteria. The motivation and design of the budgetary criterion in particular have been in the spotlight. Buiter, Corsetti and Roubini (1993) argue that the budgetary criterion is badly motivated and leads to unnecessary hardship. In their opinion, there is no case for restricting the deficit and the debt–GDP ratio to lie below any specific numerical value. They stress that from an economic point of view the nominal gross debt of general government is a concept of very little use. Instead the focus should be on the net non-monetary liabilities of the consolidated general government and the central bank, since this would be a more accurate approximation of government's wealth. As regards the deficit criterion they argue that countries with higher real growth rates can afford higher deficit ratios. De Grauwe (1996b) explains that the theory of the optimum currency areas cannot be readily used to justify the convergence criteria. In his view optimal currency areas are not created as such, but emerge gradually. Therefore, he is of the opinion that more emphasis should be put on strengthening the institutional framework for monetary and economic policy.

All in all, the need for testing inflation, interest rate and exchange rate convergence is not controversial. In our view, however, the budgetary convergence criterion too is based on sound logic. The budgetary criterion provides a concrete yardstick by which to assess objectively whether a given Member State has achieved a sufficient degree of fiscal convergence. In retrospect, it can be concluded that the convergence process was driven by the criteria, especially the one on the budgetary position. The convergence criteria can be regarded as a useful measure for judging whether a country is pursuing a sound stability-oriented macroeconomic policy. They also serve as a visible standard against which anyone can assess policy, thus helping to strengthen policy discipline. None the less, it is self-evident that not all aspects of sustainable convergence can be expressed in a limited number of statistics. Regarding this, the Treaty points out that factors other than those laid down in the criteria need to be taken into account when assessing the sustainability of convergence.

2. REASSESSMENT OF THE MAY 1998 DECISIONS

The inflation criterion

At the time of the assessment in March 1998, the most recent twelve-month period for which harmonized inflation figures were available was February 1997–January 1998, the so-called reference period. As can be seen from Table 3.1, the three Member States with the lowest inflation in the reference period were Austria (1.1 per cent), France (1.2 per cent) and Ireland (1.2 per cent). This results in a reference value for the EU of 2.7 per cent: the reference value is calculated as the unweighted average of at most the three Member States with the lowest inflation plus 1.5 percentage points. For 1998 the reference value for the EU amounts to 2.2 per cent, given the inflation outcomes of Germany (0.7 per cent), France (0.7 per cent) and Austria (0.8 per cent). Hence the reference value decreased in the course of 1998

Table 3.1 Inflation and long-term interest rates in the EU (%)

	Inflation[a]			Long-term interest rates		
	1996	97:02 -98:01	1998	1996	97:02 -98:01	1998
Belgium	1.8	1.4	0.9	6.5	5.7	4.8
Denmark	2.1	1.9	1.3	7.2	6.2	4.9
Germany	1.2	1.4	0.7	6.2	5.6	4.6
Greece	7.9	5.2	4.5	14.4	9.8	8.5
Spain	3.6	1.8	1.8	8.7	6.3	4.8
France	2.1	1.2	0.7	6.3	5.5	4.6
Ireland	2.2	1.2	2.1	7.3	6.2	4.8
Italy	4.0	1.8	2.0	9.4	6.7	4.9
Luxembourg	1.2	1.4	1.0	6.3	5.6	4.7
Netherlands	1.4	1.8	1.8	6.2	5.5	4.6
Austria	1.8	1.1	0.8	6.3	5.6	4.7
Portugal	2.9	1.8	2.2	8.6	6.2	4.9
Finland	1.1	1.3	1.4	7.1	5.9	4.8
Sweden	0.8	1.9	1.0	8.0	6.5	5.0
UK	2.5	1.8	1.5	7.9	7.0	5.5
Euro area[b]	2.2	1.5	1.1	7.2	5.9	4.7
EU[b]	2.4	1.7	1.3	7.5	6.1	4.9
Reference values[c]						
Euro area	2.7	2.7	2.2	8.5	7.8	6.6
EU	2.5	2.7	2.2	9.1	7.8	6.6

Notes:

[a] Harmonized Indices of Consumer Prices (HICP) figures.

[b] Weighted average.

[c] Inflation: Unweighted average of inflation in the three Member States with the lowest inflation plus 1.5 percentage points on the basis of twelve-month moving averages. Long-term interest rate: Average of the long-term interest rates in the three Member States with the lowest inflation plus 2 percentage points on the basis of twelve-month moving averages.

from 2.7 per cent to 2.2 per cent. The disinflation process in Europe therefore continued during the interim period. However, despite lower inflation rates on average in 1998, inflation rates in individual countries diverged more than

Figure 3.1 Inflation and long-term interest rate dispersion
(Standard deviation in percentage points)

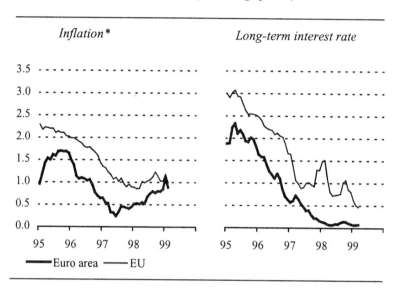

Note: * Harmonized indices of Consumer Prices (HICP) figures.
       For 1995 interim indices are used.

in 1997. This point is illustrated by Figure 3.1. In the period 1995–98 the dispersion of inflation reached very low values in 1997, but rebounded in 1998. With respect to the performance of individual countries relative to the reference rate, it is interesting to note that in 1998 inflation in some countries was equal (Portugal) or very close (Ireland, Italy) to the reference value. One year earlier in the reference period, inflation rates were at least 0.9 percentage point below the reference value. Going back to 1996, Portugal, Spain, Italy and Greece exceeded the reference value, in the latter three countries by more than 1 percentage point. This underlines the opinion at the time that inflation in these countries came down only recently and hence that convergence was still fragile (De Nederlandsche Bank, 1998). All in all, inflation outcomes in 1998 do not change the assessment made in March 1998: only Greece had an inflation rate above the reference value in both years.

The long-term interest rate criterion

The reference value for the long-term interest rate criterion is calculated as the (unweighted) average of the long-term rates in the three Member States with the lowest inflation plus 2 percentage points. It comes out at 7.8 per cent, calculated as the average of the long-term interest rates of Austria (5.6 per cent), France (5.5 per cent) and Ireland (6.2 per cent). For 1998, the reference value amounts to 6.6 per cent, based on the long-term rates of Germany, France and Austria. As can be seen from Figure 3.1 the dispersion with respect to the long-term interest rate declined spectacularly in the years to 1998. The dominant perception of financial markets was that the EMU project and the perceived composition of the euro area (that is including Italy) were fully credible. With the benefit of hindsight, it can be concluded that the interest rate criterion was not very discriminating. In the following interim period from 3 May 1998 to 31 December 1999, despite turbulence in global financial markets, only a small divergence occurred but basically the convergence process continued. It can therefore be argued that Stage Three of EMU started *de facto* in May 1998. Like the inflation criterion, compliance with the interest rate criterion was the same in 1998 as in the reference period a year earlier. Hence the original assessment (related to 1997) is also valid for 1998: only Greece exceeded the reference value, albeit to a lesser extent than in the reference period.

The budgetary criterion

Under the provisions of the Treaty, the Ecofin Council has to determine, based on a recommendation from the Commission, whether or not a budget deficit is excessive. This decision should be based on the following two criteria (Article 104(2) EC Treaty):

1. whether the ratio of the planned or actual government deficit to gross domestic product exceeds a reference value; and
2. whether the ratio of government debt to gross domestic product exceeds a reference value.

The reference values, as defined in the Treaty's Protocol 5 on the excessive deficit procedure, are 3 per cent for the government deficit and 60 per cent for government debt. It can be shown that, based on a nominal GDP growth of 5 per cent per year, the debt ratio converges asymptotically to 60 per cent of GDP in case of a government deficit of 3 per cent of GDP, thus providing some internal consistency between the deficit and debt criterion. In order to avoid an excessive deficit, the government deficit and debt must in principle not exceed respectively 3 and 60 per cent of GDP. However, regarding the government deficit, Article 104(2a) of the Treaty allows for two exceptions. The first is when 'the ratio has declined substantially and continuously and reached a level that comes close to the reference value' and the second when 'the excess over the reference value is only exceptional and temporary and the ratio remains close to the reference value'. Furthermore, regarding the government debt, Article 104(2b) stipulates that a debt ratio above 60 per cent of GDP is excessive 'unless the ratio is sufficiently diminishing and approaching the reference value at a satisfactory pace'.

Below we review the decisions taken by the Ecofin Council in May 1998 against the background of the budgetary figures which were available in March 1998 with respect to Member States' government deficit and debt (see Table 3.2). Furthermore, we assess budgetary developments in the interim period, that is the budgetary outcomes in 1998.

On 12 May 1997, the Ecofin Council had cleared the way for Finland and the Netherlands to join EMU by abrogating their excessive deficit. Denmark, Luxembourg and Ireland had been non-excessive-deficit countries for some time. As the budgetary outcomes for these five countries had not deteriorated since the Ecofin Council decisions, there was no reason to reconsider the budgetary positions in these countries. However, the other ten Member States still had an excessive deficit prior to the May 1998 summit. Therefore, the Ecofin Council had to consider whether the excessive deficit of these Member States could be abrogated in May 1998. The Member States under consideration could be divided in four groups, ranked by budgetary performance (see Table 3.3).

Group 1: Austria, Portugal, Spain, Sweden and the UK

Austria's general government deficit declined to 2.5 per cent of GDP in 1997. Albeit still exceeding the reference value, the debt ratio was falling slightly mainly as a result of privatization receipts, sales of financial claims and a reclassification of public companies to the private sector. Portugal had benefited considerably from the lower interest rates in the run-up to EMU, resulting in a sharp fall in interest expenditures. As a result, the government deficit declined from 6.1 per cent of GDP in 1993 to 2.5 per cent of GDP in 1997, while the debt ratio approached the reference value in 1997. Spain had managed to reduce its government deficit from 6.9 per cent of GDP in 1993 to 2.6 per cent of GDP in 1997, by lowering both government expenditure and taxation. The debt trend showed only a limited decline, while over the period 1990–97 Spanish gross debt increased in total by 24 percentage points. The United Kingdom and Sweden had made great progress in reducing their budget deficits from the high levels of the early 1990s to below the reference value in 1997. Furthermore, the UK gross debt ratio was

Table 3.2 General government finances in the EU (% of GDP)

	Budget balance					Government debt				
	1993	1997		1998		1993	1997		1998	
		a	b	a	b		a	b	a	b
Belgium	-7.1	-2.1	-1.9	-1.7	-1.3	135	122	123	118	117
Denmark	-2.8	0.7	0.4	1.1	0.8	82	65	64	60	58
Germany	-3.2	-2.7	-2.7	-2.5	-2.1	48	61	62	61	61
Greece	-13.8	-4.0	-3.9	-2.2	-2.4	112	109	109	108	107
Spain	-6.9	-2.6	-2.6	-2.2	-1.8	60	69	68	67	66
France	-5.8	-3.0	-3.0	-2.9	-2.9	45	58	58	58	59
Ireland	-2.7	0.9	1.1	1.1	2.3	96	66	61	60	52
Italy	-9.5	-2.7	-2.7	-2.5	-2.7	119	122	122	118	119
Luxembourg	1.7	1.7	2.9	1.0	2.1	6	7	6	7	7
Netherlands	-3.2	-1.4	-0.9	-1.6	-0.9	81	72	71	70	68
Austria	-4.2	-2.5	-1.9	-2.3	-2.1	63	66	64	65	63
Portugal	-6.1	-2.5	-2.5	-2.2	-2.3	63	62	62	60	58
Finland	-8.0	-0.9	-1.2	0.3	1.0	58	56	55	54	50
Sweden	-12.2	-0.8	-0.7	0.5	2.0	76	77	77	74	75
UK	-7.9	-1.9	-1.9	-0.6	0.6	49	53	52	52	49
Euro area	-5.5	-2.5	-2.5	-2.4	-2.1	67	75	75	74	73
EU	-6.1	-2.4	-2.3	-1.9	-1.5	65	72	72	71	70

Note:
Column a: Figures according to March 1998 Notification.
Column b: Figures according to March 1999 Notification.

less than 60 per cent of GDP, while the Swedish debt ratio had been declining since 1994.

Group 2: Germany and France
The effects of German reunification dominated budgetary developments in Germany in the 1990s. Of particular importance was the take-over of the outstanding debt of the Treuhand by the federal government in 1995, which raised the debt ratio by roughly 10 percentage points (De Nederlandsche Bank, 1998). The trend in the German government's budget deficit diverged from that in most other Member States. While nearly all Member States benefited from lower interest expenditures, the German government was

Table 3.3 Survey of deficit and debt performance in 1997

	Debt ratio		
	Moderate and declining	Moderate and rising	High but declining
Deficit <= 3% of GDP	Austria Portugal Spain Sweden UK	Germany France	Belgium Italy
Deficit > 3% of GDP			Greece

faced with rising interest expenditure partly associated with the take-over of the Treuhand debt. Non-interest expenditures were substantially reduced, with government investment severely affected. As a result Germany's government deficit undershot the reference value by 0.3 per cent of GDP, while the debt ratio amounted to 61.3 per cent of GDP according to the available figures of March 1998.

France's deficit in 1997 exactly equalled the reference value. There had been fairly significant recourse to one-off and self-reversing measures[4] in order to achieve this figure. For example, the French state received a self-reversing deficit-reducing capital transfer of 0.5 per cent of GDP from France Télécom in exchange for taking over future pension liabilities. The gross debt ratio, although increasing since 1993, was below the reference value in 1997.

Group 3: Belgium and Italy
The level of government debt in Belgium was more than double the reference value in 1997. However, the gross debt ratio had declined by 13 percentage points since 1993, when it peaked at 135 per cent of GDP. Stock-flow adjustments contributed to this reduction by 3.5 percentage points of GDP in 1996, mainly reflecting the impact of financial operations as the sale of assets by the government and the central bank. Belgium's budgetary deficit reached a maximum of 7.1 per cent of GDP in 1993. Since then, a gradual but steady consolidation process has achieved a significant reduction in the deficit. According to the available figures of March 1998, the deficit amounted to 2.1 per cent of GDP in 1997. More than half of the deficit reduction between 1993 and 1997 was attributable to lower interest

expenditures. There had also been a slight increase in the already very high level of taxation, while the Belgian government had reduced non-interest expenditures to a limited extent, involving a further cut in the already relatively low level of investment expenditure.

Just as in Belgium, the level of government debt in Italy was more than double the reference value in 1997. The reduction in the budget deficit was of a very recent date, namely 1997. Of the progress made since 1993 in reducing the deficit (6.8 per cent of GDP), four percentage points was registered in 1997. Italy also benefited substantially from the fall in interest rates which had taken place since 1995. This fall was partly a reflection of market expectations that Italy would be one of the founding members of EMU. Between 1993 and 1997 interest expenditures fell by 2.6 per cent of GDP. There was a slight lowering of taxation, while government expenditure was sharply reduced. However, in 1997 the downward trend in the deficit was helped – much more so than in other Member States – by one-off measures amounting to some 1 per cent of GDP in 1997. The so-called euro tax, which the Italian government promised to return in later years, formed an important part of these one-off measures. In addition, self-reversing measures amounting to 0.3 per cent of GDP were taken, which will require compensating measures when their effects unwind. An issue which also drew a lot of attention in the run-up to the May 1998 decisions was the Italian budgetary phenomenon of the so-called *residui passivi*. These *residui passivi* consisted of expenditures which were approved by parliament but for which the cash resources had not yet been released due to the strict cash policy of the Italian Treasury. As the amount of outstanding *residui passivi* had risen to 8.7 per cent of GDP in 1997 in the run-up to EMU, some observers feared that they could threaten Italy's public finances in the future when the blocked cash entitlements were released. Another important issue for Italian public finances was the high sensitivity of government expenditures to interest rates changes. In the early 1990s two-thirds of Italian government debt had a residual maturity of less than one year (EMI, 1998). Although this share was reduced to 49 per cent in 1997, government finances remained sensitive to interest rate movements, more so than in other Member States with high government debt ratios. For example, in Belgium only a quarter of government debt had a residual maturity of less than one year.

Group 4: Greece
In Greece the general government deficit amounted to 4.0 per cent of GDP in 1997 and thus exceeded the reference value. Since 1993, when the deficit still stood at 13.8 per cent of GDP, it had fallen continuously, although it had still not approached the reference value. Since GDP had been growing at rates between 2 and 3 per cent over several years, the excess over the

reference value could not be regarded as 'exceptional' or 'temporary'. The reduction in the deficit had been the result of both a decline in interest and other expenditures and of an increase in effective taxation, especially as a result of improved tax collection. The gross debt ratio was at 108 per cent of GDP, well above the reference value and had scarcely fallen from its level in 1993 (111 per cent of GDP).

The May 1998 decisions
Based on a recommendation of the European Commission, the Ecofin Council finally decided in May 1998 to abrogate the excessive deficits for Belgium, Germany, Spain, France, Italy, Austria, Portugal, Sweden and the United Kingdom (groups 1, 2 and 3). As a consequence, only Greece still had an excessive deficit after the decisions taken in May. Among the 11 participating countries, only three (France, Luxembourg and Finland) had a gross debt ratio in 1997 which did not exceed the reference value. For other Member States, reference had to be made to the qualification that their debt ratios were 'sufficiently diminishing and approaching the reference value at a satisfactory pace' (Article 104(2b) EC Treaty). In the case of Germany, gross debt even slightly increased in 1997, but this was at least partly attributable to the effects of German reunification.

The interim period
Although 11 countries qualified for the budgetary criterion, it was obvious that convergence in the field of public finances was still rather fragile in a number of Member States (De Nederlandsche Bank, 1998). Therefore, it is worthwhile to compare the preliminary deficit figures used in May 1998 with the revised figures available. The two sets of figures display only minor differences (Table 3.2). Only in the case of Finland a slight increase of the 1997 deficit was there, while Denmark's surplus was revised downwards. The revised 1997 figures for Belgium, Greece, Ireland, Luxembourg, the Netherlands, Austria and Sweden were more favourable than the preliminary ones. In general, government budget balances improved further in 1998. As a result, the average budgetary deficit in the euro area declined from 2.5 per cent of GDP in 1997 to 2.1 per cent in 1998. Only in Luxembourg and Austria did the budgetary outcomes worsen somewhat in 1998. However, compared to the original deficit figures on which the May 1998 decisions were based, the picture still remained more favourable even in these two countries.

    Does this mean that public finances as far as budgetary deficits are concerned are on a sounder footing in the interim period compared to May 1998? For a fair judgement, one has to evaluate the development of the underlying budgetary positions. One way to do this is to adjust ordinary deficit figures for cyclical developments, that is, to calculate cyclically adjusted deficits. Table 3.4 compares the cyclically adjusted deficits in 1997 and 1998 according to the methodology used by the European Commission (European Commission, 1995). It is quite striking to note that, although budgetary outcomes taken at face value were more favourable in 1998 compared to 1997, cyclically adjusted deficits deteriorated in 1998 in several Member States. As a result the average cyclically adjusted budget balance slightly decreased in the euro area in 1998. Furthermore, the favourable development of budgetary deficits in 1998 was also highly attributable to lower interest rates as interest expenditures fell in most Member States as a percentage of GDP. This fall was partly a more or less 'earned' reward for some Members States more credible and sounder budgetary policies which reduced the risk premium. However, this is not the whole story as across the board interest rates were at historically low levels. The so-called cyclically adjusted primary balance excludes interest payments and therefore gives the best indication of the underlying budgetary position. Table 3.4 shows that, except for Germany and Finland, the cyclically adjusted primary balance deteriorated in all euro area Member States in 1998. This illustrates that although economic growth was quite strong and interest rates were rather low in 1998, in general budgetary positions did not achieve a sounder footing.

The exchange rate criterion

Compliance with the exchange rate criterion required ERM membership for at least two years. During the reference period the exchange rate must have fluctuated within the normal ERM fluctuation margins without devaluation against the currency of any other Member State and without major tensions. Although the ERM margins for most currencies were widened from ±2¼ per cent to ±15 per cent a reasonable interpretation of 'normal fluctuation margins' must imply that the exchange rate has remained within, or at least close to, the ±2¼ per cent margin. The requirement of absence of major tensions refers to the possibility of interventions or (substantial) interest rate adjustments. From Table 3.5 it follows that at the time of the assessment in March 1998 Italy and Finland had not been ERM members for the full two-year period. The Irish punt had fluctuated outside the ±2¼ per cent margin, which was partly determined by the trend in the pound sterling. Sweden and the United Kingdom were not members of the ERM. Greece joined the ERM on 16 March 1998. The conclusion of the Ecofin Council was that in all Member States except Greece, Sweden and the UK, exchange rate developments were not incompatible with the exchange rate criterion.

Table 3.4 Cyclically adjusted budget balances (% of GDP)

	1997	1998	Change*	Of which:	
				primary balance	interest payments
Belgium	-1.6	-1.4	0.2	-0.2	-0.4
Denmark	-0.6	-0.3	0.3	-0.2	-0.5
Germany	-2.2	-2.0	0.2	0.1	-0.1
Greece	-3.5	-2.4	1.1	0.6	-0.5
Spain	-1.7	-1.4	0.3	-0.2	-0.5
France	-2.4	-2.8	-0.4	-0.6	-0.2
Ireland	0.9	0.8	-0.1	-0.9	-0.8
Italy	-2.4	-2.3	0.1	-1.6	-1.7
Luxembourg	3.3	1.7	-1.6	-1.5	0.1
Netherlands	-0.9	-1.6	-0.7	-1.1	-0.4
Austria	-1.4	-2.1	-0.7	-0.7	0.0
Portugal	-2.0	-2.2	-0.2	-1.1	-0.9
Finland	-1.0	0.2	1.2	1.4	0.2
Sweden	0.2	2.1	1.9	1.1	-0.8
UK	-2.4	0.0	2.4	2.2	-0.2
Euro area	-2.0	-2.1	-0.1	-0.6	-0.5
EU	-2.0	-1.6	0.4	0.0	-0.4

Note: * Difference of 1998 and 1997 columns; minus sign implies a decrease.
Source: European Commission (1999).

The exchange rate of euro area currencies in the interim period
The stability of the euro area currencies within the ERM offers an indication of the success of EMU. Turbulence in international financial markets used to cause tension in the ERM by lifting the exchange rate of the Deutschmark and the other core currencies while pressing down the exchange rates of the peripheral currencies. In the interim period, exchange rate convergence was supported by the pre-announcement of the bilateral exchange rates to be used in determining the euro conversion rates. In May 1998 these rates were set equal to the ERM central rates for the participating countries.[5] The result was a smooth path of convergence (Figure 3.2). Indeed, from the decision on EMU participation until the start of monetary union and the launch of the euro no disturbances in ERM exchange rates happened, even though

Table 3.5 Exchange rates

	ERM member over past 2 years[a]	Fluctuation margin against other ERM currencies[b]	Money market interest rate differential against DM[c]
Belgium	Yes	-3.0; 2.5	-0.1; 0.5
Denmark	Yes	-3.4; 1.2	0.2; 1.1
Germany	Yes	-2.9; 2.2	n.a.
Greece	No	n.a.	n.a.
Spain	Yes	-2.1; 3.5	1.1; 5.2
France	Yes	-3.5; 0.6	-0.1; 0.9
Ireland	Yes	-4.8; 12.5	1.7; 3.2
Italy	25-11-96	-3.0; 2.5	2.1; 4.2
Luxembourg	Yes	-3.0; 2.5	-0.1; 0.5
Netherlands	Yes	-2.8; 2.8	-0.7; 0.2
Austria	Yes	-2.9; 2.2	-0.2; 0.4
Portugal	Yes	-2.3; 3.5	1.2; 4.6
Finland	14-10-96	-1.1; 3.6	-0.3; 0.1
Sweden	No	n.a.	n.a.
UK	No	n.a.	n.a.

Notes:
[a] No devaluation in ERM has taken place over the last two years before the examination (March 1996-February 1998). Therefore, no seperate column has been created in the table for this aspect of the exchange rate criterion. On 25-11-96 Italy again became a full member of the ERM after having indefinitely suspended foreign exchange intervention on 17-9-92.
[b] For each currency participating in the ERM a lower and upper limit has been set for the exchange rate against each other ERM currency in the reference period (expressed as a percentage point deviation from the bilateral central rates). The table shows the lowest of the lower limits and the highest of the upper limits. The movement against the Irish punt has been omitted, since otherwise the figures would mainly reflect the exchange rate movement of the Irish punt. n.a. = not applicable.
[c] This column shows for each Member State participating in the ERM the lower and upper limit for the 3-month interest rate differential against the German interest rate. n.a. = not applicable.
Source: EMI (1998).

international financial markets were very turbulent during the summer and autumn of 1998. In this period, the exchange rates of the currencies of the participating Member States were determined for over 95 per cent by the establishment of the EMU and the euro (De Grauwe, Dewachter and Veestraeten, 1998). It is illustrative that Finland, the only Scandinavian country participating in EMU, was hardly touched by the turbulence in financial markets, whereas the two Scandinavian 'outs', Sweden and Denmark, experienced downward pressure on their exchange rates. Also the collapse of the Italian government and the subsequent participation of the Communist Party in the Italian government did not cause uncertainty in financial markets. All in all, exchange rate developments suggest a strong market confidence in EMU. Markets also reacted favourably to the decisions on which countries were to participate in EMU.

Figure 3.2 Deviations from the DM-exchange rates
(weekly averages, %)

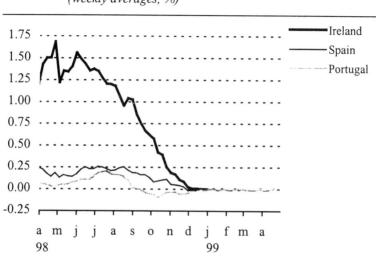

Legal convergence

The requirements on legal convergence are contained in Articles 108 and 109 of the EC Treaty. Article 108 lays down that national central banks must be completely independent when carrying out their ESCB-related tasks. Article 109 requires that, before the ESCB is established, legislation and other provisions relating to national central banks should be compatible with the EC Treaty and the ESCB Statute.

National central bank independence has institutional, personal and financial implications. Institutional independence implies that third parties are not allowed to approve, suspend, overrule or shelve decisions of national central banks. For example, governments are not allowed to issue instructions to national central banks. Personal independence requires that the term of office of the president and the other board members of the national central banks is at least five years. In addition, they can only be removed from office if they are no longer fulfilling the conditions required for the performance of their duties or if they are being guilty of serious misconduct. Regarding financial independence, it is stipulated that a national central bank must have enough financial resources to duly perform its ESCB tasks.

For the purpose of integrating national central banks into the ESCB, it is important to guarantee that the central bank legislation does not create any obstacles that might hinder national central banks in carrying out their ESCB-related functions. A governor of a national central bank cannot be obliged to take specified positions in the context of his or her membership of the Governing Council of the ECB.

The Convergence reports by the EMI and the European Commission and the reports of several national central banks identified a number of imperfections. By 1 January 1999, however, the central banks' independence and integration into the ESCB had been satisfactorily embodied in the national legislation of all 11 countries that have adopted the euro.

3. FUTURE APPLICATION OF THE CRITERIA

In the future the convergence procedure will be used to assess whether other EU Member States may adopt the euro. At present none of the remaining four EU countries (Denmark, Greece, Sweden and the United Kingdom) has plans to apply as early as 2000 but Greece, for example, is determined to apply for EMU membership in 2001. Taking a longer view, other countries may join the European Union in the future and consequently may wish to join the euro area as well. Hence, the qualification procedure will have to be applied again. Basic principles, such as equal treatment and transparency, imply that future assessments should be done in a similar way as the one in March 1998. On the one hand, the Treaty does not have separate provisions for the qualifying procedure after the start of Stage Three. On the other, it is also possible that future situations will be substantially different from that before the start of Stage Three. In any case it is vital that potential participants can enter the euro area as smoothly as possible without watering down the criteria. Below, we discuss the lessons that can be drawn from the assessment in March 1998 and, for the budgetary criterion, the experience with Ecofin Council decisions in the excessive deficit procedure, which has run annually from 1994 onwards.

Future interpretation of the inflation and long-term interest criteria

Three obvious options for calculating the reference value of the inflation criterion are the following:

1. the unweighted average of the inflation rates in the three countries with the lowest inflation within the European Union plus 1½ percentage points.
2. the euro area average (weighted).
3. the unweighted average of the inflation rates in the three countries with the lowest inflation within the euro area plus 1½ percentage points.

The first option is exactly equal to the definition of the reference value in the Treaty. Option 2 recognizes that the euro area is now a fact and may be considered as the core to which potential entrants must converge. In that option the weighted euro area average could be the reference value. The third option is to restrict the calculation to the members of the euro area rather than the EU. The three reference values can be found in Table 3.1. For 1996 they are not much different, ranging between 2.2 and 2.7 per cent. For 1997 and 1998, however, the difference is substantial: the euro area average comes out more than a percentage point lower than the other two options. However, if outliers in terms of inflation performance are excluded from the calculations, which is possible under the Treaty, the difference is less significant. For future years it may well be the case that in quantitative terms the options are nearly equivalent. The assessment in March 1998 applied the inflation criterion in a straightforward way, although other inflation indicators were taken into account. Therefore it seems preferable to apply option 1 to future entrants. Completely analogous to the inflation criterion, we argue that the same rule should be used in assessing future compliance with the interest rate criterion.

Future interpretation of the budgetary criterion

The interpretation of the budgetary criterion in future examinations may be based, from the viewpoint of continuity, on all previous examinations by the Ecofin Council which have taken place since 1994 in the so-called excessive deficit procedure. From these examinations it is clear that for government deficits the reference value of 3 per cent of GDP is a strict limit. The room for manoeuvre allowed in the Treaty has thus far not been used. For government debt values exceeding 60 per cent of GDP however, the case is less clear. Looking back, debt in countries with debt-to-GDP ratios over 100 per cent has not been judged excessive. This raises the question of how future cases should be dealt with.

To this end we examine the available evidence – final data, but no forecasts or projections for future years – by looking at so-called positive test cases. A country in a specific year of examination is considered a positive test case if (i) the deficit is below 3 per cent of GDP, (ii) the ratio of debt to GDP is above 60 per cent and (iii) the Ecofin Council deemed the deficit not excessive. Including the assessment in March 1998, 17 such cases can be identified and are listed in Table 3.6.[6]

Table 3.6 Future interpretation of debt criterion

Country (year t)[a]	Deficit ratio year t[b] (% of GDP)	Debt ratio year t[b] (% of GDP)	Number of years to reach 60% of GDP[c]
Ireland (1993)	2.3	99.0	30
Ireland (1994)	2.3	89.8	26
Ireland (1995)	2.4	85.5	27
Denmark (1995)	1.4	71.9	7
Ireland (1996)	0.9	72.8	6
Denmark (1996)	1.6	70.2	7
Netherlands (1996)	2.4	78.5	22
Belgium (1997)	2.1	122.2	33
Denmark (1997)	-0.7	65.1	1
Germany (1997)	2.7	61.3	7
Spain (1997)	2.6	68.8	20
Ireland (1997)	-0.9	66.3	2
Italy (1997)	2.7	121.6	61
Netherlands (1997)	1.4	72.1	7
Austria (1997)	2.5	66.1	12
Portugal (1997)	2.5	62.0	5
Sweden (1997)	0.8	76.6	7

Notes:
[a] A country (with specific year) is listed in this table if the deficit is below 3% of GDP and debt exceeds 60% of GDP, while it is judged by the Ecofin Council that the deficit in that year is not excessive.
[b] Figures as known at the time of the examination by the Ecofin Council.
[c] Technical calculations based on a constant deficit (the deficit in year t) and constant nominal GDP growth of 5% per annum.

For each positive test case the number of years to reach a debt ratio of 60 per cent of GDP is calculated. Underlying these simple and mechanical calculations is the assumption of a constant deficit at the level prevailing in the year used in the examination and, for reasons of simplicity and transparency, a constant rate of nominal GDP growth of 5 per cent per annum and no stock-flow adjustments, in all cases. Treating the debt ratio and the number of years to reach 60 per cent of GDP as a pair of observations for each positive test case, it is possible to depict all positive test cases as is done in Figure 3.3. For example, consider the two right-most points representing the test cases of Italy (1997) and Belgium (1997). The suggested interpretation is that, assuming unchanged fiscal policy, Italy is allowed to converge to 60 per cent of GDP in approximately 60 years while Belgium is allowed 'only' a little over 30 years, although the difference in the debt ratio is less than 1 percentage point. Points depicted relatively high in Figure 3.3 correspond to cases in which a country is allowed a relatively long time to converge.

The final step is to derive a so-called implicit reference curve. In our case, we draw the curve as close as possible to the upper-most points of the figure since we are looking for the 'loosest' interpretation, not a kind of average interpretation. Berndsen (1997) shows that this curve is non-linear. From Figure 3.3, it follows that the examination of Germany and Italy over the year 1997 results in the loosest reference curve.[7] The constant deficit corresponding to the implicit reference curve is 2.7 per cent of GDP. Hence this value for the deficit may be viewed as a lower bound for future application of the debt criterion. However, it is important to note that in the actual Ecofin decision additional commitments were negotiated for some countries with very high debt ratios. The results of these negotiations have not been incorporated in the method because of their forward-looking nature. Italy and Belgium have committed themselves to primary surpluses (budget balance excluding interest payments) of 5.5 and 6 per cent of GDP respectively. If they pursue policies in accordance with their commitments, they will move to the south-west in Figure 3.3 and converge towards the 60 per cent of GDP level much quicker than the reference curve would suggest.

Based on the track record of the Ecofin Council so far, we therefore conclude that highly indebted countries (debt ratio over 60 per cent of GDP) may comply with the budgetary criteria. Although the deficit criterion has been applied strictly, it seems that the debt criterion is no longer really binding: past misbehaviour over a longer term (that is, debt over 100 per cent of GDP) is therefore to a large extent discounted in favour of present, only recently established good behaviour: a relatively high fiscal deficit of 2.7 per cent is sufficient to pass the test.

Figure 3.3 Implied reference curve*

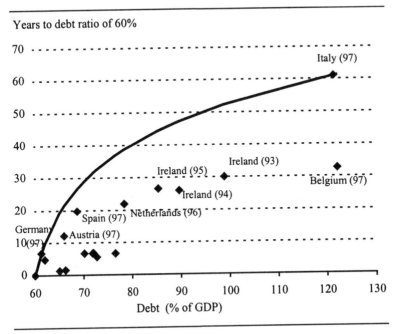

Note: * Based on data in Table 3.6.

Future interpretation of the exchange rate criterion

As in the case of the inflation and long-term interest rate criteria, there is not just one obvious way for the future interpretation of the exchange rate criterion. Basically, there are two options:

1. require both ERM-II membership for two years and respecting the 'normal' fluctuation margins without severe tensions (in particular no devaluation) in the review period.
2. 'actual' stability of exchange rate against the euro over two years.

Option 1 is the exchange rate criterion as it is formulated in the Treaty, where ERM-II is substituted for ERM-I. It combines the requirement of formal ERM-II membership with a yardstick for assessing actual exchange rate stability. Option 2 could be considered an effective weakening of the criterion, since the requirement of ERM-II membership is deleted. This leaves option 1, but with a realistic interpretation of its different aspects. In this respect, it is recalled from Section 2 that in May 1998 Member States were allowed to join EMU without literal compliance with the exchange rate criterion. It seems reasonable to regard ERM-II membership a prerequisite, but the two-year period is of less importance if there is substantial evidence of actual exchange rate stability. In particular, exchange rates should have fluctuated within or close to the ±2¼ per cent margin. The fact that Denmark has agreed to the narrow fluctuation margins of ±2¼ per cent within the formal band of ±15 per cent indicates that it interprets the exchange rate criterion in this way.

4. CONCLUSION

This chapter reflects the long-term logic behind the May 1998 decisions on participation in EMU. It concludes that – taking into account all available information one year later – the same countries would form a monetary union. Our assessment of inflation, interest and exchange rate performances in the interim period confirms the success of EMU. In sharp contrast to earlier similar episodes, the turbulence in global financial markets that occurred during the summer and fall of 1998 did not result in severe tensions in euro area financial markets. Therefore, it can be argued that the *de facto* start of Stage Three of EMU was in May 1998.

On the future interpretation of the convergence criteria it turned out that the inflation and interest rate criteria can be applied as before. The exchange rate criterion needs a minor adaptation: the requirement of ERM-II membership should replace the ERM-I requirement. For future applicants the crux will probably be to pass the budgetary test. In this chapter, a coherent method is worked out to assess budgetary performance in the light of former decisions of the Ecofin Council. Drawing on past decisions it follows that the deficit requirements are hard and the debt requirements are relatively soft: a deficit exceeding the 3 per cent reference value will probably disqualify a Member State from joining EMU, unless it results from either an unusual event outside the control of the country concerned or a severe economic downturn. As our analysis suggests, countries with a debt ratio over 60 per cent can be regarded as being in compliance with the budgetary criterion if the debt ratio is declining and the deficit is equal or below 2.7 per cent of GDP.

NOTES

1. Belgium, Germany, Spain, France, Ireland, Italy, Luxembourg, the Netherlands, Austria, Portugal and Finland.
2. See Szász (1999) for the ins and outs of the political and economic backgrounds of EMU.

3. In the period from 25 March until 2 May, governments had to decide their positions. Several, among them the German, French and Dutch governments, took advice from their respective central banks and consulted their national parliaments. See Deutsche Bundesbank (1998), Banque de France (1998) and De Nederlandsche Bank (1998).
4. One-off measures are defined as budgetary measures which affect budgetary outcomes in one year but which do not have a rebound in later years. Self-reversing measures are defined as budgetary measures which affect budgetary outcomes in one year at the expense (or benefit) of future budgetary situations.
5. Since the Danish krone, the Greek drachma and the pound sterling (all ECU component currencies) would not be converted into the euro, it was not possible to announce in advance the irrevocable euro conversion rates for the participating currencies.
6. Negative test cases (a country has the predicate 'excessive deficit' although deficit and debt are below their respective reference values) did not emerge in the period 1994–98 (and are not likely to emerge).
7. In the case of Germany it was explicitly recognized that the level of debt exceeded 60 per cent of GDP as a result of the assumption of debt directly related to German reunification.

PART TWO

Analysis of the Euro Area

4.   The Real Economy of the Euro Area

Ronald Albers, Martin Bijsterbosch and Focco Vijselaar

The emphasis in this chapter is on the performance of the real economy of the group of countries which in 1999 joined the euro area. This covers both long-term trends in economic growth, inflation and labour market performance, and short-term cyclical movements. Our analysis has an empirical and to a large extent descriptive character.

The first section of this chapter primarily focuses on price indicators for the euro area. After a brief look at nominal convergence between national economies, it highlights some stylized facts in the nominal sphere of the euro area as a whole. In the second section, we examine the degree of business cycle correspondence in the euro area and we discuss the relevance of this issue for monetary policy. In the final section, we discuss labour market developments, with an emphasis on structural unemployment. The focus in all these areas is on the extent to which the economies in the recently established euro area have become integrated and which structural problems remain to be overcome. In the final section we draw some conclusions.

1. PRICE INDICATORS

This section examines inflation convergence in the euro area and presents an overview of the available short-term price indicators for the euro area as a whole. It focuses on the general economic properties of these variables and presents some stylized facts. The first half of this section deals mainly with the available price indicators at the consumer level. The second part discusses price indicators at an earlier stage of the production cycle, which could be used to assess consumer price developments in the future. An analysis of the leading indicator properties of these and other variables with respect to inflation is presented in Chapter 5.

*Figure 4.1 Average inflation and inflation dispersion in the euro
            area, 1970-98 (%)*

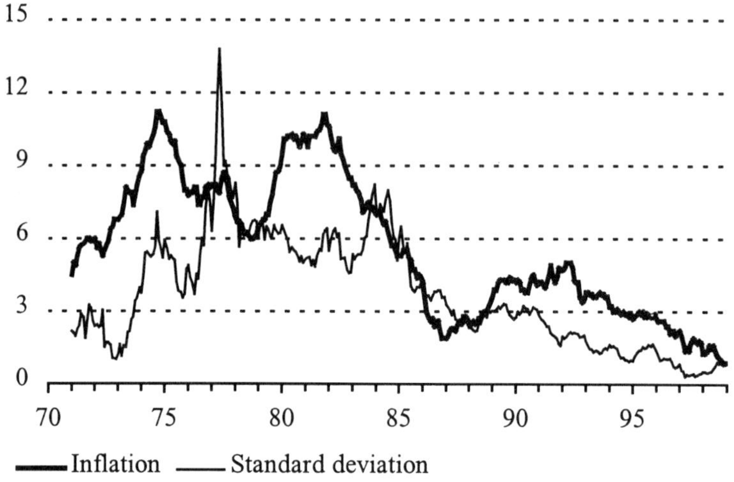

Inflation convergence

Since 1970, inflation rates of the group of countries that joined the euro area
in 1999 have converged considerably to a relatively low level (Figure 4.1).
This disinflation process was most evident during the 1980s, after the second
oil price shock had increased inflation to an average of around 10 per cent.
Except for an interruption around the beginning of the 1990s, the disinflation
process continued gradually in that decade, and in 1997 the average inflation
rate in the euro area reached the upper limit of price stability.[1] The
convergence of inflation is largely attributable to decelerating price increases
in countries with traditionally higher inflation rates, notably in Italy, Spain
and Portugal.

Structural changes seem to have contributed to the disinflation process,
especially during the 1990s. These changes relate to the disciplinary effect of
deregulated capital markets and increased international competition as a
result of the liberalization of trade flows. In addition, the sheltered sector of
the euro area economy witnessed a decline in the inflation rate due to the
tendency towards privatization and deregulation. The removal of different
kinds of indexation mechanisms may have led to a structural decline in the
upward pressure of the wage formation process on inflation. Finally, the
disinflation process may have been fostered by a greater emphasis on price

stability in macroeconomic policy and an increased degree of independence of central banks in the countries of the euro area.

HICP is relevant price index for euro area

Given the definition of price stability adopted by the ECB, which is based on the harmonized index of consumer prices (HICP), the MUICP (Monetary Union Index of Consumer Prices) and its sub-components play a major role in the analysis of inflation in the euro area. The MUICP is based on the aggregation of HICPs of individual member states and is published on a monthly basis. Moreover, member states publish consumer prices based on national definitions. The key difference between the national Consumer Price Index (CPI) and the HICP is that the latter is based on a smaller consumer basket in order to harmonize the national baskets. Excluded items are owner-occupied housing costs, education and healthcare spending. However, by eliminating these items from the HICP service inflation might be underestimated in the harmonized index as compared to the national index. These differences in coverage mainly explain the discrepancies between harmonized and national inflation rates. Although the ECB's definition of price stability is formulated in terms of harmonized consumer prices, the national CPIs continue to play an important role as a short-term indicator, as in most member states the national CPIs are released earlier than the HICPs and they tend to provide a reliable early indication of the harmonized figures in that month.[2]

Short-term movements in HICP due to limited number of sub-indices

The MUICP is usually broken down along two different lines: by consumption categories and by sectors. The first breakdown is based on the COICOP classification (Classification of Individual Consumption by Purpose) as defined by Eurostat (ESA95). Table 4.1 provides an overview of the contributions of the COICOP categories to HICP inflation in the euro area. In terms of weights in the index, three spending categories stand out as the most important. These are 'food and non-alcoholic beverages', 'housing and related expenses' and 'transport'. Among the categories with the largest weights, these three components also tend to exhibit the largest price fluctuations measured by their respective standard deviations. Therefore, these three components play a major role in explaining short-term inflation developments.

Table 4.1 COICOP breakdown of HICP inflation (%)

	Weight*	1996	1997	1998
1. Food and non-alcoholic beverages	18.5	1.8	0.9	1.4
2. Alcoholic beverages and tobacco	4.4	2.6	3.5	2.6
3. Clothing and footwear	8.9	1.9	1.0	1.0
4. Housing; water, electricity, gas and other fuels	15.8	2.8	2.8	1.0
5. Furnishing and household equipment	8.1	1.9	0.9	1.1
6. Health (paid by consumer)	0.9	2.9	4.5	3.9
7. Transport	16.2	2.7	1.5	0.2
8. Communications	1.9	2.2	-1.4	-1.0
9. Recreation and culture	9.8	1.2	1.3	0.9
10. Education (paid by consumer)	0.5	3.5	2.2	2.6
11. Hotels, cafes and restaurants	9.0	2.6	2.0	2.2
12. Miscellaneous goods and services	6.0	2.3	1.5	0.9
Overall index	100.0	2.2	1.6	1.1

Note: * 1998 consumer spending weights; the 1996 figures exclude France
on the sub-index level.

Tradables and non-tradables inflation: no convergence

The second breakdown is along sectoral lines, which is perhaps more suitable from an economic-analytic point of view. This breakdown basically comprises five components of HICP ('processed food', 'unprocessed food', 'energy', 'non-energy industrial goods' and 'services'), from which three additional items can be derived (Table 4.2). These three items are 'food' (from 'unprocessed food' and 'processed food'), 'industrial goods' (from 'energy' and 'non-energy industrial goods') and 'goods' (from 'food' and 'industrial goods').

Non-tradables or services inflation is generally higher than tradables or goods inflation. This stylized fact is also observed in the euro area, as is shown in Figure 4.2.[3] With the exception of two periods following the oil price shocks in the 1970s, which fostered tradables inflation and left non-tradables inflation relatively unaffected, inflation in the sheltered sector has been substantially higher than price increases in the open sector of the economy. These sectoral inflation differentials can be explained by the so-called Balassa–Samuelson hypothesis (Balassa, 1964; Samuelson, 1964), which states that technological progress is more rapid in the traded goods

Table 4.2 Sectoral breakdown of HICP inflation (%)

	Weight*	1996	1997	1998
Goods	65.4	1.8	1.1	0.6
Food	22.9	2.0	1.4	1.6
Unprocessed food	9.4	1.9	1.4	2.0
Processed food	13.5	2.0	1.4	1.4
Industrial goods	42.5	1.7	1.0	0.1
Energy	8.8	2.4	2.8	-2.6
Non-energy	33.7	1.5	0.5	0.9
Services	34.6	3.1	2.4	2.0
Underlying inflation				
Excl. seasonal food and energy	86.9	2.2	1.5	1.3
10% trimmed mean	90.0	2.3	1.6	1.3
Overall index	100.0	2.2	1.6	1.1

Note: * 1998 consumer spending weights.

sector than in the non-traded goods sector. The relatively rapid productivity growth in the tradables sector will exert an upward influence on nominal wages in the entire economy, because wage claims in the non-tradables sector tend to follow those in the tradables sector. This dual productivity growth generates an inflation differential between sectors, which tends to increase aggregate inflation. This also suggests that inflation tends to be higher in catch-up economies, such as Portugal and Spain. If this is true, inflation differentials within the euro area may persist in the future (Alberola and Tyrväinen, 1998). This will complicate the conduct of monetary policy, which is not able to reduce inflation differences between countries or sectors.

Here, economic policies at the national level must come into the play. For example, governments could pursue structural policies in order to foster productivity growth in the services sector. Moreover, policies aimed at increasing wage differentiation might loosen sectoral wage linkages. This may reduce inflation pressures generated by wage claims in the services sector. A second explanation for the higher inflation rate in the services sector may be the relatively high incidence of regulated prices in this sector. This explanation is complementary to the Balassa–Samuelson thesis, which relates to market-determined prices. Examples of generally regulated prices

*Figure 4.2 Tradables and non-tradables inflation in the
euro area, 1970-98 (%)*

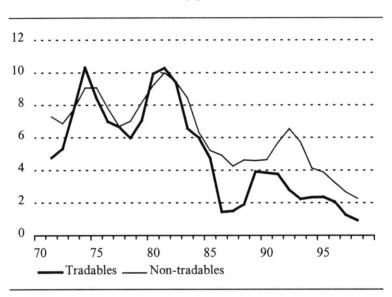

are housing rents or healthcare prices. These components generally tend to
exhibit above-average price increases.

Core inflation

In addition to the consumer price inflation measures presented above, the
concept of underlying or core inflation is often used by central banks to
capture the general trend in inflation more accurately. An important
limitation of the headline rate is its susceptibility to specific, one-off
disturbances, which are unrelated to the inflationary process. In constructing
an underlying inflation measure, a number of different approaches can be
adopted. The most common approach used by central banks is based on
adjustment by exclusion. In this technique the most volatile sub-components
(usually unprocessed food, energy and/or policy-induced price changes) are
removed from the aggregate price index by attaching zero weights to them
while rescaling the sub-indices that are retained. A second approach is based
on the removal of outliers by using statistical techniques. This involves, for
example, the calculation of trimmed means or weighted medians (see, for
example, Cecchetti, 1997).[4] A third, more recent approach explicitly refers to
economic theory, and defines underlying inflation as that component of

headline inflation which has no long-run impact on real output growth (Quah and Vahey, 1995; Fase and Folkertsma, 1997; Gartner and Wehinger, 1998).

For the euro area, only underlying inflation measures based on the first two approaches are calculated on a regular basis by the ECB (Table 4.2). The first is the MUICP excluding seasonal food and energy and the second is a 10 per cent trimmed mean inflation rate. However, due to the short history of the series it is too early to know whether these series provide valuable additional information.[5]

Prices at an earlier stage of the production cycle

In addition to consumer price developments, the analysis of price developments of goods and services at an earlier stage of the production cycle may help assess the direction of consumer price inflation in the future (see also Chapter 5). These are, among others, producer price statistics, commodity price indices and labour costs. These indicators at the euro area level should be treated with caution as they have a varying degree of coverage and comparability. However, improvements can be expected as a result of the Regulation on the European System of National and Regional Accounts 1995 (ESA95) and of the Regulation on Short-Term Statistics from 1999 onwards. In the remaining part of this section, we show economic characteristics of some of these variables at an area-wide level.

Producer selling prices (PPI) are relatively close to consumer prices in the production cycle.[6] Therefore, producer prices may contain information on consumer price developments in the near future. This is confirmed in Chapter 5, which deals with the leading indicator properties of different variables with respect to inflation in the euro area. In contrast to the strong correlation between the PPI and the CPI, the relation between commodity prices and the CPI is quite weak.[7] Another important feature of price dynamics is the different degree of volatility of price series depending on the stage of the production cycle. In general, price volatility in earlier stages of the production cycle is higher than at the end (Van Gelderen, 1913). Price rigidity at the consumer level appears to be a common characteristic of many European economies (Van Bergeijk, Haffner and Waasdorp, 1993).

Price indicators for the labour market

As to the labour market, the most relevant price indicator is unit labour costs (ULC).[8] Figure 4.3 shows the evolution of ULCs and of producer prices in the industrial sector of the euro area. The shaded areas in the figure are periods of economic slowdown; the boundaries of these areas are based upon

Figure 4.3 Unit labour costs and producer prices in the euro
area, 1980-98 (annual change, %)

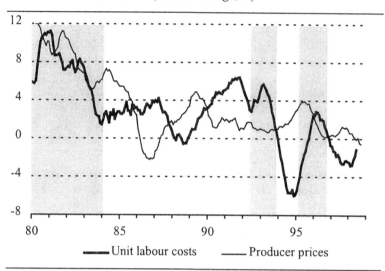

Note: Shaded areas denote periods of economic slowdown.

the turning points in the industrial production cycle. Developments in ULCs
in the euro area appear to be highly sensitive to the business cycle. As soon
as the economy enters a period of economic slowdown, labour productivity
growth falls and ULCs tend to accelerate. In the literature, the procyclical
behaviour of labour productivity has been explained by technological shocks,
labour hoarding and increasing returns to scale during a cyclical upturn (Heer
and Linnemann, 1998).

Although changes in labour productivity growth tend to account for short-
term fluctuations in ULCs, wage costs are also determined by movements in
contractual wages. A key empirical question is the cyclical behaviour of real
wages, as both procyclical and countercyclical behaviour can theoretically be
justified. Standard textbook models usually imply countercyclical wages by
assuming that firms are on a downward-sloping labour demand schedule and
that nominal wages are slow to adjust during downturns. On the other hand,
real wages might be procyclical because of the presence of countercyclical
mark-ups or imperfect competition.[9] In addition, increasing labour market
tightness during upturns might account for a (lagged) procyclicality of real
wages. The existing empirical evidence on this subject is clearly mixed
(Abraham and Haltiwanger, 1995; Brandolini, 1995).

Figure 4.4 Cyclicality of real wages in the euro area, 1985-98
(standardized cyclical components)

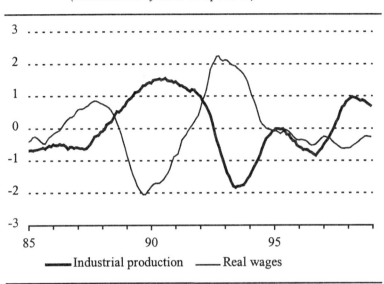

A brief look at the cyclicality of real wages in the euro area is presented in Figure 4.4, which shows the detrended and normalized components of industrial production (as a proxy for the economic cycle) and of real hourly wages.[9] These cyclical components were obtained after filtering out the trends of the deseasonalized series, based on an HP filter as used in Section 2. Clearly, the cyclical trough from the beginning of the 1990s was preceded by a cyclical upturn in real wage growth. However, in other periods, such as the second half of the 1980s, the relationship seems less straightforward. The maximum correlation coefficient (in absolute terms) between the cyclical components of industrial production and real wages was found at a lead of five months and was −0.53 over the period 1985–98. The correlation coefficient without a lead or lag appeared to be −0.41. These findings indicate that real wages in the euro area might be countercyclical. The recession at the beginning of the 1990s has shown that exuberant wage increases can contribute to the severity of an economic downturn.

2. SYNCHRONICITY OF BUSINESS CYCLES

The prospects for EMU have been hotly debated. Much of the discussion has dealt with risks stemming from lack of fiscal discipline, structural rigidities in European labour and product markets, and asymmetric shocks in participating countries (see, for example, Bayoumi and Eichengreen, 1996; Feldstein, 1997; Kenen, 1995; Obstfeld, 1998; Obstfeld and Peri, 1998; Von Hagen and Eichengreen, 1996). This section focuses on the latter risk. To that end, we investigate the synchronicity of business cycles of E(M)U member states. Synchronicity of business cycles might provide evidence on the relative importance of asymmetric shocks – as only in absence of significant asymmetric shocks would we expect to find a high degree of synchronicity.

Synchronicity of business cycles is an important prerequisite for a smooth functioning of EMU. If cyclical divergences are substantial, it will be hard to adopt a monetary policy stance that suits both the euro area as a whole and the participating countries individually. This could lead to a sub-optimal outcome for the common monetary policy through economic and political tensions (Von Hagen, 1997). If, on the other hand, cyclical divergences are only slight, then the loss of independence in monetary policy matters may not constitute a great cost to the participating countries.

The US is often considered the archetypal case of a well-functioning monetary union and is therefore sometimes used as a benchmark for EMU (Bayoumi and Eichengreen, 1993; Bayoumi and Prasad, 1997; Chamie, Deserres and Lalonde, 1994). The mean cross correlation of output of 19 individual states in the US amounted to 0.75 over the period 1978–92 (Hess and Shin, 1998). This compares to 0.63 for the mean cross correlation of GDP of EMU countries over the same period, providing a snapshot of the degree of cyclical convergence reached in Europe. A more thorough analysis of cyclical convergence in Europe is presented below.

Identifying business cycles

Following Jacobs (1997), we define business cycles as more or less regular patterns in fluctuations in economic activity. In this chapter, business cycles are determined for production at constant prices in manufacturing industry (called industrial production henceforth).[11] Though manufacturing output accounts for only about a fifth of GDP in most industrialized countries, it accounts for a larger part of cyclical fluctuations in GDP. Cycles in industrial production can thus be more clearly observed than in GDP data. Furthermore, data on industrial production are available on a monthly rather than a quarterly basis. Lastly, data on quarterly GDP are not available for a relatively large number of relevant countries before 1980, whereas most countries do have monthly data on industrial production starting from the early 1970s. The use of industrial production data thus enables us to examine the impact of the oil crises.

'The' business cycle is an elusive concept which is hard to determine empirically. Following standard practice, time series of aggregate economic fluctuations may be decomposed into four components: a trend, a cycle, seasonal fluctuations, and an irregular error term (Zarnowitz, 1992). The method of trend determination is a critical factor in the estimate of the 'cyclical' component, which remains after filtering out the trend of a deseasonalized series. In order to examine the sensitivity of our results to the choice of filter, we have used two methods of trend determination: a segmented linear trend as applied by Berk and Bikker (1995), and several Hodrick–Prescott (HP) filters (Hodrick and Prescott, 1997).[12] The results proved to be highly robust for the specific detrending method used (Vijselaar and Albers, 1999). We present the results using a HP filter with a relatively high value of the smoothing parameter λ of 10^6, which renders a relatively stable pattern of the estimated trend.

A point to note is that business cycles of countries can coincide, even if trend growth rates differ substantially. Thus, divergences in absolute growth rates need not imply major differences in growth cycles. Recent developments in Germany and the Netherlands are a case in point. Germany has had a significantly lower rate of GDP growth over the past six years than the Netherlands, whereas the degree of cyclical co-movement has remained high (Vijselaar and Albers, 1999).

Results

We measure the degree of synchronicity from the contemporaneous correlation between a country's business cycle and that of the euro area. The euro area aggregate is used as benchmark, because monetary policy of the ECB is directed at the euro area as a whole. In order to avoid an overestimation of the correlation coefficient, we have to exclude the individual country from the aggregate if the country is participating in EMU. This implies that the coherence with the euro area will be larger than suggested by the correlation coefficients – in particular for large countries. Hence, our results underestimate rather than overestimate the degree of convergence in the euro area.

Figure 4.5 shows the reference cycle for industrial production in the euro area covering the period 1973–98. An alternation of major and minor cycles is apparent. Table 4.3 gives a chronology of turning points for all identified cycles. Peaks for major cycles are in 1974, 1979 and 1990, and troughs in 1975, 1983 and 1993. It is too early to decide whether the upper turning point identified in early 1998 constitutes the top of a major or a minor cycle. The average duration of an expansion (28.2 months) clearly exceeds that of

Figure 4.5 Manufacturing production reference cycle,
1973-98 (standard deviations)

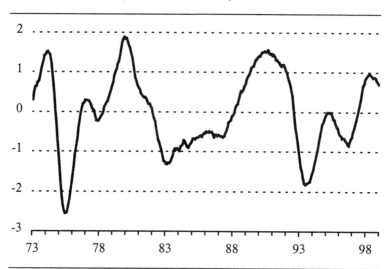

Table 4.3 Growth cycle turning points for the euro area:
Industrial production, 1973-98

Peak	Trough	Duration peak to peak (months)
1974:2	1975:6	-
1976:2	1977:11	34
1979:11	1983:2	35
1986:4	1986:8	77
1990:8	1993:6	52
1995:5	1996:9	57
1998:3		34

a downturn (19.8 months), a well-known characteristic of post-war business cycles in other advanced economies (Zarnowitz, 1992).

Table 4.4 shows the contemporaneous business cycle correlations of individual countries with the euro area. Most EMU participants have a business cycle that is highly synchronous with that of the euro area. Germany shows a much lower correlation coefficient over the last sub-period. This can be attributed to a phase shift, triggered by German reunification (Vijselaar

Table 4.4 Contemporaneous correlation coefficients of industrial production in the euro area[a]

	1973-97	1979-97	1987-97
Austria	0.87	0.88	0.86
Belgium	0.89	0.87	0.91
France	0.97	0.96	0.97
Germany[b]	0.75	0.72	0.58
Ireland	0.55	0.55	0.52
Italy	0.79	0.75	0.67
Luxemburg	0.67	0.59	0.88
Netherlands	0.91	0.90	0.95
Portugal	0.69	0.67	0.83
Spain	0.71	0.80	0.82
Greece	0.74	0.82	0.78
Sweden	0.29	0.46	0.57
United Kingdom	0.58	0.58	0.56
United States	0.60	0.45	0.20

Notes:
[a] Denmark and Finland are not included due to lack of data for the 1970s.
[b] Before 1991: West Germany.

and Albers, 1999). The correlation coefficients of Spain and Portugal increase over time, whereas Italy shows a reverse development. No clear-cut answer can be given why this is the case. Spain and Portugal may have gained from their accession to the EU in 1986, which intensified trade and financial links with the rest of the euro area. Moreover, though all three countries frequently devalued against the deutsche mark, only the Italian lira suspended from ERM following the currency crises of 1992–93. Ireland shows a somewhat lower synchronicity with the euro aggregate, despite membership of ERM since 1979 – a pattern which is consistent over time. This may be attributed to the relatively close trade links of Ireland with the UK and the US. Moreover, the catch-up effect in Irish economic growth in the 1990s may cloud the picture as well.

As to the out-countries, only Greece shows a high degree of synchronicity. The correlation coefficients for Sweden and the UK are somewhat lower. The US and euro area cycles are clearly not synchronous in the two sub-periods. Synchronicity over the whole period (1973–97) is still considerable, which can probably be explained by the impact of the oil crises that affected all industrial countries simultaneously. The low degree of synchronicity with the US provides a check that the coherence between cycles is a European rather than a more widespread phenomenon.

Thus, even though cyclical divergences among participating states can and no doubt will occur, the integration of the EMU group in its present composition is such that it is in no immediate danger of breaking down due to major divergences in growth paths. These conclusions corroborate findings by others (Artis and Zhang, 1997; Christodoulakis, Dimelis and Kollintzas, 1995).

Some qualifications are in order. As Bayoumi and Eichengreen (1996) point out, with the approach chosen here it cannot be ascertained whether observed output movements reflect disturbances or responses. Attempts to distinguish between demand and supply shocks using VAR models indicate that there is evidence of a core and periphery distinction within the euro area (Bayoumi and Eichengreen, 1993). However, studies which specify various types of shocks (such as monetary and non-monetary shocks on the demand side) find a less clear-cut core–periphery distinction, although the symmetry of shocks across EMU countries does not appear to be particularly strong (Bhattacharya and Binner, 1998; Chamie, Deserres and Lalonde, 1994). Given the inherent problems of robustness with VAR models and the different results presented in the studies mentioned above, it remains an open question whether or not differences in the nature of (asymmetric) shocks are important for the euro area economy.

The evidence given here indicates that even the most pronounced asymmetric shock of the past decades – German reunification – had no major impact on the degree of cyclical convergence in Europe. Moreover, the inclusion of the 'periphery' countries (Ireland, Italy, Portugal and Spain) in EMU seems to make no substantial difference to the degree of cyclical convergence.[13] To the extent that the ECB takes the business cycle into account, its policy should not be different from what it would have been with a monetary union consisting of fewer countries. In this respect, we might thus be optimistic about the prospects for EMU.

As arguably the most important out-country, the UK has a clearly different cyclical pattern than the euro area. If the UK still had a different cyclical pattern upon entering EMU, this would complicate the conduct of monetary policy by the ECB. To the extent that monetary policy influences the business cycle, a more synchronous British business cycle could be achieved if the UK joined ERM-II, reducing the costs of entering EMU. On the other hand, as Frankel and Rose (1997) argue, participation in EMU itself may lead to further business cycle symmetry by boosting trade integration. Countries which join EMU may therefore satisfy optimum currency area criteria *ex post* better than *ex ante*.

3. LABOUR MARKET

In contrast to the substantial degree of cyclical convergence noted in the previous section, the labour market in the euro area is still highly segmented. The existence and persistence of substantial real wage differentials among participating countries and the consistently low degree of migration across national borders testify to this segmentation (OECD, 1999b). The development of both employment and unemployment in the euro area is the net result of often divergent movements within individual countries, which to a large extent are driven by country-specific institutional factors. Since the early 1970s, unemployment figures in the euro area have risen considerably. The development of unemployment has compared unfavourably to North America and Japan. The same is true of employment growth. In the absence of successful remedies the large number of unemployed in combination with an ageing population will increase the burden on the working population going into the next century. The existing structural rigidities have given rise to a large number of labour market policy actions and recommendations to reduce the large social costs of high unemployment (OECD, 1994a,b). In general, the key objective of labour market reform is to increase the flexibility of the labour markets. Our main concern here, however, is with monitoring actual labour market performance in the euro area, rather than with policy recommendations.[14]

Development of unemployment

Table 4.5 presents unemployment rates for the euro area and its 11 constituent countries. It gives evidence of the high level of broad inactivity in the euro area, which has increased substantially since the early 1970s. Unemployment rates show persistent differences in levels among countries. Some mainly large countries (including Germany, France and Italy) show persistently high and rising unemployment rates during the 1990s. Other countries, including Ireland, the Netherlands and Spain, have made considerable progress in reducing inactivity during the last decade, although in most cases the level of unemployment is still high. A drawback of the official unemployment data is that they tend to underestimate the broad level of inactivity, due to factors such as early retirement, training schemes and discouraged workers (OECD, 1995; Conference Board Europe, 1997).

The net participation rate is a concept that yields better comparable measures of the degree of inactivity. Table 4.6 presents estimates of the net participation rate of the labour force in EU Member States according to two definitions. The first definition refers to all jobs, while the second definition excludes small jobs of fewer than 11 hours a week.[15] There is a considerable

Analysis of the Euro Area

Table 4.5 Unemployment rates, 1960-98 (%)

	1960-73	1974-80	1981-90	1991-97	1998
Belgium	2.1	5.6	9.7	8.8	8.8
Germany*	0.7	2.9	6.0	7.9	9.4
Spain	2.6	6.5	18.5	21.1	18.8
France	2.0	4.7	9.2	11.5	11.7
Ireland	5.6	8.3	14.7	13.4	7.8
Italy	5.1	6.3	8.8	10.8	12.2
Luxembourg	0.0	0.9	2.5	2.6	2.8
Netherlands	1.1	5.4	8.5	6.2	4.0
Austria	1.7	1.8	3.4	3.9	4.7
Portugal	2.4	6.1	7.0	6.0	4.9
Finland	2.0	4.6	5.3	14.2	11.4
Euro area	2.4	4.9	9.1	10.7	10.9
Denmark	1.1	4.9	7.4	8.0	5.1
Greece	4.6	2.1	6.4	8.7	9.6
Sweden	1.9	1.9	2.7	8.0	8.2
United Kingdom	1.9	4.3	9.8	9.0	6.3
EU	2.3	4.6	9.0	10.3	10.0
US	4.9	6.8	7.1	6.2	4.5
Japan	1.3	1.9	2.5	2.8	4.1

Note: * 1960-90: West Germany.
Sources: EU countries: Eurostat; US and Japan: OECD.

differentiation of participation rates among countries, which does not fully mirror differences in headline unemployment. For instance, the German labour market performance with respect to the net participation rate is better than its unemployment record. Note that the incidence of small part-time jobs accounts for only a small part of the variation in net participation rates among EU Member States, with the notable exception of the Netherlands, where the difference between the two measures is by far the largest for the euro area economies, reflecting a high incidence of part-time work. In the Netherlands a continued rise in part-time employment was accompanied by sizeable reductions in registered unemployment during the 1990s. One should, however, be cautious in drawing too firm a lesson for policy since the example of the Netherlands also indicates that in terms of the net

Table 4.6 Net participation rate of population aged 15-64, 1997 (%)

	Employed total	Employed	Employed < 11 h/wk
Belgium	67	66	1
Germany	64	61	2
Spain	48	47	1
France	59	58	1
Ireland	56	55	1
Italy	51	50	0
Luxembourg	60	59	1
Netherlands	67	60	7
Austria	67	66	1
Portugal	63	63	1
Finland	62	60	2
Euro area	58	57	1
Denmark	76	71	5
Greece	55	55	0
Sweden	67	65	2
United Kingdom	70	66	4
European Union	60	58	2

Source: Eurostat, *Labour Force Survey.*

participation rate the labour market performance of the country is not much better than that of other euro area economies.

Structural unemployment

A key concept in the analysis of unemployment is the 'structural' rate of unemployment. As noted above, a well-known phenomenon of European economies and of the euro area as a whole is the persistent upward trend in unemployment since the early 1970s, reaching a higher level after each recession. In explaining the observed pattern of rising actual (and almost certainly also structural) unemployment rates, attention in the literature has focused on the combination of a sequence of adverse (external) shocks and labour market rigidities, leading to unemployment persistence or hysteresis (Blanchard and Summers, 1987; Blanchard and Katz, 1997; Røed, 1997).[16]

The factors behind structural unemployment include institutional and demographic factors, such as the age structure of the labour force, labour mobility, schooling and skills levels, insider–outsider problems, the incentive structure posed by the social security system, minimum wage legislation, the strictness of employment protection, trade union power, and the degree of flexibility of labour market regulations. An important explanation for hysteresis effects is that a long period of high unemployment tends to lead to the long-term unemployed either losing their skills or becoming less effective in their search for jobs, leading to a higher rate of structural unemployment.

In the course of the 1990s various labour market reform measures have been initiated to reduce the level of structural unemployment. These include liberalization of wage formation, increased working-time flexibility, reductions of the level and duration of unemployment benefits, reductions of high marginal effective tax rates on low-income labour, job-search assistance and an easing of employment protection legislation. These efforts, however, have not yet led to a generally accepted 'best-practice' approach and progress has been uneven both between countries and between different policy areas (OECD, 1997c).

The rate at which the labour market exerts no upward or downward pressure on the inflation rate is called the non-accelerating inflation rate of unemployment (NAIRU). The NAIRU is an operationalization of the concept of structural unemployment which is of particular interest in the context of monetary policy (Gordon, 1997). Obtaining empirical estimates of the NAIRU is fraught with difficulties because of persistence effects and because estimates are characterized by large margins of error (Staiger, Stock and Watson, 1997). We made rough estimates of the level of the NAIRU in the euro area for a number of periods using the following specification. Changes in world commodity prices were added to the regression to control for the effects of external supply shocks:

$$\Delta \pi_t = \alpha + \beta U_{t-i} + \gamma X_{t-i} + \varepsilon \qquad (4.1)$$

where π is inflation, U is the unemployment rate and X is the percentage change in world commodity prices. Adding a lagged term of changes in the unemployment rate, following Franz and Gordon (1993), enables us to test the significance of so-called hysteresis effects, that is, the phenomenon that negative shocks to unemployment tend to produce permanent increases in the unemployment rate:

$$\Delta \pi_t = \alpha_1 + \beta_1 U_{t-i} + \gamma_1 \Delta U_{t-i} + \delta X_{t-i} + \varepsilon' \qquad (4.2)$$

A value of the hysteresis coefficient φ ($\varphi = \gamma_1/(\gamma_1 + \beta_1)$) of 1 indicates full hysteresis (a change in unemployment is fully reflected in a subsequent rise in structural unemployment). If $\varphi = 0$ there is no hysteresis, while a value of φ between 0 and 1 implies partial hysteresis.

Table 4.7 NAIRU estimates for the euro area (%)

Euro area[a]	1972-79	1980-90	1991-98
NAIRU	5.1	9.2	10.1
95% confidence interval	3.3 - 6.9	8.1 - 10.3	7.6 - 12.6
φ	0.77	0.87	0.78
Individual member countries		1997 [b]	1996 [c]
Belgium		11.6	7.7
Germany		9.6	8.9
Spain		19.4	18.0
France		10.2	9.7
Ireland		11.0	11.4
Italy		10.6	9.7
Luxembourg		-	1.7
Netherlands		5.5	6.3
Austria		5.4	6.0
Portugal		-	5.8
Finland		11.3	10.2

Sources: [a] Own estimates; [b] OECD; [c] IMF (1999).

The top panel of Table 4.7 presents estimates of the NAIRU in the euro area between 1972 and 1998 for three sub-periods. The table shows almost a doubling of structural unemployment since the 1970s, to around 10 per cent in the most recent sub-period. These figures highlight the extent to which labour market problems burden the economy of the euro area. Persistence effects are found to be large, but full hysteresis is rejected.[17] In other words, a large part of but not the entire rise in structural unemployment in the euro area during the 1980s and 1990s can be ascribed to hysteresis.

The bottom panel of Table 4.7 shows recent OECD and IMF estimates of the NAIRU for individual countries in the euro area. The considerable differences in the level of structural unemployment among member states stand out. In the course of the 1990s a number of big countries experienced further increases in headline (and probably also structural) unemployment while other, mainly small, countries performed significantly better and registered declines in unemployment rates (IMF, 1999).[18] To the extent that these differences reflect the outcome of different labour market policies among countries, this suggests that structural reforms of the labour market have favourable effects on structural unemployment. It is very difficult, however, to assess the quantitative impact of specific policy measures.

Our analysis thus confirms the generally supported notion that unemployment in the euro area is mainly of a structural, not a cyclical, nature, which implies that demand management can do little to improve the situation. This underscores the need to tackle the problem with structural labour market reforms, whereby progress so far has been uneven among countries.

Figure 4.6 Labour market and cyclical fluctuations in the
euro area, 1985-98

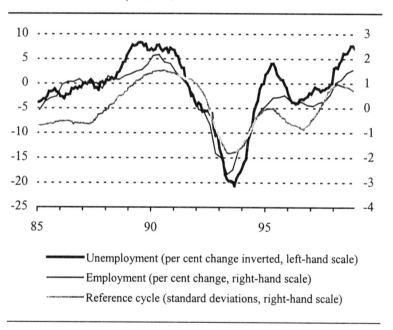

Unemployment (per cent change inverted, left-hand scale)
Employment (per cent change, right-hand scale)
Reference cycle (standard deviations, right-hand scale)

Cyclical behaviour of labour market variables

Turning to the cyclical as opposed to the structural behaviour of labour market variables, changes in employment, unemployment and the number of unfilled vacancies show a high degree of correspondence with the reference

Figure 4.7 Employment and unfilled vacancies in the euro area,
*   1989-98*

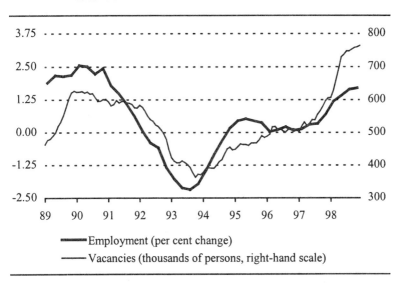

Employment (per cent change)
Vacancies (thousands of persons, right-hand scale)

Note: Due to missing data on vacancies for France, Italy and Ireland the euro
area series for both variables were computed excluding these counties.

cycle for the euro area (Figure 4.6). The behaviour of these three variables is
roughly procyclical, although it appears that labour market response is
asymmetric in various stages of the cycle. In the early phase of an upswing
an increase in employment growth and a decline in unemployment tend to
occur with a lag. In the beginning of the downturn, unemployment declines
with a shorter lag. This asymmetric pattern may reflect the fact that
enterprises react quicker to nominal wage rigidities in a downturn than in an
upturn. This suggests that wage responses to a cyclical downturn should be
swift, in order to be able to mitigate the negative impact on employment.
Over the cycle, the number of unfilled vacancies closely follows employment
growth (Figure 4.7). This pattern is consistent with labour hoarding theories
of the business cycle (Millard, Scott and Sensier, 1999).

4. CONCLUSIONS

The real economies of the 11 countries of the euro area have converged to a large extent. This convergence is evident with respect to inflation rates and the high degree of business cycle conformity. At the same time, some divergence of inflation rates among participating countries will probably remain, due to differences in cyclical position and catch-up effects. With respect to the labour market, however, hardly any convergence has taken place as is evident from the substantial and persistent differences in participation rates among countries. The high level of structural unemployment (estimated to be around 10 per cent) and substantial labour market rigidities remain major economic challenges facing the euro area.

APPENDIX 4.A. DATA SOURCES

The time series used were taken from a variety of official sources. These include data from national statistical agencies and Eurostat and data published by national central banks, the ECB and the European Commission. An absolute scarcity of real economy statistics and problems with the comparability of data across countries pose a number of problems, which at the time of writing are particularly severe in the area of labour market statistics. In addition, differences in coverage and definitions, the base-year used, the method of seasonal adjustment, frequency and timeliness of publication hamper the computation of euro area aggregates. In addition, structural breaks in the series compound the difficulties with obtaining data which cover a sizeable time span. At the time of writing, harmonized Eurostat figures on real economy variables were mainly limited to inflation and unemployment data, while national accounts data were being revised in the run-up to the introduction of the new European System of Accounts (ESA95) in all EU Member States as of 1999. A problem with the available harmonized series is that they tend to have a short history. In order to compute euro area aggregates we used an 80 per cent threshold value: if for a certain indicator figures are available which cover 80 per cent of the total weight, a euro area average has been computed. For the various time series considered, we used different weighting schemes to compute euro area aggregates. Table 4.A1 presents the weights for GDP, industrial production, and private consumption (used to weight consumer price inflation).[19]

Table 4.A1 Country weights

	GDP	Industrial production	Private consumption
Belgium	3.9	3.4	4.0
Germany	30.6	34.9	30.0
Spain	10.2	9.7	10.5
France	21.2	19.2	21.0
Ireland	1.1	1.5	1.0
Italy	20.3	19.3	21.2
Luxembourg	0.2	0.2	0.3
Netherlands	5.5	4.6	5.5
Austria	3.1	3	2.9
Portugal	2.3	2.6	2.3
Finland	1.6	1.6	1.4
Euro area	100.0	100.0	100.0
Euro area	78.8	81.7	78.4
Denmark	1.6	1.3	1.4
Greece	1.8	1.1	2.1
Sweden	2.3	2.2	2.0
United Kingdom	15.5	13.7	16.2
European Union	100.0	100.0	100.0

Source: Eurostat, *Statistics in Focus.*

NOTES

1. See Chapter 9 for the ESCB's definition of price stability.
2. For more information on improving the quality and comparability of consumer price indices, see Eurostat and University of Florence (1996).
3. Figure 4.1 is based on a disaggregation of implicit consumption deflators of Germany, France, Italy, Spain, the Netherlands and Belgium.
4. A trimmed mean involves the removal of outliers in the cross-sectional distribution of price changes, usually by trimming a percentage of the tails of the distribution. A weighted median is the central point in the price distribution, that is, half of the weighted prices rise less and the other half more than the central rate. The difference with a simple weighted average is that the weighted median accords a progressively lower weight to more extreme values towards the ends of the distribution of price changes.
5. For a study on the added value of different underlying inflation indicators for the Netherlands, see Bijsterbosch (1998).

6. The series we use are based on an aggregation of industrial domestic selling prices and are calculated on a monthly basis. It is recognized that this is an imperfect measure, as price movements of goods that are exported to a member state within the euro area are not taken into account. However, to take account of this, detailed data on producer export prices would be needed which are not available.

7. While the maximum correlation coefficient between the CPI and the PPI was found to be 0.86 (at a lead of one month), the maximum correlation coefficient between the CPI and the HWWA commodity price index (in euros) is 0.25 (also at a lead of one month). The maximum correlation coefficient between the PPI and the HWWA index is 0.54 (at a lead of two months). These correlations refer to the period January 1982–December 1998.

8. The ULC series used here are based on the industrial sector only, in view of measurement problems of productivity growth in the service sector. ULCs are calculated on a quarterly basis.

9. Mark-ups might be countercyclical as firms may reduce mark-ups in booms to build up the customer base or because the ability of firms to collude may be greater during downturns (Rotemberg and Woodford, 1991).

10. Real wages were deflated by using national CPIs.

11. Though not presented here, GDP data were analysed as well. The results were similar to those of the analysis with industrial production data.

12. The HP filter contains a 'penalty' parameter, λ, that determines the extent to which the trend tracks the development of the original series. The higher λ, the more stable the remaining trend, and the less erratic the residual cycle. The standard value for λ when using monthly data is 14,400, which, however, yields a relatively volatile trend component.

13. This conclusion is corroborated by the finding that exclusion of the 'peripheral' countries from the benchmark does not significantly change the results.

14. The exact level of the unemployment rate depends on the definitions used (OECD, 1997d). Movements over time, however, show much the same pattern, irrespective of which set of unemployment data is used.

15. Because of problems with the measurement of small part-time jobs the comparability of the figures on the net participation rate of people working 11 hours or more is probably highest.

16. So-called 'skill-biased' technical change has been found to account for an important part of wage inequality increases in Europe, but it is unlikely to be a major factor behind the rise in total unemployment (Berman, Bound and Machin, 1998).

17. The estimated level of the NAIRU in the euro area compares unfavourably to the 5–6 per cent recently found by Gordon (1997) for the United States. In addition, Franz and Gordon (1993) find a much lower value of the persistence term φ of around 0.38 for the United States in the period 1973–90.

18. In future research, a closer examination of the structure of unemployment at a disaggregate level would be in order, taking into account factors such as skill differentiation across and within industries, the evolution of the age composition of the labour force, and the duration of unemployment. For lack of adequate data, such analyses were beyond the scope of this contribution.

19. The differences between GDP and industrial production weights reflect differences in industrial structure. Base years used are 1994 purchasing power parity quantity weights as published by Eurostat (1997). Purchasing power parity weights are to be preferred over current exchange rate weights since they take into account existing differences in price levels and make it possible to clearly distinguish volume and price movements (Winder, 1997a). Regular updating of the weights as new figures become available is advisable to avoid the compounding of index number problems.

5. Indicators for Inflation

Niek Nahuis and Carlo Winder

The principal and overriding objective of the ESCB is to maintain price stability in the euro area. This objective is specified as a year-on-year increase of the Harmonized Index of Consumer Prices (HICP) for the euro area of below 2 per cent. In addition to the definition of price stability, the monetary policy strategy of the ESCB consists of two key elements (see also Chapter 9). The first one is that a prominent role is attributed to money, recognizing that inflation is essentially a monetary phenomenon in the long run. Money will not be the sole guide for the monetary policy of the ESCB, however. Therefore, as the second element of its strategy, the ESCB will monitor a range of economic and financial indicators in order to assess monetary developments in the euro area (ECB, 1999d). The evaluation of these indicators will be based on their expected influence on future price developments, recognizing that price stability is a medium-term concept. Hence, monetary policy must have a medium-term focus.

A key question is how to assess monetary developments in the euro area and, in particular, prospective inflationary pressures. One option is to use large-scale macroeconometric models for forecasting and simulation exercises (see Box 5.1). An advantage of this approach is that in principle the whole economy is modelled, so that the relevant interactions and feedback mechanisms between the key macroeconomic variables are accounted for. Drawbacks are that building large-scale macroeconometric models is very time-consuming and that a large number of specific assumptions have to be made (Sims, 1980). As an alternative, one may opt for a more limited set-up, focusing on the specific issue to be addressed. In the present context, this boils down to an assessment of the inflationary prospects. In this regard, one may try to identify a set of indicators which possess leading indicator properties with respect to future inflation. One can also analyse equilibrium concepts like the NAIRU. In the same vein, the Non-Accelerating Inflation Rate of Capacity Utilization (NAIRCU) can be defined. If capacity utilization is higher than the NAIRCU, inflation is expected to accelerate.

Box 5.1 EUROMON: a multicountry model for Europe

One of the trends in structural model building over the past decades has been the growing interest in multicountry modelling. This development is related to the increased degree of interdependence between national economies and the importance of international policy coordination. Within Europe, the establishment of EMU has given an impetus to modelling the interdependencies between European countries. Obviously, a tool is needed for monetary and fiscal policy analyses, both at a national and an area-wide level. A multicountry model yields also the opportunity to trace the differences and similarities between the individual countries, for instance in terms of monetary transmission mechanisms and responses to external shocks. Against this background, the Econometric Research and Special Studies Department of De Nederlandsche Bank developed a structural multicountry model for Europe, EUROMON. A first version was presented in Boeschoten et al. (1996), while the most recent version is documented in De Bondt et al. (1997).

In the present version of EUROMON eight European countries are modelled, namely Germany, France, Italy, Spain, the Netherlands, Belgium, the UK and Denmark. A distinctive feature of EUROMON compared to existing multicountry models is that the model structure of the large countries is the same as those for the smaller countries, so that fiscal and monetary policy issues can be analysed in a fairly detailed way. Another important feature of EUROMON is that portfolio models are used to describe the private sector's financial asset holdings. This approach enables a fuller analysis of monetary policy transmission, since substitution processes between different types of financial assets are endogenised and non-labour income flows are explicitly related to the stock of financial assets. For a comprehensive discussion the reader is referred to De Bondt *et al.* (1997).

For an adequate assessment of the monetary developments it is advisable not to restrict oneself *a priori* to one of these methodologies. The use of different tools yields useful information and leads to a more comprehensive picture of the monetary developments in the euro area. At present, this argument is particularly relevant since the establishment of EMU constitutes a structural change. In line with the Lucas critique it is an open question whether econometric relationships remain valid after the start of Stage Three, since significant changes are likely to occur in the economic, monetary and financial environment. In this chapter we will therefore follow two approaches to assess inflationary prospects in the euro area. First, we will analyse the leading indicator properties of a series of potential indicators with respect to future inflation. Next, we will estimate the NAIRCU for the euro area.

1. LEADING INDICATORS OF INFLATION

Data and methodology

In this section we assess the usefulness of ten potential indicators of future inflation. These variables can be classified into four categories:

- variables that have a more or less direct impact on the development of consumer prices, like the nominal effective exchange rate of the euro and producer prices;
- variables reflecting current or future tensions in the real part of the economy, which may lead to higher inflation. We consider the output gap (see also Bolt and Van Els, 1998) and the business cycle indicator constructed by De Nederlandsche Bank (Berk and Bikker, 1995). We measure the output gap here as the differential between industrial production and its trend, identified with the aid of the HP filter;
- monetary aggregates: M1, M3 and credit to the private sector.[1] These variables have a less direct impact on inflation than the variables in the former two categories (European Central Bank, 1999d). Under the assumption that the monetary indicators possess leading indicator properties for future inflation, it is therefore to be expected that the lead-time of monetary aggregates will be longer;
- financial market prices: the long-term interest rate (yield on ten-year government bonds), the yield spread (the differential between the long-term interest rate and the three-month interest rate) and share prices. These variables partly reflect expectations of future inflation held by private agents. A change of these expectations will generally be manifested quickly in financial prices (see also Berk, 1998b).

Our dataset refers to aggregates of the five largest countries of the euro area (Germany, France, Italy, Spain and the Netherlands).[2] We employ monthly data and the sample period is 1975:1–97:12. Inflation is measured as the percentage change of consumer prices on an annual basis. We also use the year-on-year growth rates for the potential indicators, except the output gap,

Box 5.2 Possible pitfalls of VAR analyses

From a methodological point of view, it is useful to dwell for a moment on possible pitfalls with the interpretation of the results of a VAR analysis. Absence of predictive power does not necessarily mean that the indicator is of no use to monetary authorities. It may simply reflect that the indicator is already used in conducting monetary policy. This can be illustrated with the following example taken from Woodford (1994). Suppose that inflation is determined by a relationship of the form

$$\pi_{t+1} = s_t + u_t + \varepsilon_{t+1}$$

with π_{t+1} inflation in period $t+1$, s_t an indicator observed at date t, u_t a control variable of the monetary authorities chosen at date t, and ε_{t+1} a mean-zero random variable not forecastable at date t. The variables on the right-hand side of the equation are assumed to be mutually independent. The variance of inflation is minimized by the policy rule $u_t = -s_t$. If this rule is followed, a regression of inflation on the indicator (or on the control variable) will asymptotically yield a zero coefficient. Obviously, it would be incorrect to advise the authorities to stop monitoring the indicator, since the optimal choice of the control variable depends on the value of the indicator. If the empirical results indicate absence of causality, the recommendation must be that the monetary authorities should continue their policy. If in the past the indicator was actively used, they must maintain this policy. If the indicator was not used, the absence of causality is an indication not to incorporate this information. In other words, monetary authorities should maintain the status quo.[3]

the business cycle indicator, the long-term interest and the yield spread, for which the levels have been analysed.

In order to analyse the leading indicator properties of the variables mentioned above, we use a Vector Auto-Regression (VAR) modelling strategy. VAR models can be seen as reduced form specifications of an underlying large structural model and are especially useful to investigate the dynamic interactions between the variables (Zellner and Palm, 1974). Here we analyse bivariate VAR models. For each indicator, we consider a system of two equations, in which both inflation and the indicator are related to their realizations.[4] The VAR framework allows us to assess the predictive performance of the indicators with respect to future inflation in two ways (see Box 5.2). First, using Granger causality tests, we examine whether there is evidence of causality between inflation and the indicator. Second, we analyse the impulse response function of inflation resulting from a shock in the indicator.

Within the conceptual framework of VAR modelling it is important to take proper account of the time series properties of the data, as they determine the precise form of the VAR model to be examined. In particular, careful attention has to be paid to issues of stationarity and cointegration, which are crucial to the validity of statistical inference. In the empirical analysis, we therefore first test for non-stationarity of the variables. We find that inflation displays non-stationary behaviour. In case of stationarity of the indicator, a VAR model for the change in inflation and the level of the indicator is investigated. If the indicator is non-stationary, cointegration with inflation may occur, that is, a long-run relationship between the two variables is present. If cointegration cannot be rejected, the VAR model is reformulated as a Vector Error Correction (VEC) model. This model is a system of two equations which relate the changes of inflation and the indicator to the error correction term and lagged changes of inflation and the indicator. If cointegration is rejected, a VAR model for the changes in both inflation and the indicator results. Hence, three cases can be distinguished:

A. Indicator is stationary. A VAR model for the change in inflation and the level of the indicator is investigated.
B. Indicator is non-stationary; cointegration between inflation and the indicator is present. In this case a VEC model has been analysed.
C. Indicator is non-stationary; cointegration between inflation and the indicator is absent. In this case, a VAR model for the changes in both inflation and the indicator has been examined.

Empirical results

As a first step in the empirical analysis we tested for (non-)stationarity of the individual series and the possible existence of a long-run relationship with inflation. Table 5.1 summarizes the findings. The results of this (co)integration analysis are discussed in detail in the appendix. The integration analysis shows that most variables, including inflation, are non-stationary. The only variables which prove to be stationary are the output gap, the business cycle indicator and the yield spread, leading to the conclusion that these variables are not apt as indicators of future inflation, since the random walk behaviour of inflation cannot be related to the development of these indicators. The other seven potential indicators display

Table 5.1 Summary of findings of the (co)integration analysis

Variable	Stationarity	Cointegration with inflation	Resulting model type*
Inflation, π	No	-	-
Narrow money, $\dot{M}_1$	No	No	C
Broad money, $\dot{M}_3$	No	No	C
Credit, $C\dot{R}$	No	Yes	B
Long-term interest rate, r_l	No	No	C
Yield spread, $r_l - r_s$	Yes	-	A
Nom. eff. exchange rate, $\dot{e}_{eff}$	No	Yes	B
Producer prices, $\dot{p}_a$	No	Yes	B
Share prices, $\dot{p}_{eq}$	No	No	C
Output gap, GAP	Yes	-	A
Business cycle ind., $CONJ$	Yes	-	A

Note: * A: VAR model for the change in inflation and the level of indicator;
B: VEC model;
C: VAR model for change in both inflation and the indicator.

non-stationary behaviour. The cointegration analysis to investigate whether for these variables a long-run relationship with inflation exists, shows that in three out of the seven cases (credit to the private sector, nominal exchange rate changes and producer price changes) cointegration is present. The long-run relationships found are plausible from an economic point of view. As shown in the appendix, a one-percentage point higher growth of credit to the private sector will ultimately lead to a 1.1 percentage points higher inflation. An appreciation of the euro of 1 per cent leads in the long-run to a 0.5 percentage points lower inflation rate, while an increase of producer prices will have an almost equiproportional impact on inflation.

The results of the integration and cointegration analysis determine the precise form of the VAR model, which must be used to investigate the causal relationships between inflation and the potential indicators. The conclusions are summarized in the final column of Table 5.1. For the output gap, the business cycle indicator and the yield spread, a VAR model for the change in inflation and the level of the indicator needs to be considered (case A). A VEC model has to be analysed (case B) for credit growth and the relative change in the effective nominal exchange rate and of the producer prices. For the remaining four potential indicators a VAR model for the change in inflation and the change in the indicator is considered.

The estimated VAR and VEC models are used to determine the causal relationships, if any, between inflation and the indicator. Several possibilities may arise. The indicator may have predictive power with respect to future inflation, but it may also be possible that inflation leads the development of the indicator. Inflation and the indicator may also affect each other with a lag (bidirectional causality). Obviously, if a variable has predictive power for future inflation, it is also important to know whether we have a feedback from inflation on the development of the indicator. In case of a VEC model, causality may be effective via the deviations from the long-run relationship (long-run impact) and/or via the lagged changes of the variables (short-run impact). In our analysis, separate tests for both types of causality are carried out. The combined hypothesis of causality via both the long-run relationship and the short-run adjustment processes is also tested. If cointegration is not present, there is no steady state relationship between inflation and the indicator, and causality can only manifest itself via the short-run adjustment processes.

Table 5.2 presents the values of the Wald statistics for the null hypothesis that causality is not present, together with their *p*-values. Probabilities lower than 0.05 imply that the null-hypothesis has to be rejected, and hence, that causality is present. Strong evidence of causality from the indicator to inflation is found for the variables, which are cointegrated with inflation (credit growth and changes of the nominal effective exchange rate and of producer prices). The relevant channel of causality concerns particularly the deviations from the long-run relationships. In all three cases a highly significant value for the Wald statistic is found. Only in the case of changes in producer prices is causality via short-run adjustment processes significant. An interesting result is that feedback causality from inflation to these indicators is not present, though producer prices constitute a borderline case.

The other potential indicators may only affect inflation temporarily. For none of these variables do we find evidence of significant causality from the indicator to inflation. In three cases (M1, M3 and the long-term interest rate), the empirical results indicate that inflation causes the development of these indicators. For the remaining four potential indicators (yield spread, share prices, output gap and the business cycle indicator) no significant causality is found at all, casting doubts on their usefulness for the monetary authorities. In summary, only three variables appear to possess useful leading indicator properties with respect to future inflation, namely credit growth, changes in the nominal effective exchange rate and producer prices changes. These variables are cointegrated with inflation with a plausible long-run relation-

Table 5.2 Results of causality analysis

	k^a	Indicator causes inflation			Inflation causes indicator		
		Total^b	Long run^c	Short run^d	Total^b	Long run^c	Short run^d
$\dot{M}_1$	(4)	-	-	6.71 (0.08)	-	-	10.01 (0.02)
$\dot{M}_3$	(4)	-	-	6.44 (0.09)	-	-	11.62 (0.01)
$\dot{CR}$	(2)	9.43 (0.01)	12.81 (0.00)	1.68 (0.20)	3.01 (0.22)	1.62 (0.20)	0.90 (0.34)
r_l	(2)	-	-	2.58 (0.11)	-	-	12.24 (0.00)
$r_l - r_s$	(2)	-	-	1.42 (0.23)	-	-	0.42 (0.52)
$\dot{e}_{eff}$	(2)	7.32 (0.03)	12.14 (0.00)	0.85 (0.36)	2.57 (0.28)	3.37 (0.07)	0.46 (0.50)
$\dot{p}_a$	(3)	33.07 (0.00)	10.30 (0.00)	18.9 (0.00)	7.77 (0.05)	3.01 (0.08)	3.94 (0.14)
$\dot{p}_{eq}$	(2)	-	-	1.22 (0.27)	-	-	3.23 (0.07)
GAP	(4)	-	-	3.22 (0.36)	-	-	4.37 (0.22)
CONJ	(5)	-	-	8.87 (0.11)	-	-	8.77 (0.12)

Notes:
Wald-statistics; p-values in parentheses. The tested hypothesis is absence of causality.
[a] The order of the VAR model in levels.
[b] Distribution $\chi^2(k)$.
[c] Distribution $\chi^2(1)$.
[d] Distribution $\chi^2(k-1)$.

ship, while there is strong evidence of unidirectional causality from the indicator to future inflation. These three indicators will therefore be analysed further below.

Further analysis

From a policy point of view it is not only important to know which variables are leading indicators with respect to future inflation, but also to have an impression of their lead time. The question therefore arises how quickly inflation will react to a shock in the indicator. Our cointegration results, for instance, show that a 1 percentage point higher growth of credit to the private sector ultimately leads to a 1.1 percentage points higher inflation rate. The question naturally arises what 'ultimately' means and with what speed the adjustments will take place. We address these questions using impulse response simulations.

Figure 5.1 presents the impulse response functions, which show the effects of a one standard error shock in the indicator on inflation and the indicator itself. We use a time horizon of 60 months. For the case of credit growth, however, we employ a horizon of 200 months, since the adjustment processes are not fully realized after 60 months. The figure shows that the impact on inflation resulting from the shock in the indicator is distributed rather smoothly over time. For the credit growth case, for instance, inflation will be 0.1 percentage points higher after 12 months. The impact on inflation is gradually rising and after 24 months one-third of the ultimate effect will be realized. Figure 5.1 shows also that the adjustment processes in case of a shock in the other two indicators take place more quickly.

In order to analyse the lead time of the three indicators in more detail, we have calculated which part of the ultimate change in inflation resulting from the shock in the indicator will be realized for several choices of the time horizon. Table 5.3 reports these shares for the 3, 6, 12 and 24 months time horizons, while the last column gives the median lag, that is, the number of months needed to accomplish 50 per cent of the total change in inflation.

The growth of credit to the private sector appears to be an indicator of inflation in the longer term. Even after 24 months only 26 per cent of the ultimate change of inflation is effected and the median lag is equal to 4½ years. The other two indicators have a much more direct impact on inflation. In the case of a shock in the nominal effective exchange rate, more than 50 per cent of the total change in inflation is realized within 12 months, while a change in the producer prices has an even more immediate impact on inflation. After three months more than 60 per cent of the total change in inflation is already realized, while the total adjustment has been completed after one year. For the median lag a value of only two months is found, so that producer price changes have a lead time which is rather short. The impulse response analysis thus suggests that the growth of credit to the private sector is a leading indicator for longer-term inflationary prospects. Nominal effective exchange rate changes are useful for medium-term

purposes, while producer price changes are appropriate as a short-term
indicator of future inflation developments.

Figure 5.1 Results of impulse response simulations (%)*

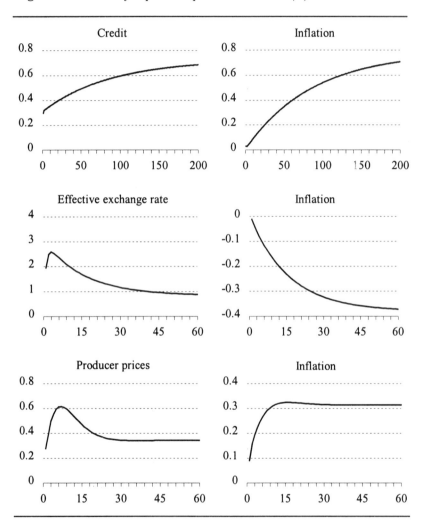

Table 5.3 Realized part of total adjustment of inflation for
different time horizons (%)

	3 months	6 months	12 months	24 months	Median lag*
$C\dot{R}$	5	8	14	26	54
$\dot{e}_{eff}$	16	31	54	80	10
$\dot{p}_a$	62	84	102	102	2

Note: * Months. Shocks in percentage changes.

2. ESTIMATING THE NAIRCU

This section deals with the usefulness of capacity utilization as a measure of inflationary pressure. This variable is related to the output gap and the business cycle indicator, which have been analysed above. The focus here is different, however. Instead of evaluating leading indicator properties we estimate an equilibrium rate of capacity utilization, which is defined as the level that is consistent with a stable inflation rate. This so-called NAIRCU (non-accelerating inflation rate of capacity utilization) was first introduced by McElhattan (1978).

Data for capacity utilization of the available production installations are compiled by national statistical agencies on the basis of quarterly surveys among industrial firms. Due to the short reporting lag and the high correlation with industrial production, capacity utilization plays a major role in the analysis of short-term economic trends (Corrado and Mattey, 1997). Because of the relation with production, capacity utilization can be considered as a proxy of the demand for the goods of a country. A change of capacity utilization implies a shift of the aggregate demand curve.

In a small open economy, capacity utilization of the main trading partners is also relevant, because imports can reduce bottlenecks. This implies that the relation between demand and inflation is weaker in a small open economy, like the Netherlands, than in a relatively closed economy like the euro area.

Research on the NAIRCU mainly deals with the United States. McElhattan (1985) estimates the NAIRCU in the US to be approximately 82 per cent, but with a fairly wide 95 per cent confidence interval of 5 percentage points. More recent studies, such as Bauer (1990), Garner (1994) and Emery and Chang (1997), find similar results. Bauer finds a NAIRCU of 81.4 per cent for the sample period 1953–89. Using different sample periods his point estimate lies between 80 and 81.9 per cent, while the confidence interval ranges from 4.3 to 4.9 per cent. Garner estimates the NAIRCU for different periods between 1963 and 1993. His estimates of the Stable Inflation Rate of Capacity Utilization vary from 80.8 to 82.9 per cent. Emery and Chang find an estimate of the NAIRCU that ranges from 81 to 83.2 per cent. However, they do no take supply variables into account, resulting in a bias towards zero of the estimated coefficients. By contrast, Franz and Gordon (1993) do not find a significant NAIRCU for the US. They equate the NAIRCU with the mean of capacity utilization, which is 81.7 per cent in the period from 1973 to 1990. They also estimate a NAIRCU for Germany. Here their NAIRCU is significant at a level of 84.7 per cent for this period. This study is the only one that concentrates on a European country. Nowadays the euro area is the relevant area for the monetary policy of the ESCB, so there remains a gap in the empirical literature. This section tries to fill this void.

Data and model specification

Empirical research on the NAIRCU essentially uses a standard natural rate version of the Phillips curve, to which typically supply variables have been added.[5] Following Gordon (1997) our model consists of three elements: (i) the inertia in the price adjustment process; (ii) the demand indicator and (iii) supply variables.

The inclusion of lagged inflation rates in the model reflects inertia in the price adjustment process. The basic idea is that this accounts for the entire process of dynamic price adjustment consisting of both the formation of expectations and delayed effects of real factors.[6] Here we focus on capacity utilization as the demand indicator. Besides the demand variable, we also include variables related to the supply side of the economy. The supply side also influences the inflation rate and ignoring this would lead to a bias in the estimated coefficients of the other variables. To take account of this we add to our model two variables that influence the costs of manufacturers. These are the price of raw materials (expressed in ecus) and the exchange rate of the ecu versus the dollar.

As a preliminary analysis we run unit root tests for all variables. Consumer prices, prices of raw materials and the ecu-dollar exchange rate are I(2). These variables will enter the equation as the first difference of the annual change. Capacity utilization is I(0), implying that it fluctuates around a constant long-term average (no time trend). The considerations above lead to the following empirical specification:[7]

$$\Delta\pi_t = \Sigma\beta_i\Delta\pi_{t-i} + \gamma(CU_t - CU^*) + \Sigma\delta_i\Delta p_{rm,t-i} + \Sigma\phi_i\Delta e_{t-i} + \varepsilon_t \qquad (5.1)$$

where: π inflation rate
       CU capacity utilization rate
       CU^* NAIRCU
       p_{rm} annual change in the price of raw materials
       e annual change in ecu-dollar exchange rate
       Δ difference operator

Empirical results

Estimation of (5.1) by non-linear least squares yields directly the NAIRCU, along with its standard error.[8] We estimated (5.1) both for the euro area and for a narrower aggregate, which we will label the core group, for which longer time series are available.[9] The core group comprises Belgium, France, Germany and the Netherlands. This enables us to estimate the equation for the core group using quarterly data from 1980 onward, whereas for the euro area the sample period starts in 1987. Table 5.4 presents the results.

The highly significant coefficients of the deviations of capacity utilization from its natural rate indicate the importance of capacity utilization as a determinant of inflation. This close relationship is probably a result of the low degree of openness of these two areas. Imports are thus limited, so the link between production and demand at home should be close.

One other main finding is the relatively narrow confidence interval around the NAIRCU estimates. For the euro area the 95 per cent confidence interval of the NAIRCU ranges from 81.5 to 83.3 per cent. The width of the confidence interval for the NAIRCU for the core group is comparable to that of the euro area.[10] These intervals are considerably smaller than the intervals found by McElhattan (1985) and Bauer (1990), which are 4–5 per cent.

The inertia effect is limited in the core group and the euro area. For the core group we are even unable to reject the hypothesis that the lagged inflation rates are jointly zero. As a result, the long-term effects, which include the inertia effect and the short-term effect of $(CU-CU^*)$ on inflation are almost equal. The (long-term) effect can be illustrated as follows: an increase of 1 per cent of capacity utilization for one quarter leads to an increase in the inflation rate of 0.05 per cent in the euro area and 0.07 per cent in the core group. So if this increase lasts for 20 quarters the inflation rate in the euro area will be permanently 1 per cent higher. The difference of the impact on inflation of capacity utilization between the core group and the euro area suggests that the short-term supply curve in the group core is flatter than the euro area (Lucas, 1973). A possible explanation for this difference could be the greater credibility of monetary policy in the countries of the core group, which results in a larger impact on output of unexpected price movements. Furthermore, because capacity utilization is a survey outcome,

Analysis of the Euro Area

Table 5.4 Empirical results

	Core group 1980:3-96:4			Euro area 1987:2-96:4		
		t-stat[a]	p-value		t-stat[a]	p-value
(CU-CU*)	0.047	4.7	0.000	0.067	5.4	0.000
NAIRCU	84.7	0.5		82.4	0.5	
$\Delta p_{rm,t}$	0.012	5.1	0.000	0.009	2.9	0.004
$\Delta p_{rm,t-1}$	0.007	3.9	0.002	0.007	5.4	0.004
Δe_{t-1}	0.033	5.9	0.000	0.021	3.3	0.000
L-t effect[b]	0.050			0.068		
Test $\beta_i = 0$[c]		1.3	0.308		2.5	0.048
R^2(adj)	0.72			0.55		
LM test	10.53		0.032	3.44		0.487

Notes:
[a] Newey-West t-statistics. Standard error for NAIRCU.
[b] Permanent effect on inflation of a one per cent increase in capacity utilization for one quarter (including inertia).
[c] Test of the hypothesis that all β_i are zero. F-statistic.

some measurement errors can be expected. Aggregation of individual country data reduces the variation of these errors, so the downward measurement error bias is smaller.

The level of the NAIRCU of the euro area turns out to be almost equal to that of the US. Due to the higher average level of capacity utilization in the core group its NAIRCU is 84.7 per cent, compared to the euro area's NAIRCU of 82.4 per cent. Two explanations for this difference could be given. The first is that the countries of the core group use the available production capacity more efficiently. The second is that the difference is the result of (unknown) cultural habits, which result in a more pessimistic view of entrepreneurs in South European countries.

The stability of the NAIRCU in the euro area

The relation between capacity utilization and inflation may change over time. Some authors conclude that the relation between capacity utilization and inflation has become more diffuse since 1982 (Cecchetti, 1995; Emery and Chang, 1997). They argue that because the share of the manufacturing sector in the economy in total output has declined, capacity utilization refers to an increasingly smaller part of the economy. Therefore, capacity utilization may become less representative of economy-wide developments. Another explanation they give is the increased openness of the economy and the decrease in trade barriers. Imports may relieve domestic demand pressures more often than before. Both factors could lead to a weakening of the relation between capacity utilization and inflation.

A related question is the stability of the level of the NAIRCU. For the United States there is no convincing evidence of a substantial shift of the NAIRCU (Garner, 1994; Gordon, 1998). However, innovations, better management techniques and the improved functioning of product and labour markets may have led to a more efficient use of the capital stock. Furthermore, increased competition, for example stimulated by the establishment of the internal market and the deregulation of product markets, may have strengthened this process by reducing entrepreneurs' pricing power. Consequently, entrepreneurs may start to increase prices by a higher level of demand than in the past. These factors could have lead to an upward shift of the NAIRCU.

We test the stability over time of the relationship between capacity utilization and inflation by dividing the sample period into two equal parts denoted by the subscripts 0 and 1 in specification (5.2). This results in the following equation:

$$\Delta \pi_t = \Sigma \beta_i \Delta \pi_{t-i} + \Sigma \delta_i \Delta p_{rm,t-i} + \Sigma \phi_i \Delta e_{t-i} + \varepsilon_t$$
$$+ \gamma_0 (CU_t - CU_0^*) \qquad\qquad (5.2a: 1980:3-88:4)$$
and $\qquad\qquad + \gamma_1 (CU_t - CU_1^*) \qquad\qquad (5.2b: 1989:1-96:4)$

This equation allows different values of the parameters γ and CU^* across the two periods and gives an impression of the stability of the NAIRCU. Because of the greater data availability, this exercise has been done for the core group only. Table 5.5 reports the results.

Our results indicate that the NAIRCU is relatively stable over time. For the US a similar result is obtained by Gordon (1998), who found a relatively stable NAIRCU compared to the NAIRU, despite the considerably greater variance of capacity utilization compared to that of unemployment. Unfortunately, he gives no explanation for this difference. The effect of capacity utilization on inflation also hardly changes between the two sub-samples. The 95 per cent confidence interval for the second sample remains small, approximately between 2.0 and 2.8 per cent.

The results give some insight into the processes that are expected to influence the relationship between demand and inflation. First, although trade

Table 5.5 The NAIRCU in the core group

		1980:3-88:4			1989:1-96:4	
		t-stat*	*p*-value		*t*-stat*	*p*-value
(CU-CU)*	0.046	2.5	0.016	0.050	5.1	0.000
NAIRCU	84.5	0.7		84.8	0.6	

Note: * Newey-West *t*-statistics. Standard error for NAIRCU.

flows of individual countries have increased considerably over the last 20 years, the greater part of these flows consists of intra-European trade. As a consequence, the link between demand and production in the euro area as a whole is still very close. However, the openness of the euro area and the US is comparable, so the difference in confidence intervals between these areas remains puzzling. Second, the argument that the declining share of the industry has weakened the relationship seems at first glance not very solid. As in the US, the service sector of the euro area has grown significantly, but the relationship between demand and inflation has hardly changed. However, the transformation to a services economy has proceeded further in the US so this effect may become more appreciable in the (near) future. A further possibility is that our sample is too short to pick up such an effect.

Our findings for the euro area and the core group suggest that the relationship between capacity utilization and inflation is stable. Capacity utilization appears to be a useful indicator for assessing the inflation risks stemming from the demand side of the economy.

Inflation between 1987 and 1998

Next, we examine whether the empirical results are useful in explaining the actual development of inflation in the euro area. Figure 5.2 shows the dynamic simulated equation and two components, measuring respectively the effect of the demand variable and the effect of the supply variables on inflation. Figure 5.2 illustrates that capacity utilization explains most of the movements in inflation, while the impact of the supply variables is mostly temporary.

Finally, we plot in Figure 5.3 actual inflation, capacity utilization and the NAIRCU for the period 1987–98. The 95 per cent confidence interval, which

Figure 5.2 Demand and supply effect on euro area inflation (%)

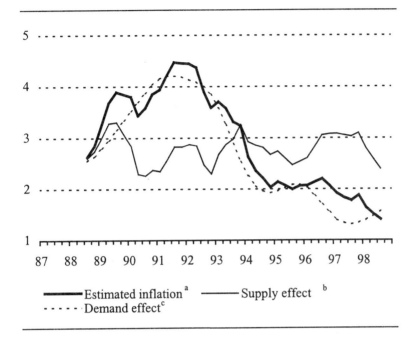

Notes:

$$^a \quad \pi_t = \Sigma\beta_i\Delta p_{t-1} + \gamma(CU_t - CU^*) + \Sigma\delta_i\Delta\pi_{rm,t-1} + \Sigma\phi_i\Delta e_{t-i}$$

$$^b \quad \pi_t = \Sigma\beta_i\Delta p_{t-1} + \Sigma\delta_i\Delta\pi_{rm,t-1} + \Sigma\phi_i\Delta e_{t-i}$$

$$^c \quad \pi_t = \Sigma\beta_i\Delta p_{t-1} + \gamma(CU_t - CU^*)$$

ranges from 81.5 to 83.2, is shown as well. Comparing Figures 5.2 and 5.3 shows that the fit of actual and estimated inflation is quite good. Furthermore, the latter figure makes clear that turning points in inflation can be detected. In 1987 the economic situation in Europe improved and producers expanded their production, capacity utilization climbed and exceeded the NAIRCU. Inflation also increased. During the period of high growth at the end of the 1980s and the beginning of the 1990s, capacity utilization stayed above its equilibrium. In this period inflation increased almost continuously. The rise in inflation stopped when utilization dropped below the NAIRCU in 1992. Capacity utilization stayed below its equilibrium from that time until 1995. In this period inflation showed a downward trend. Then, in 1995, utilization exceeded the NAIRCU for a short period and also the decline of inflation stagnated. The next year, however,

Figure 5.3 Inflation, NAIRCU and capacity utilization (%)

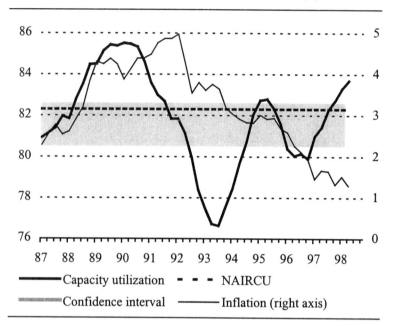

growth prospects deteriorated and utilization again fell below the NAIRCU, resulting in downward pressure on prices. In 1997 the economic outlook became more favourable and capacity utilization rose and passed the NAIRCU in 1998. However, as Figure 5.2 shows, inflation remained subdued due to a supply shock (declining energy prices). Recent data reveal that capacity utilization is dropping below the NAIRCU again, implying some downward pressure on prices in early 1999.

3. CONCLUSIONS

This chapter has considered two approaches to assessing inflationary prospects in the euro area. First, we analysed the leading indicator properties of a set of potential indicators with respect to future inflation. The empirical evidence shows that three variables, namely, growth of credit to the private sector, changes of the nominal effective exchange rate of the euro and producer price changes, are particularly useful for the monetary authorities in their monetary policy evaluation. The three indicators appear to be cointegrated with inflation with a plausible long-run relationship, while there is strong evidence of unidirectional causality from the indicator to future inflation. Impulse response simulations to determine the lead time of these indicators showed that credit growth is a leading indicator of longer-term inflationary prospects. The nominal effective exchange rate changes are useful for medium-term purposes, while producer price changes are appropriate as a short-term indicator of future inflation.

In the second part of the chapter we analysed the usefulness of capacity utilization as a measure of inflationary pressures. There exists a close relationship between industrial production and capacity utilization so the latter can be seen as an indicator of demand of goods in a country. In this context, we estimated the NAIRCU, that is, the level of capacity utilization that is compatible with the absence of inflationary pressures. The empirical analysis yields a value of the NAIRCU equal to 82.4 per cent, with a narrow 95 per cent confidence interval ranging from 81.5 to 83.3 per cent. A possible explanation for the close connection between capacity utilization and inflation is the limited openness of the euro area, so little is bought in neighbouring countries. Further, our results indicate that the level of the NAIRCU and the impact of capacity utilization on inflation are relatively stable over time. Therefore the deviation of capacity utilization from the NAIRCU can be a useful indicator of inflationary pressures from the demand side. Visual inspection showed that turning points in the inflation rate during the last decade could be detected with help of the NAIRCU. Over the past decade the relatively low levels of capacity utilization exercised a substantial downward pressure on the inflation rate in the euro area.

APPENDIX 5.A. FURTHER STATISTICAL RESULTS

This appendix discusses the results of the (co)integration analysis of the time series examined in Section 5.1. The first step consists of a test of non-stationarity of the series by applying the standard Dickey–Fuller procedure. As recommended by Dickey and Pantula (1987), we first test the null-hypothesis that the series are integrated of order 2, that is, whether differencing twice is necessary to obtain stationarity, and next investigate the null of integratedness of order 1. Table 5.A1 reports the results.

Table 5.A1 shows that all variables are non-stationary with the order of integration equal to 1. Exceptions are the output gap, the business cycle indicator and the yield spread, which are stationary. Notice that the finding that the yield spread is stationary, while the long-term interest rate is non-stationary, indicates that cointegration between the short- and long-term interest rates is present. Notice also that the growth rates of M1, M3 and credit to the private sector follow non-stationary processes. This implies that

Table 5.A1 Results of integration analysis

Variable	I(2) vs I(1)	I(1) vs I(0)	Conclusion
Inflation, π	-5.15*	-0.60	I(1)
Narrow money, M_1	-13.95*	-2.05	I(1)
Broad money, M_3	-16.37*	-1.69	I(1)
Credit, CR	-7.97*	-2.27	I(1)
Long-term interest rate, r_l	-6.11*	-0.99	I(1)
Yield spread, $r_l - r_s$	-14.43*	-3.31*	I(0)
Nom. eff. exchange rate, e_{eff}	-9.38*	-1.93	I(1)
Producer prices, p_a	-6.08*	-0.62	I(1)
Share prices, p_{eq}	-11.43*	-1.78	I(1)
Output gap, GAP	-12.43*	-5.45*	I(0)
Business cycle ind., $CONJ$	-4.17*	-4.21*	I(0)

Note: * indicates significance at 5% level.

that the levels of these variables are integrated of order 2, a finding that is corroborated by the results reported in Winder (1997b).

For the seven potential indicators that follow a non-stationary process, cointegration with inflation may occur; that is, a linear combination of the two variables is stationary. Cointegration is tested for by applying the Johansen procedure (Johansen, 1991). The results for Johansen's trace test and (if cointegration is present) the long-run relationship, are given in Table 5.A2.

The growth rates of credit to the private sector, the changes of the nominal effective exchange rate and producer price changes appear to be cointegrated with inflation, with long-run relationships that are plausible from an economic point of view. Remarkably, for both M1 and M3, cointegration with inflation is rejected. This does not necessarily imply, however, that monetary aggregates are not useful for monetary policy purposes. Economic theory for instance indicates that the relevant variable to be considered is excess money supply, that is, monetary expansion that is not accounted for by the explanatory variables of the demand for money (Fase and Winder, 1998). In line with the Woodford critique, it can also be argued that the monetary authorities have actually used the information in these variables in a successful way. This argument is particularly relevant since the Bundesbank, the central bank of the anchor country in the ERM, consistently pursued a policy of monetary targeting and to a large extent determined the stance of monetary policy in Europe.

Table 5.A2 Results of cointegration analysis

Variable	Johansen trace test	Long-run relationship
Narrow money, M_1	19.71	-
Broad money, M_3	14.95	-
Credit, CR	20.63*	$\hat{\pi} = 1.08\,CR$ (4.01)
Long-term interest rate, r_l	10.58	-
Nom. eff. exchange rate, e_{eff}	24.76*	$\pi = -0.46\,e_{eff}$ (2.86)
Producer prices, p_a	26.70*	$\pi = 0.91 p_a$ (13.90)
Share prices, p_{eq}	15.49	-

Note: * indicates significance at 5% level; *t*-values in parentheses. All variables are percentage changes, except the long-term interest rate.

NOTES

1. The data on the monetary aggregates concern M1H and M3H, since data on the fully harmonized definitions of the monetary aggregates, which have been introduced recently, are not available for the whole sample period considered here.
2. These countries account for about 85 per cent of total area-wide output, so it is reasonable to expect that the results give a representative picture for the euro area as a whole. Aggregate data for the five countries are constructed using the method discussed in Winder (1997a).
3. For a more extensive discussion, the reader is referred to Woodford (1994).
4. The order of the VAR model, that is, the maximum lag of the variables included, is determined with the Schwartz criterion.
5. This methodology is also applied in Bolt and Van Els (1998). However, they use the output gap as demand variable.
6. In the 1960s and 1970s incorporating the history of inflation was often seen as modelling adaptive expectations. Gordon argues that inertia reflects the entire adjustment process existing of the lagged effects of the adjustments in wage and price contracts and the forming of (rational) expectations.
7. The standard specification is: $\Delta\pi_t = \alpha + \Sigma\beta_i\Delta\pi_{t-i} + \gamma CU_t + \Sigma\delta_i\Delta p_{rm,t-i} + \Sigma\phi_i\Delta e_{t-i} + \varepsilon_t$. The absence of inflationary pressures from capacity utilization implies that the NAIRCU equals $-\alpha/\gamma$. We obtain eq. (5.2) by substituting $-\alpha/\gamma$ (=CU^*) directly into the above equation.
8. In eq. (5.1) the coefficients of the lagged levels of inflation add up to one, since this equation is expressed in first differences. This is a necessary condition for calculating a natural rate, because otherwise there would be a trade-off between inflation and the demand indicator.
9. Our euro area aggregate consists of Belgium, France, Germany, Ireland, Italy, the Netherlands, Portugal and Spain. Austria, Finland and Luxembourg are excluded because

of data problems. The core group accounts for more than 60 per cent of the euro area's GDP.

10. The results turn out to be robust for a specification where the supply variables are substituted for producer prices (not presented).

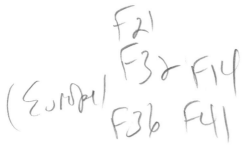
6. External Economic Relations of the Euro Area

Irene de Greef, David Hofman and Niek Nahuis

The birth of the euro has first of all consequences for the relations among the participating countries. It will further the process of economic integration, as described in Chapters 4 and 7. Accordingly, trade and financial flows among the participating countries will lose their international character and will become regional instead. The economic processes associated with the establishment of a monetary union will thus strengthen the perception of the euro area as a single economic entity. This entity will be of large economic significance, representing around 16 per cent of global GDP. The founding of the European Monetary Union will therefore also have a significant impact on relations with non-euro area countries. Crucially, attention in international policy debates will shift towards the euro area and away from the individual countries that constitute the area. The fact that the participating countries now share one currency might be regarded as facilitating international coordination of exchange rate policies by reducing the number of authorities involved. For that reason EMU has already sparked new life into the discussion on the desirability of such coordination (see Chapter 11). Similarly, EMU brings a new focus to the international debate on relative current account positions, because an important macroeconomic policy tool, monetary policy, will now be in the hands of a single policy maker. Debates such as the 'burden sharing' discussion following the crisis in Asia and other emerging markets in 1997 and 1998 might become more common.

In this chapter we analyse the euro area's economic relations with the rest of the world, in particular the United States and Japan. First we discuss the euro area's openness, using indicators such as the volume of trade and capital flows and the existence of institutional and other barriers. Next we consider the euro area current account position from a theoretical point of view. Building on this we finally develop empirical models of the current account for the euro area as well as the United States and Japan.

1. OPENNESS

Openness may refer to both flows of goods and services (foreign trade) and financial flows (international capital mobility). In fact, trade and capital flows are two sides of the same coin. This is particularly evident from the various ways of calculating the current account. The current account may be alternatively defined as the sum of net exports (including net factor income and net transfer payments), the difference between national saving and domestic investment, or as the change in net foreign assets. Whilst the first approach emphasizes transactions with foreigners relating to current production of goods and services, the latter stresses the use of international capital markets for consumption smoothing, given the intertemporal budget constraint. Therefore, factors that affect national saving–investment balances also have an impact on international trade flows, and vice versa. For example, a reduction in institutional barriers to capital mobility may contribute to a greater incidence of (politically sensitive) current account imbalances.

Foreign trade

When considered individually, most euro area countries are relatively open to international trade (Table 6.1). This holds particularly true when trade in both goods and services is considered. However, to facilitate comparison with the euro area, for which an aggregate for trade in services is not available, this section will focus on openness with respect to trade in goods only. In accordance with the theory that smaller countries tend to trade more because of the more limited scope for division of labour and specialization on the national level, the smaller economies in the euro area are most open to trade in goods; openness in Belgium and Ireland even exceeds 50 per cent of GDP. While the degree of openness is substantially lower in the larger economies, openness in the four largest economies nevertheless still ranges between 18 and 20 per cent.

For all euro area countries, however, a large share of trade reflects intra-euro area trade, which cancels out if the area as a whole is studied. The relative importance of international trade for the economy of the euro area is thus significantly smaller than for the individual countries. The euro area is – in line with its size – a much more closed economy. Exports of goods of the euro area amount roughly to 12 per cent of GDP and imports to 11 per cent.[1] Despite being more closed than its constituent countries, the euro area is, with an average openness of 11.4 per cent, substantially more open than the United States and Japan. It should be stressed, however, that comparisons of trade ratios both across countries and across time should be treated with caution due to difficulties with the international comparability of price levels and divergent price developments between sectors within a country (Van Bergeijk and Mensink, 1997).

Table 6.1 Openness to trade[a] (average 1993-97, % of GDP)

	Goods and services[b]	Goods[c]	Of which: outside euro area	Barriers to trade and investment[d]
Euro area		11.4	11.4	1.5
Germany	23.0	20.1	11.3	1.8
France	22.5	18.1	9.2	1.1
Italy	21.8	18.4	9.5	1.1
Austria	39.2	26.8	10.3	1.9
Belgium[e]	66.1	57.7	22.4	1.4
Finland	33.2	26.9	18.1	1.8
Ireland	70.8	56.1	38.4	1.1
Netherlands	49.9	40.4	18.0	1.1
Portugal	30.6	26.6	9.5	2.3
Spain	23.7	18.2	7.8	1.6
United States	11.6	9.4		1.2
Japan	9.1	7.8		1.8

Notes:
[a] Openness = ½ * (exports + imports) / GDP.
[b] Source: IMF, *International Financial Statistics*, National Accounts definition. Currently, reliable data on extra euro area trade in goods and services are not available.
[c] Merchandise goods only; source: IMF, *Direction of Trade Statistics*
[d] Scale 0–6 from least to most restrictive; source: OECD.
[e] Including Luxembourg.

The difference in openness between the euro area and the United States may to some extent be explained by the larger weight of services in the American economy. By their very nature, goods cross borders more easily than services, which are often non-tradables. In nominal terms the increase was even more pronounced because prices of services have risen faster than prices of goods. As a consequence of the home bias of the service sector, the increase in its importance has tended to weigh down the relative importance of trade flows for these economies. This effect explains the fact that, in most countries, openness in terms of trade relative to GDP improved relatively slowly over the past decades although international trade grew very rapidly.

At present the process of increasing importance of services has advanced furthest in the US. In 1994, the percentage contribution of services to GDP amounted to 71 per cent for the US, but around only 63 per cent for both the euro area and Japan.[2] This suggests that openness, measured in terms of merchandise trade, may constitute a relative underestimation of the international integration of the industrial sector of the US (or alternatively, a relative overestimation of that of the euro area). Remarkably, despite Japan's higher income level, the weight for services in the Japanese economy equals that of the euro area. Given the fact that the Japanese economy is smaller than that of the euro area, a higher degree of openness would be expected in Japan. In reality, however, Japan is substantially more closed than the euro area, especially with regards to imports.

The euro area's main trading partners

Table 6.2 specifies the composition of the import and export flows of goods by country of origin/destination. Around 25 per cent of euro area trade is with the other EU member states. Most prominent among them is the UK, which is the single largest trading partner of the euro area with export and import shares approaching 18 per cent and 16 per cent respectively. The second most important trading partner of the euro area is the United States. Euro area trade with Japan is considerably less important. However, the relative importance of the Asian region in euro area trade has increased dramatically over the past decade and is now more important than trade with the NAFTA countries. In particular, a large share of euro area imports is of Asian origin. Ties with Central and Eastern Europe also strengthened over this period, albeit somewhat less impressively. To date Central and Eastern Europe has primarily gained weight as a market for euro area exports, rather than as a source of imports.

Foreign direct investment

With the exception of Ireland, a significant part of the euro area's cross-border investment flows consists of investment in other euro area countries, particularly in the case of inward foreign direct investment (Table 6.3). The individual euro area countries are thus generally more open than the euro area as a whole.

Unlike openness to foreign trade, openness to foreign direct investment does not seem related to size. While smaller countries have a more limited

Table 6.2 Trading partners of the euro area (% of extra euro area merchandise trade)

	1983-87		1993-97	
	Exports	Imports	Exports	Imports
Other EU[a]	26.5	22.1	25.8	22.7
of which UK	17.5	14.7	17.6	15.7
Other Western Europe[b]	10.0	8.4	8.7	8.7
Central and Eastern Europe	8.3	9.9	12.2	11.1
South Mediterranean[c]	7.6	7.7	6.9	5.9
NAFTA[d]	17.8	16.1	15.1	16.0
of which US	15.6	13.6	13.0	14.3
Latin America	3.7	5.4	4.6	4.1
Asia	9.8	14.3	16.9	22.6
of which Japan	2.5	6.9	3.9	7.7
of which China and Hong Kong	2.1	2.0	3.9	4.8
Other countries	16.1	16.2	9.9	8.7

Notes:
[a]   UK, Denmark, Greece and Sweden.
[b]   Norway, Switzerland and Iceland.
[c]   Morocco, Algeria, Tunesia, Libya, Egypt, Israel, Turkey, Malta, Cyprus
      and Gibraltar.
[d]   US, Canada and Mexico.

scope for division of labour and specialization, other factors, such as differences in investment climate, apparently also play a role. In this context it should be noted that the euro area is characterized by a net outflow of foreign direct investment. This has given rise to a recurring debate on the relative merits of the euro area's investment climate, notably in Germany.

None the less, from a global perspective the euro area still attracts more foreign direct investment than Japan. Note that while the United States is less open than the euro area in terms of foreign trade, it is more open in terms of foreign direct investment. Overall openness may therefore not be very different, as foreign trade and foreign direct investment are to some extent substitutes.

Table 6.3 Openness to foreign direct investment
(average 1991-95, % of GDP)

	Outward		Inward		Openness[a]	
	Total	Outside euro area	Total	Outside euro area	Total	Outside euro area
Euro area		0.73		0.53		0.63
Germany	1.09	0.53	0.18	0.08	0.64	0.31
France	1.79	1.21	1.47	1.02	1.63	1.12
Italy	0.65	0.37	0.33	0.16	0.49	0.27
Austria	0.74	0.50	0.50	0.22	0.62	0.36
Belgium[b]	2.54	-0.47	4.23	1.30	3.39	0.42
Finland	1.30	1,02	0.69	0.56	1.00	0.79
Ireland	0.67	0.67	2.51	2.44	1.59	1.56
Netherlands	4.17	2.73	2.25	1.27	3.21	2.00
Portugal	0.49	0.12	1.80	0.87	1.15	0.50
Spain	0.64	0.46	1.88	0.85	1.26	0.66
United States	0.93		0.59		0.76	
Japan	0.51		0.03		0.27	

Notes:
[a] Openness = ½ * (outward + inward).
[b] Including Luxembourg.
Source: IMF, *International Financial Statistics* and OECD (1999b).

Barriers to trade and investment

When discussing openness to imports and FDI it is useful, in addition to actual flows, also to consider (potential) barriers to trade. The last column in Table 6.1 shows a measure for barriers to trade and investment, which is calculated by the OECD. This aggregate measure takes account of tariffs, non-tariff barriers (NTBs), regulatory and administrative barriers, discrimination by nationality, and barriers to foreign ownership of businesses. As can be seen from the table, there are considerable differences between European countries in this regard. Germany has relatively high barriers and appears to be as closed as Japan. Other European countries, notably France, Italy, the Netherlands and Ireland are very open and do even better than the United States. On average the euro area appears to be somewhat more closed than the US, but substantially more liberal than Japan.

Obviously, such an overall indicator may hide different patterns for different classes of barriers. When the average level of tariffs and measures of pervasiveness of non-tariff barriers to trade are compared internationally, OECD statistics (OECD, 1997a) tend to show that these are higher in the European Union than in the US and Japan. According to these measures of barriers to trade Japan is even most open. But this picture changes drastically when invisible barriers to trade, such as national regulatory standards and legal or factual discrimination against foreign products or entrepreneurs, are also considered. The survey by the International Institute for Management Development (IMD, 1997), which captures these barriers in addition to tariffs and NTBs, ranks Japan as being most protectionist, while most euro area countries rank somewhere in the middle.[3] The US is in this survey more open than the four largest euro area countries. Thus invisible barriers appear to be substantially lower in the euro area and the US than in Japan. A similar pattern applies to formal rules on FDI, of which there are relatively few in most countries of the euro area and the US when compared to Japan (OECD, 1997b).

Measuring capital mobility

Over the past two decades a worldwide liberalization of international capital movements has taken place. Institutional barriers to cross-border capital flows were brought down particularly quickly in the 1980s, for example as measured by the capital control index of Broer and Jansen (1998). As part of this process the European Union put directives in place to bring about the complete liberalization of capital markets within the European Union by 1 July 1990.[4] With the exception of Luxembourg most euro area countries still have some restrictions in place with regard to capital movements to and from non-EU members. None the less, the euro area countries are among the most liberalized countries in the OECD (OECD, 1997b).

There are two main approaches to measuring actual capital mobility in the literature. One is based on the volume of capital flows by comparing saving and investment rates, the other on the price of capital by comparing expected yields on financial assets (Obstfeld, 1986). The first approach originates with Feldstein and Horioka (1980), who argued that 'with perfect capital mobility, there should be no relation between domestic saving and domestic investment: saving in each country responds to the worldwide opportunities for investment while investment in that country is financed by the worldwide pool of capital' (p. 317). In contrast, saving necessarily equals investment in

Analysis of the Euro Area

any country in a world of immobile capital. To test these propositions Feldstein and Horioka used a regression equation of the form:

$$(I/Y)_i = \alpha + \beta(S/Y)_i \qquad (6.1)$$

where $(I/Y)_i$ is the ratio of gross domestic investment to GDP in country i, $(S/Y)_i$ is the corresponding ratio of gross domestic saving to GDP. A low estimated coefficient on saving, β, was interpreted as a sign of high capital mobility, whereas a high coefficient supposedly signalled the lack thereof. Contrary to expectations, Feldstein and Horioka found that saving and investment were generally highly correlated during 1960–74, with no indication that this relationship weakened over time. However, as the subsequent literature on this subject has made clear, the results of such tests need to be interpreted with care. While a lack of correlation between saving and investment is a sure sign of capital mobility, a high correlation need not be caused by capital immobility. Several alternative explanations have been put forward for the consistently high saving–investment correlations found in empirical research, even if there is substantial mobility of financial capital.[5]

The second approach to measuring capital mobility relies on the concept of interest rate parity. The idea behind this line of research is that in a world characterized by perfect capital mobility assets with the same risk characteristics have the same expected return. Part of this research has focused on testing covered interest parity, by comparing nominal interest rates in different financial centres when contracted in a common currency, such as the interest rate on dollar CDs sold in New York and those sold in the eurodollar market in London (Obstfeld, 1994). Other studies have attempted to test uncovered interest parity, that is, the equality of expected rates of return regardless of exchange rate risk (Frankel and MacArthur, 1988; Berk and Knot, 1999). The problem with such undertakings is that they generally require auxiliary assumptions regarding the formation of – unobservable – exchange rate expectations, the effects of which cannot be disentangled from the overall results of the tests.

Euro area capital mobility

One may assume that in combination with the revolutionary developments in communication and information technology the abolition of numerous capital market restrictions caused a sharp increase in capital mobility among the member countries of the OECD in the years following on Feldstein and Horioka's sample period (1960–74). We have therefore updated the original study, using a larger sample of countries. Table 6.4 presents our results.

Table 6.4 Cross-section saving-investment regressions, 1960-96

Equation: $(I/Y)_i = \alpha + \beta (S/Y)_i$

	OECD		Euro area	
Period	β	R^2	β	R^2
1960-64	0.91	0.91	0.74	0.85
	(0.06)		(0.10)	
1965-69	0.82	0.83	0.53	0.46
	(0.08)		(0.18)	
1970-74	0.87	0.81	0.41	0.25
	(0.09)		(0.20)	
1975-79	0.73	0.46	0.07	-0.12
	(0.17)		(0.35)	
1980-84	0.61	0.50	0.46	0.09
	(0.13)		(0.33)	
1985-89	0.63	0.73	0.84	0.72
	(0.08)		(0.17)	
1990-94	0.60	0.67	0.57	0.20
	(0.09)		(0.32)	
1992-96	0.60	0.55	0.75	0.18
	(0.11)		(0.42)	

Note: Standard errors in parentheses. Euro area does not include Luxembourg
(10 countries). For data sources see Appendix 6.A.

Like Feldstein and Horioka, we find that until the mid-1970s the estimated coefficients on saving are significantly different from zero, though on the whole not from unity. From the mid-1970s onwards the estimated coefficients for the OECD decline, particularly in the second half of the 1970s and the first half of the 1980s. Moreover, from the first half of the 1980s onwards the estimated coefficients are in general significantly less than unity. Therefore, these results tentatively suggest an increase in capital mobility in the OECD area as a whole from the late 1970s onwards. Our results indicate that this increase in capital mobility took place in the euro area long before that in the OECD as a whole. The estimated coefficient on saving plunges as early as the second half of the 1960s. From the second half of the 1970s onwards β is no longer statistically different from zero. Note, though, that these results are less reliable than those for the OECD due to the fact that the sample is very small.

Studies of the behaviour of relative rates of return confirm that capital mobility has increased since the early 1970s (Obstfeld, 1994), though for the OECD area as a whole perhaps not much beyond the wave of financial deregulation in the 1980s (Berk and Knot, 1999). In contrast, in the euro area the convergence of nominal long-term interest rates has made great strides since the 1980s. Using principal component analysis, Fase and Vlaar (1998) find that by 1996 close to 80 per cent of long-term interest rate movements in the six core countries of the EU (Belgium, France, Germany, Italy, the Netherlands and the United Kingdom) could be explained by the first principal component, against around 30 per cent in 1980. In fact, interest rate convergence made such progress in the 1990s that by May 1998 the long-term interest rate convergence criterion for participation in EMU had lost much of its discriminating power (Chapter 3). This suggests that in the euro area capital mobility increased even in the 1990s, though a reduction of exchange rate volatility and a greater degree of coordination of monetary policy among the countries concerned may also have played a role, particularly in the period leading up to EMU.

2. DETERMINANTS OF THE CURRENT ACCOUNT

Figure 6.1 shows the actual development of the euro area current account over the last 20 years, together with the current accounts of the United States and Japan. Despite fairly persistent variations of up to two percentage points of GDP, the euro area current account appears to revert to a mean slightly above 0 per cent of GDP (−1¼ per cent of GDP for the US and 2 per cent of GDP for Japan).

Broadly speaking, there are two approaches to the current account, namely the macroeconomic approach and the more traditional trade approach. The macroeconomic view is based on intertemporal models of the open economy. In these models agents optimize their consumption plans, subject to an intertemporal budget constraint. They use the international capital markets to smooth their consumption. In this approach the current account may be defined as saving minus investment or, alternatively, the change in net foreign assets. A current account surplus implies that a nation is accumulating claims on foreigners, while a deficit means that a country is on balance selling or borrowing assets abroad. In the steady state, the actual stock of net foreign assets equals its long-run equilibrium value. Note that this does not imply that the current account is equal to zero in the steady

*Figure 6.1 Current account developments in the euro area, the
United States and Japan, 1979–98
(% of GDP, four-quarter moving average)*

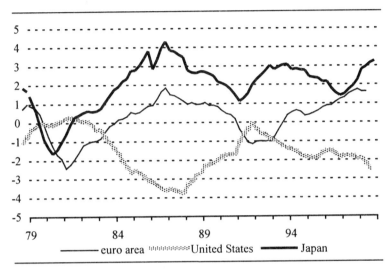

Note: The euro area aggregate is the sum of the current accounts of the
individual countries.
Source: IMF.

state. Current account imbalances may be a permanent feature of the global
economy when growth rates differ among countries.

Masson, Kremers and Horne (1994) show that the equilibrium value of net
foreign assets is in fact determined by factors that also determine the
macroeconomic saving and investment balance, namely government debt and
demographic variables. In the short run, shocks may cause saving and
investment, and therefore the current account, to deviate temporarily from its
steady state level. In this approach, such shocks are typically related to
business cycle developments. By contrast, the trade view defines the current
account as exports minus imports. Consequently, it stresses factors connected
to differences in current production and competitiveness, in particular
exchange rate developments. In the remainder of this section we will discuss
the various long-term and short-term determinants – government debt, age
structure of the population, stance of the business cycle, and exchange rates –
in more detail. These variables will be incorporated in a full-scale model of
the current account in Section 6.3.

Government finances

Government finances in the three main economic blocs have undergone some wide swings in the past 20 years. For example, while Japan enjoyed sizeable budget surpluses in the late 1980s and early 1990s, its government finances deteriorated dramatically in the remainder of the 1990s due to various spending packages in support of the ailing economy.

By contrast, the United States and the euro area experienced budget deficits throughout the 1980s and managed important improvements in government finances from the early 1990s onwards. The US has even arrived at a budget surplus. In Europe this achievement was in large measure driven by the requirements for participation in the monetary union as laid down in the Maastricht Treaty. Provided that Ricardian equivalence does not fully hold, as many policy makers and standard textbook models assume, government saving should be positively related to national saving and government debt should be inversely related to net foreign assets. Masson, Kremers and Horne (1994) and Masson and Knight (1986) among others have found that this is indeed the case.[6]

Demography

Through their effect on saving and investment decisions demographic developments may also influence net foreign assets and the current account. With regard to saving, an economy characterized by a higher ratio of elderly people will generally have a higher level of net foreign assets than one with a relatively young population. The reason is that elderly people have accumulated assets during their working life in order to finance their retirement. Put differently, as young and elderly people tend to save less than those of working age, an increase in the number of youth and old-aged relative to the working population would be associated with a deterioration of the current account if unmatched by developments in trading countries. However, the tendency of young people to dissave may to some extent be compensated by those of working age, in so far as the latter may accumulate additional savings for their children, for example to provide for their educational expenses. Thus, the overriding influence of a shifting age structure on saving would seem to be captured by the proportion of the elderly in society. The impact of demographic developments on investment is less clear-cut. On the one hand, greying will probably result in a lower rate of economic growth and therefore a lower rate of investment. On the other hand, ageing of the pool of workers will bring with it an increase in labour costs, thereby stimulating a switch to more capital-intensive methods of production, and thus higher capital investment. On balance, the impact of demographic change on net foreign assets and the current account appears to be dominated by its effects on saving (Higgins, 1997).

As is evident from Table 6.5, the process of greying advances more quickly in Japan and the euro area than in the United States.

Table 6.5 Elderly dependency rates*

	1990	2010	2030
Euro area	21.0	27.5	42.5
Austria	22.4	27.7	44.0
Belgium	22.4	25.6	41.1
Finland	19.7	24.3	41.1
France	20.8	24.6	39.1
Germany	21.7	30.3	49.2
Ireland	18.4	18.0	25.3
Italy	21.6	31.2	48.3
Luxembourg	19.9	25.9	44.2
Netherlands	19.1	24.2	45.1
Portugal	19.5	22.0	33.5
Spain	19.8	25.9	41.0
United States	19.1	20.4	36.8
Japan	17.1	33.0	44.5

Note: * Population aged 65 and older as a percentage of population aged 15–64.

Business cycle developments

Of a more short-term nature is the impact of the international business cycle. Berk (1997) finds that international business cycles tend to be initiated in the economy of the United States. In the early stages of an international business cycle domestic demand in America and therefore American demand for imports will grow faster than global demand for imports. Thus, the US current account will deteriorate at this stage, to improve again once the upturn of the global economy gets under way.[7] Given that the European business cycles generally lag behind that of the United States, both domestic demand in Europe and the European demand for imports tend to lag behind its exports. This might explain why the euro area current account generally runs counter to that of the United States (Figure 6.1), and why it leads the economy as a whole.[8]

Exchange rate movements

Another potential determinant of current account developments of a more short-term nature is the nominal exchange rate. A depreciation of the home currency will increase the price competitiveness of the producers of the home country and worsen that of foreign suppliers. In theory, therefore, a depreciation of the currency will lead to an increase in exports and a decrease in imports – and thus to an improvement of the current account. There are, however, at least two caveats to the working of this basic mechanism.

First, in the short run, J-curve effects are commonly observed phenomena. That is, changes in relative prices resulting from depreciation initially have an adverse effect on the current account, as physical trade flows are slow to react to price changes. Clostermann (1996) finds some evidence for J-curve effects in Germany. This is broadly in line with findings for the United States (Meade, 1988; Backus, Kehoe and Kydland, 1994). All these studies, however, also find that J-curve effects are relatively modest and short-lived.

Second, and more important, pricing strategies of exporters and/or importers may weaken or prevent real effects of exchange rate changes even in the longer run. Costs associated with entering or leaving foreign markets and costs associated with expanding or contracting sales in a (foreign) market may induce exporters to hold their prices steady in terms of the foreign currency. In the event of this so-called 'pricing to market', exporters will allow exchange rate changes to be absorbed by their sales margins. The incentive for this type of behaviour will typically be stronger when exchange rate changes are perceived by firms as temporary deviations from some longer-term equilibrium level.[9] In addition, the speed of price adjustment will typically depend on market structure and degree of competition (Van Bergeijk and Haffner, 1996). There is considerable evidence suggesting that pricing-to-market plays an important role in practice. The fact that the 'law of one price' does not hold (except for certain highly homogeneous products) is well known in the economic literature. Engel (1993) finds that the consumer price of a good relative to a different good within the same country tends to be considerably less variable than the price of that good relative to a similar good in another country. One implication of this result is that exchange rate developments are not expected to lead to substantial inflation differentials and that, as a consequence, real and nominal exchange rates are – at least to some extent – expected to move together. This phenomenon is indeed often observed (Krugman, 1989; Faruqee, 1995) and it is certainly also apparent in the exchange rate of the euro over the past 20 years, as can be seen from Figure 6.2 which shows the development of the effective exchange rate of the euro in both a nominal and a CPI-deflated version. It is clear that both the nominal and the CPI-based rates show an almost

Figure 6.2 Nominal and real effective exchange rates of the euro (1990=100, monthly average)

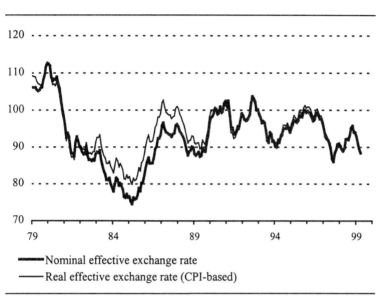

Nominal effective exchange rate

Real effective exchange rate (CPI-based)

Source: BIS.

identical pattern. As explained above, this almost perfect correlation could be read as an indication of muted or absent effects of exchange rate changes on national price levels and as a confirmation of the pricing-to-market hypothesis. In this light, one would not expect the developments in the (real) exchange rate to have a major direct impact on the current account.

3. EMPIRICAL MODELS OF THE CURRENT ACCOUNT

Based on the discussion above, this section presents empirical models of the current accounts of the US, Japan and the euro area.[10] Our model consists of two building blocks written out below in equations (6.2) and (6.3).

$$NFA^*_t = \gamma + \alpha DEBT_t + \beta DR_t \tag{6.2}$$

$$CA_t = \psi + \theta(NFA_{t-1} - NFA^*_{t-1}) + \Sigma\gamma_i\Delta DEBT_{t-i} + \Sigma\delta_i\Delta NFA_{t-i}$$
$$+ \Sigma\phi_i\Delta DR_{t-i} + \Sigma\zeta_i GAP_{t-i} + \Sigma\phi_i COMP_{t-i} + \varepsilon_t \tag{6.3}$$

where:

CA	current account, expressed as a ratio of GDP ($=\Delta$NFA)
NFA	net foreign assets, expressed as a ratio of GDP
$NFA*$	equilibrium level of net foreign assets
$DEBT$	government debt, expressed as a ratio of GDP
DR	dependency ratio minus the dependency ratio of the two other areas combined
GAP	output gap
$COMP$	competitiveness indicator

First, we estimate (6.2), which describes the long-run equilibrium value of net foreign assets. This equilibrium value is determined by demographics and government debt. The demographic variable is defined as the people aged 65 and over expressed as a ratio of the people aged between 15 and 64 minus this ratio of the other two countries combined. This last correction is made because the accumulation of net foreign assets depends not only on the age structure of the home country, but on that of the trading partners as well. Government debt is included because a deficit reduces national savings and therefore the accumulated assets position.

Second, we integrate this long-run relation into a dynamic model and add short-run determinants, which may cause the current account to temporarily deviate from its steady-state level. This results in (6.3). If equilibrium holds, *NFA* equals *NFA**. If actual net foreign assets differ from their equilibrium level the current account will be influenced by an adjustment process, the speed of which is determined by the parameter θ. If θ is less then unity the adjustment process will take place over multiple periods. There are three kinds of short-run determinants: (i) the lagged first differences of the variables appearing in the long-run relation are included, that is, ΔDR, ΔNFA and $\Delta DEBT$. The second variable is equal to the current account while the third equals the budget deficit of the government; (ii) the output gap is included as business cycle variable; (iii) the deviation of the nominal exchange rate from purchasing power parity is taken as competitiveness indicator. An increase in the indicator implies an improvement in competitiveness.

In sum, (6.3) shows that current account dynamics are driven by temporary factors and the adjustment process of the actual net foreign assets position to its equilibrium level.

The long-run relationship

If two or more series are non-stationary, there is a possibility that a linear combination of these non-stationary series may be stationary, or I(0). Such a linear combination (cointegrated relation) may be interpreted as a long-run equilibrium relationship between the variables.[11] So in a preliminary analysis we test for non-stationarity of the variables appearing in (6.3), net foreign assets, the dependency ratio and government debt, using the augmented Dickey–Fuller test. The outcomes indicate that all but one series are integrated of order 1. Only the dependency ratio of Japan appears to be integrated of order 2. Masson, Kremers and Horne (1994) found a comparable result, and argue that this may be the result of interpolation of the population statistics and the relatively small sample size. Like them, we proceed on the assumption that the dependency ratio of Japan is integrated of order 1.

We use the Johansen approach to estimate the equilibrium relation, because of the relatively short sample (1958–96). This approach has a relatively high power to reject non-stationarity and is the efficient way to estimate the long-run equilibrium relations (Gonzalo, 1994).[12] The results are shown in Table 6.6. Columns 2–4 report the test on the number of cointegrating vectors. Columns 5–7 give the long-run relationship.

Table 6.6 Empirical results: long-run analysis[a]

	Number of cointegrating vectors[b]			Long-run relation $NFA^* = \alpha DR + \beta DEBT + \gamma$		
	0	1	2	DR	DEBT	γ
US	39.7[c]	8.6	0.0	5.91 (7.4)	-0.20 (2.6)	24.38
Japan	45.6[c]	7.8	0.1	1.79 (3.4)	-0.71 (15.7)	34.78
Euro area	43.8[c]	11.8	1.0	4.85 (17.5)	0.58 (25.6)	-47.13

Notes:
[a] Sample period 1958–96; *t*-statistics in parentheses.
[b] Likelihood ratio.
[c] Denotes rejection at 1% level.

The hypothesis of no cointegrated relation is rejected for all three countries, but we cannot reject the hypothesis of one cointegrated relation, so we conclude that one equilibrium relation exists in each of the cases. All equations imply that the relative age structure is an important determinant of net foreign assets. The coefficient of the dependency ratio has in all equations the right sign and is significant. The influence of government debt on net foreign assets is somewhat less clear. For the United States and Japan we find that an increase in government debt lowers the equilibrium value of net foreign assets as suggested by theory. However, for the euro area the debt coefficient has the wrong sign. This is an indication that one or more explanatory variables may be missing in the specification, for example a variable capturing the level of capital controls.[13] This remains a topic for further research.

The complete model

Now, we can estimate the whole model. We use the estimated long-run equilibrium relation found in (6.2) to calculate $(NFA-NFA^*)$. We then estimate the adjustment parameter and the coefficients of the short-run determinants in (6.3). Table 6.7 reports the results of our preferred regressions.

The adjustment parameter θ determines how quickly deviations from the long-run equilibrium value of net foreign assets are corrected. In all countries this parameter is significant, indicating a tendency to equilibrium. In the euro area the process of adjustment to the equilibrium level of net foreign assets is considerably faster than in both the US and Japan. In the euro area the adjustment process lasts less than five years whereas in the other two countries the process takes more than ten years.

As expected, the government budget has a negative short-run effect. However, in Japan the effect is rather small and not significant. In the euro area and especially the US the deficit has a much larger effect on the current account. The lagged changes of net foreign assets are also significant, so the current account is partly determined by an autoregressive process.

Surprisingly, the output gap seems not important in the US and Japan. Only in the euro area does there exist a significantly negative effect of the output gap on the current account.[14]

The evidence on the influence of the competitiveness indicators is mixed. For the euro area and the US an improvement in competitiveness *vis-à-vis* Japan leads to a higher current account balance in the same year. The current account of the US improves one year after an increase in competitiveness *vis-à-vis* the euro area. For Japan and the euro area our results indicate the existence of a J-curve effect with respect to competitiveness *vis-à-vis* the US: after an increase in competitiveness the current account first deteriorates, and then improves the next year. For the euro area the total effect on the current account is very small. For Japan changes in competitiveness *vis-à-vis* the euro area have a puzzling effect.

Table 6.7 Empirical results: dynamic models[a]

	Japan		US		Euro area	
Adj. speed θ	-0.06	(2.3)	-0.09	(2.4)	-0.22	(5.6)
ΔNFA_{t-1}	0.60	(3.6)	0.61	(4.0)	0.28	(3.5)
ΔNFA_{t-2}			0.18	(1.3)		
$\Delta DEBT_{t-1}$	-0.03	(0.7)	-0.24	(3.7)	-0.12	(8.0)
$\Delta DEBT_{t-2}$			-0.15	(2.7)	-0.07	(4.0)
ΔDR_{t-1}			1.19	(3.0)		
ΔDR_{t-2}					-0.90	(5.6)
$COMP_t$ vs US	-0.01	(0.9)[b]			-0.04	(4.5)
$COMP_{t-1}$ vs US	0.04	(2.1)[b]			0.05	(8.7)
$COMP_t$ vs euro area	-0.04	(3.9)				
$COMP_{t-1}$ vs euro area	0,00	(0.2)	0.02	(3.9)		
$COMP_t$ vs Japan			0.02	(2.2)[b]	0.02	(4.0)
$COMP_{t-1}$ vs Japan						
GAP_t	-0.01	(0.5)			-0.09	(2.7)
GAP_{t-1}			-0.04	(0.8)		
Intercept	0.53	(3.8)			0.47	(4.8)
DW[c]	2.10		2.07		2.03	
R^2(adj)	0.71		0.85		0.80	
B-G LM(1)[c]	0.40	0.52	1.53	0.22	0.21	0.65
B-G LM(2)[c]	1.90	0.38	1.57	0.46	2.23	0.33
ARCH LM(1)[c]	1.25	0.26	0.40	0.53	0.08	0.78
Jarque-Bera[c]	0.07	0.97	1.64	0.44	1.49	0.47

Notes:

[a] Sample period 1958–96; *t*-statistics in parentheses. COMP, deviation of the nominal exchange rate from PPP, defined in such a way that an increase in COMP implies an increase in competitiveness of the home country.

[b] I(1), therefore the first difference is taken.

[c] DW stands for Durbin-Watson statistic. B-G LM(1) and B-G LM(2) are Breusch-Godfrey statistics, testing for first- and second-order autocorrelation respectively. ARCH LM(1) tests for first-order autoregressive conditional heteroscedasticity. Jarque-Bera statistic tests for normality of the residuals. For the last four test statistics the first column reports the value of the statistic and the second shows the corresponding *p*-value.

4. CONCLUSIONS

The euro area has a fairly low trade ratio, though slightly less so than the US or Japan. None the less, international trade issues regularly appear in the political limelight, often as a result of a widening of global current account imbalances. This must also be viewed against the background of increasing capital mobility, which has increased the scope for diverging current account developments.

Our empirical analysis shows that with regard to current account dynamics a distinction ought to be made between the long run and the short run. In the long run, government debt and demography appear to be important determinants of the current account through their effects on net foreign asset accumulation. For example, the persistent net foreign asset accumulation by Japan can partly be explained by the relatively rapid ageing of the Japanese population in recent decades and in the near future. The long-run equilibrium factors influence the current account through an adjustment process in which deviations of the net foreign assets position from its equilibrium value are corrected over the years. It turns out that this adjustment is twice as fast in the euro area than in the US and Japan. With the exception of Japan, the higher government budget deficits also contribute negatively to the current account in the short run. Surprisingly, the business cycle seems only of importance in explaining short-run variations of the current account of the euro area. The evidence on the effects of exchange rate developments points to the existence of a J-curve effect for Japan and the euro area.

APPENDIX 6.A. DATA SOURCES

This appendix provides the sources and discusses the construction of the data used in this chapter.

Saving and investment: OECD, *National Accounts,* Volume I: *Main Aggregates*. The OECD sample includes Australia, Austria, Belgium, Canada, Denmark, Finland, France, Germany, Greece, Iceland, Ireland, Italy, Japan, the Netherlands, New Zealand, Norway, Portugal, Spain, Sweden, Switzerland, Turkey, the United Kingdom and the United States (23 countries). The data for Germany refer to West Germany only for the period prior to 1991. Luxembourg has been excluded due to unreliability of the data.
Government debt: IMF, *International Financial Statistics*.
Current account balances: OECD, *Economic Outlook*. France, 1955–63: Mitchell (1980).

Net foreign assets: The value for end-1996 is taken from IMF, *International Financial Statistics*. The years 1955–95 are calculated on the basis of current account balances.

Dependency ratio: OECD, *Labour Force Statistics*. Definition: ratio of the population of 65 years and older to the population between 15 and 64 of the domestic country minus the corresponding ratio of the other two countries combined.

Gross Domestic Product: OECD, *Economic Outlook*.

Output gap: Difference between GDP (Y) and its trend (Y^*) calculated with help of the Hodrick–Prescott filter (λ=100); defined as $\ln(Y/Y^*)$.

Purchasing Power Parity exchange rates: 1970–96: OECD, *National Accounts, Volume I, Main Aggregates*; 1956–70: PPP values are calculated on the basis of GDP deflators with 1970 as base year.

GDP deflator: 1960–70: OECD, *National Accounts*, Volume I: *Main Aggregates*; 1955–59: IMF, *International Financial Statistics*.

Exchange rates: IMF, *International Financial Statistics*.

Competitiveness indicator (COMP): difference between PPP exchange rate (PPP) and actual exchange rate (E); defined as $\ln(PPP/E)$.

Euro area consists of Germany, France, Italy, the Netherlands and Belgium. The euro area aggregates are computed on the basis of GDP weights, where GDPs have been converted using 1994 PPP exchange rates. Sources: Eurostat, *Statistics in Focus* and OECD, *National Accounts, Volume II*.

NOTES

1. All data are calculated as averages over the period 1993–97, because export and import ratios tend to fluctuate significantly over the years. To some extent these swings reflect cyclical fluctuations. But more important and troubling are the swings due to price developments, such as commodity price developments and exchange rate volatility. These types of price developments are only to a limited extent relevant for structural, real openness. Unfortunately, there are currently no import price indices available, tailored to extra euro area trade. Therefore it is as yet not possible to deflate export and import value figures in a proper way. Hence the calculation of average figures is likely to give more reliable results, than for example the simple use of the figures for the most recent year available.
2. Figures derived and/or calculated from OECD data.
3. Because invisible barriers to trade are hard to measure in an objective way, polls among managers operating in foreign countries are used to estimate the severity of such barriers. A well-known survey of this type is the one conducted by IMD.
4. Some countries stipulated a transitional period (Bakker, 1996).
5. These include the intertemporal budget constraint or solvency constraint (Jansen, 1996), exogenous disturbances affecting the economy such as productivity shocks and population growth (Tesar, 1991), a large country effect as exogenous changes in saving in large countries may affect the world interest rate and thus investment (Baxter and Crucini, 1993) and current account targeting by governments (Bayoumi, 1990).
6. Others beg to differ. For an overview see Seater (1993).

7.   The American current account is negatively correlated with GDP. Maximum correlation is found when the current account is given a lag of two quarters over the period 1979–98.
8.   For the euro area the current account is positively correlated with GDP. Maximum correlation is found when the current account is given a lead of three quarters over the period 1979–98.
9.   A useful overview of strategic considerations underlying pricing-to-market behaviour is provided by Krugman (1989).
10. Our euro area aggregate consists of five founding members of the European Union: Belgium, France, Germany, Italy and the Netherlands. This group is chosen because of the long history of economic integration.
11. See Chapter 5 for a more detailed description of unit root tests and cointegration.
12. The number of lags in the specification and the precise form of the specification are determined with the Schwarz information criterion, which is a measure of information that strikes a balance between goodness of fit and parsimonious specification of a model.
13. The positive relation between government debt and net foreign assets was also found for Germany by Masson, Kremers and Horn (1994). They solved this by adding a demographic variable, which captures the people under 15. We also tried this approach, but found no satisfactory results.
14. To check the robustness of the findings we included the annual change of GDP instead of the output gap as an explanatory variable. Similar results were found with this specification.

(Europa)
F33 F36 F42 G10

7. The Euro and the Financial System

Henk Huisman, Jacob Meesters and Renske Oort

Compare the introduction of the euro on 1 January 1999 to the launching of a new movie. It would not be exaggerating to translate European hopes into the flashing title: 'A star is born'. Whether the euro will achieve stardom quickly remains to be seen, since history has shown that prevailing stars are quite persistent. At the beginning of this century, it took the dollar a couple of decades to grasp the lead role from the pound sterling, even though the United States was by far the largest economy. The dollar has been the dominant international currency since World War II, notwithstanding an increasing role for the German mark and the Japanese yen in financial markets during the last 20 years. The opinions about the future international role of the euro are wide-ranging, from a minor role in the shadow of the dollar via a bipolar system to even euro dominance.

Undoubtedly, the launching of the euro is an important event in financial markets. The euro builds on the economic power of almost 300 million people. The euro area is in terms of its share in world GDP comparable to the United States. The share in world trade in goods of the euro area of 11 per cent even exceeds the share of the United States (9 per cent) and Japan (8 per cent). This makes plausible an important international role for the euro in financial markets, particularly so if the United Kingdom joins EMU.

The implications of the launching of the euro for the development of the global financial system have gained much attention in recent years.[1] It is commonly understood that the euro will lead to more homogeneous and transparent European financial markets, because it will strengthen current trends of internationalization, securitization and increased competition in financial markets. These trends started a decade ago with the introduction of the Single Market and European Union regulations. The elimination of exchange risk within the euro area and the denomination of financial paper in euros should add to these developments. In turn, this will increase pressures to reduce transaction and other costs, thereby making financial markets in Europe an increasingly attractive environment for investments.

It is difficult to predict how quickly these developments will proceed. Indeed, it is a matter of much debate in the economic literature. The debate largely focuses on the issue to what extent the euro will be able to challenge the dollar as the major international currency. A related issue concerns the implications for the external value of the euro.

In this chapter, we try to answer these questions. We start with describing in more general terms the functions of an international currency (Section 1) In Section 2 we look at factors that determine the international use of currencies in general. We also present our empirical research on this topic. In Section 3, we assess the future international role of the euro by evaluating structural changes in capital markets and the banking sector in the euro area, while in Section 4 we review some quantitative estimates of the potential of the euro as an international currency. We summarize our findings in Section 5.

1. FUNCTIONS OF INTERNATIONAL CURRENCIES

An international currency used outside the issuing country performs three functions: as a means of exchange, a unit of account and a store of value. The international use of a currency is influenced by choices made by both the private sector and the official sector, for example, central banks, governments and international institutions such as the IMF. Given the importance of economies of scale and externalities, in practice just one currency dominates the international financial markets.

Separating the private sector from its official counterpart, Table 7.1 distinguishes six functions of an international currency. Although in principle the functions can be fulfilled separately by different currencies, in practice the functions happen to be strongly interrelated.

Table 7.1 Functions of an international currency

	Private	Official
Means of exchange	vehicle	intervention
Unit of account	invoicing	anchor
Store of value	portfolio management	reserves

Source: Cohen (1971).

Since the size of the official international reserves is relatively limited, it is mainly market forces that determine which currency is used most.

Ultimately, it is the size of private stocks and flows of financial assets rather than official arrangements, such as international agreements or exchange rate mechanisms, that drive the use of international currencies (Krugman, 1992). For example, the total world portfolio of international assets stood at US$ 7,585 billion at the end of 1995, five times as much as the total official foreign exchange reserves, which were US$ 1,508 billion (BIS and IMF Annual Reports, 1998). In terms of flows, the difference will be even more pronounced. Let us consider these functions in more detail and focus on current trends.

Private functions of an international currency

Vehicle currency

In most international payment transactions, currencies are not exchanged directly, but a third currency – a so-called vehicle currency – is used. The function of vehicle currency concerns payments between businesses (strongly related to the invoicing function), between businesses and banks, and – most important – between financial institutions. By far most international payments take place in the inter-bank market. Because of the large volume of financial transactions and their required speed, banks use very liquid, mature and liberalized currency markets.

Once the size of transactions of a particular currency has reached a critical mass, economies of scale start to reduce transaction costs. The relatively low transaction costs attract more users, which lowers costs further, which attracts more users, and so on. The market increases in size and becomes more and more transparent and efficient. Forward markets and new technologies and products are developed. Ultimately the currency becomes an attractive vehicle. Table 7.2 shows that the dollar is still overwhelmingly used as the vehicle currency (note that, as international transactions always involve two currencies, the percentages add up to 200 per cent).

Invoicing currency

Invoicing reflects real business activity. It often takes place in the currency of the exporter; this is known as Grassman's law (ECU Institute, 1995). However, when a large country is involved, the currency of that country is mostly used for invoicing (an exception is the Japanese yen, which is relatively little used in trade transactions). Furthermore, in the case of the invoicing of raw materials, in most instances the dollar is used, even if no American party is involved. The reasons are that the market for these

*Table 7.2 Daily volume of trading on currency markets
(distribution of currencies in %)*

	April 1989	April 1992	April 1995	April 1998
Total ($bn)	718	1076	1572	1971
Dollar	90	82	83	87
German mark	27	40	37	30
Yen	27	23	24	21
British pound	15	14	10	11
French franc	2	4	8	5
Other EMS	4	12	15	17
Swiss franc	10	9	7	7
Other	25	16	16	22
	200	200	200	200

Source: BIS (1999).

products can be characterized as having a low level of product differentiation, fierce competition and mostly a central market place. If we look at currency distribution, again a leading role for the dollar can be observed (Table 7.3). Although the United States accounts for nearly 15 per cent of world trade, almost half of all invoicing takes place in dollars. Apart from the United States, only Germany's share in total invoicing was larger than its share in world trade, mainly caused by intensive trade relations within Europe.

Portfolio investment
If a currency is regularly used in international transactions, it becomes desirable to hold certain amounts of cash or securities denominated in that currency. In addition, securities are held for portfolio investment purposes. As is the case for the decision to use vehicle currencies, economies of scale are important here. Deep and liquid financial markets lower transaction costs and increase the attractiveness of currencies for investment. Moreover, the role of monetary policy is important. The safest currency for investors is that of the country with the lowest inflation rate over time. At the same time, however, from a risk-minimizing view, diversification among several currencies is preferable over investment in just one currency.

Available data on the aggregate world portfolio indicate that the dollar has lost ground to the European currencies and the Japanese yen since the

Table 7.3 Denomination of trade contracts (% of total)

	1980	1987	1992
Dollar	56	48	48
German mark	14	16	15
Yen	2	4	5
British pound	7	6	6
French franc	6	7	6
Other	15	20	20
	100	100	100

Source: ECU Institute (1995).

Table 7.4 International bond holdings (% of total)

	1981	1985	1990	1993	1995	1997
Total ($bn)	194	558	1477	1790	2209	3328
Dollar	53	57	41	38	34	44
German mark	0	9	10	10	12	10
Yen	7	8	11	14	16	14
Other EU	20	10	19	23	25	24
Other	20	17	19	14	13	8
	100	100	100	100	100	100

Sources: ECU Institute (1995); BIS, *International Banking and Financial Market Developments* (several issues).

early 1980s. This development into a multicurrency system is also reflected in the currency distribution of international bond holdings (Table 7.4).

Official functions of an international currency

The official functions of an international currency are strongly interrelated. One reason to hold reserves is to be able to intervene, while interventions obviously influence both the level and the composition of official reserves. Likewise, the choice of an explicit exchange rate arrangement determines to some extent which currencies are used for interventions. When countries have pegged their currency unilaterally to a major currency, obviously their reserves are largely composed of that currency. The decision to peg to a particular currency is usually based on trade relations, inflation performance and/or political motives. In the mid-1970s one-third of all countries formally pegged their currency to the dollar. Since then the dollar has lost ground (to a share of about 10 per cent in 1998), particularly because an increasing number of countries have decided to let their currencies float. Besides formal pegs many other types of currency regimes exist, such as basket pegs, crawling pegs and managed floating,[2] which require the countries concerned to hold sufficiently high levels of foreign exchange reserves.

The dollar's share reached its peak in the mid-1970s. It is still by far the most important currency in total worldwide official foreign exchange reserves (Table 7.5). In the post-war period, the dollar took over hegemony from the pound sterling as the pivot of the Bretton Woods system of pegged exchange rates. After the collapse of the Bretton Woods system in the early 1970s, the dollar lost ground to the Deutsche mark, the ECU and the Japanese yen, but made a comeback in the 1990s. This comeback, however, was mainly the result of the dollar appreciation and huge interventions by the Bank of Japan (its dollar reserves increased to almost US$ 100 billion, or 7 per cent of total foreign exchange reserves in the world).

Table 7.5 Official holdings of foreign exchange (% of total)

	1951	1965	1975	1985	1990	1995	1997
Total ($bn)	n.a.	n.a.	162	383	845	1328	1554
Dollar	31	66	79	56	49	56	57
German mark	n.a.	0	9	13	17	14	13
Yen	n.a.	0	2	7	8	7	5
British pound	59	22	3	3	3	3	3
French franc	n.a.	2	1	1	2	2	1
Ecu	-	-	-	12	10	7	5
Other/not known	n.a.	10	6	8	11	11	16

Note: n.a. = not available.
Source: IMF (direct information and *Annual Reports*) and IMF (1983).

2. DETERMINANTS OF INTERNATIONAL CURRENCIES

Which factors determine whether a currency will be used internationally and under what circumstances will it be replaced as a key currency? There is no all-encompassing theoretical framework that gives a comprehensive explanation for the rise and fall of international currencies. The factors mostly referred to in economic literature[3] concern historical and political factors, inertia and other monopoly aspects, the external position, monetary policy and the development of financial markets. Let us consider these preconditions or characteristics in more detail.

Historical and political factors

According to Mundell (1983), it is a fact of historical tradition that the top · currency is provided by the top power. Indeed, throughout history it was the currency from leading economic and political powers that gained international use. Examples are wars, colonialism, treaties and aid programmes, such as the Marshall plan.

Probably the first currency to achieve the status of international currency was the Dutch guilder in the seventeenth century (Blinder, 1996). After the Napoleonic wars (1795–1815), the guilder lost ground. In the nineteenth century it was the pound sterling that took over command, a position that was sustained until the middle of the nineteenth century. This raises an obvious and interesting question: why could the pound sterling maintain its status as world currency even though the United States had become much more important than the United Kingdom since the turn of the century?

Inertia and monopoly aspects

Relative positions in the use of international currencies are slow to change. According to Bergsten (1975), it is far easier to remain a key currency than to become one and it is very difficult to stop being one. As we saw in the previous section, economies of scale and the reinforcing process lead to large, transparent and efficient markets. Alogoskoufis, Portes and Rey (1997) have described this as 'thick market externalities'. Adjustment costs play a role. It is expensive to change invoicing and accounting systems, and changing habits bear psychological costs, too. Furthermore, the recognizability of the dollar or 'greenback' in itself – that is, its 'brand name' – will help sustain its position, even if economic circumstances are not optimal. Only when the economic power of the country has diminished on several fronts, and the critical lower limit (which is hard to define) has been reached, the position of a currency as international currency suddenly collapses and another currency takes over.

External position

The relationship between the balance of payments and the internationalization of a currency is not clear-cut. On the one hand, one could argue that the dominant country has to provide the world with large amounts of its currency (it has to act as 'world banker'), so the balance of payments (excluding official reserves) would be in deficit for some time. On the other hand, it would be best for confidence in the economy if the current account were in surplus and the country a net creditor. The United States has maintained a current account deficit since 1982. Many authors regard this situation as unsustainable in the longer run (Kindleberger, 1985), since confidence in the economy could decline. Indeed, in the 1970s we have witnessed a steady decline of the dollar *vis-à-vis* the German mark. Since the beginning of the 1990s, the exchange rate is somewhat more stable. However, the developments in the value of the dollar and the external imbalances since the collapse of Bretton Woods have not been detrimental to the position of the dollar as leading international currency. Perhaps, as some observers claim, this is due to the fact that there has not been a viable alternative to the dollar.

A related factor that has been mentioned is the openness of the economy. When exports and imports are relatively small compared to total production, a country is able to determine its policies independently of other countries and external shocks. This can be favourable for economic and financial stability.

Monetary policy

For an international currency it is important that the issuing country pursue a sound monetary policy and develop appropriate institutions that produce both low inflation rates and low inflation variability. Furthermore, it is important to consider whether the issuing country is in favour of its currency becoming a widely used international currency. The Bundesbank has traditionally tried to restrain the use of the Deutsche mark as an international currency. The argument was that international use would interfere with efforts to control monetary aggregates and thus maintain price stability. Nevertheless, the Bundesbank has not been able, due to the ongoing liberalization of financial markets, to prevent a significant increase in the international use of the German mark. At present, 22 per cent of Deutsche marks circulates abroad, which is still much less than the 78 per cent for the dollar (*Economic Report of the President*, 1999).

Well-developed financial markets

Important for the internationalization of currencies are well-developed, sizeable and liquid financial markets with a wide range of financial instruments, deep secondary markets, and absence of capital restrictions. The key word here is transaction costs, as, for instance, is clearly outlined by Portes and Rey (1998). In their framework, transaction costs in foreign exchange and securities markets are the key determinant of the extent and speed of internationalization of currencies. They also stress the importance of a strong interconnection between the functions of a currency as a vehicle and as a financial asset. If a domestic financial system is efficient it attracts capital inflows, thereby increasing the liquidity of the bilateral foreign exchange markets, which makes the currency an attractive vehicle. Conversely, vehicle transactions increase foreign exchange market liquidity and lower transaction costs, such as the cost of portfolio substitution, resulting in a higher foreign exchange market turnover.

3. THE INTERNATIONAL ROLE OF THE EURO

So far we have described the functions and determinants of international currencies in general. Against this background we assess in this section the future role of the euro. Thereby we focus on the last two, primarily economic determinants: monetary policy and well-developed financial markets. The reason is that in these areas major changes have occurred with the introduction of one monetary policy and one currency. With regard to the other determinants – political factors, inertia and the external position – the monetary union and the single currency do not seem to entail fundamental changes.

Monetary policy

For the euro area, it seems fair to expect an improvement of the policy framework compared to the situation a few years ago in the individual countries, given the institutional set-up of the ESCB (see Chapters 8–10). Important also is the well-grounded independence of the ESCB. As can be seen in Box 7.1, our own empirical research points to the fact that this is a factor in determining the international use of a currency, more important than actual performance on inflation. A second aspect is the internal focus

---

Box 7.1 Empirical research on determinants of the international use
of currencies

Empirical research on the determinants of the international use of
currencies is scarce. Only Prem (1997) and Oort (1998) have done
studies of this type. They estimated the relation between the currency
composition of private and public world portfolios and its underlying
determinants, the characteristics of the issuing country.

Oort (1998) examined two dependent variables, the currency
composition of international bond issues and official foreign exchange
reserves. Data were collected for ten and seven countries, respectively,
over a 30-year period (1966–95) and were tested in a time-series cross-
section set-up.[4] The relative performances on a number of characteristics
as against other issuing countries were calculated and examined as
explanatory variables. They were mainly standard economic
determinants, since historical, political and monopoly factors are difficult
to model. In order to account for inertia, the endogenous variable was
included as an explanatory variable with a one-year time lag and for
most explanatory variables five-year moving averages were calculated.
Finally, country-specific constants were included that represent the
influence of absent country-specific variables. The main results of the
estimation were (*t*-values in parentheses):

$$IB = 0.60\ IB(t\text{-}1) + 0.00\ \pi + 0.37\ Y - 0.16\ OPEN$$
$$\quad\ (13.5) \qquad\quad (0.1) \quad\ (4.0) \quad\ (4.1)$$

300 country-year observations; adj. $R^2 = 0.935$

$$IR = 0.87\ IR(t\text{-}1) - 0.02\ \pi - 0.05\ S_\pi + 0.06\ Y + 2.83\ CBI$$
$$\quad\ (31.8) \qquad\quad (1.7) \quad\ (1.8) \quad\ (2.1) \quad\ (1.4)$$

210 country-year observations; adj. $R^2 = 0.991$

where: *IB*   share of currency in the issue of international bonds
                worldwide
        IR   share of currency in global official foreign exchange
                reserves
        π consumer price change in deviation from average for
                sample countries

S_π standard deviation of inflation in deviation from average for sample countries

Y share of GDP in OECD GDP

CBI index of central bank independence ($0 \le CBI \le 1$) in deviation from average for sample countries; based on Alesina (1989)

$OPEN$ average of imports and exports of goods and services as a percentage of GDP in deviation from OECD average

Of all the examined explanatory variables, the lagged endogenous variable and economic size proved to outrank the other determinants by far. The high coefficients of the lagged endogenous variables indicate that the composition of private and official portfolios adjust very slowly to changes in the characteristics of the issuing countries. The monetary determinants (inflation, inflation variability and central bank independence) and the openness of the economy gave fairly good results in some cases, but their coefficients are negligible. A remarkable outcome is the fact that central bank independence seems to be more important than actual performance on inflation.

Two other features are noteworthy, too. First, the difference between the two coefficients of the lagged variable, 0.60 for the international bonds and 0.87 for the official foreign exchange reserves, shows that private markets adjust quicker (or less slowly) than official institutions, as was to be expected intuitively. Second, in the long term the relation between currency shares in world portfolios and GDP shares in total OECD GDP seems to be quite strong, especially for international bond issues. This can be made clear by rewriting the equations in a steady-state form:

$$IB = 0.01\,\pi + 0.94\,Y - 0.40\,OPEN$$
$$IR = -0.17\,\pi - 0.39\,S_\pi + 0.42\,Y + 21.09\,CBI$$

As regards the issue of international bonds, the relation between the share of currencies and the countries' share in GDP is almost one to one. In official foreign exchange reserves, the GDP share accounts for almost half of the currency's share.

of monetary policy. Given the fact that the euro area as a whole is less open than the individual participating countries, the ESCB may display more 'benign neglect' in its exchange rate policy than has been the case in the pre-

EMU era (see Chapter 11). Therefore, it is likely that the correlation between euro and US money market interest rates and bond yields will decline. In view of risk-minimizing considerations, this could imply a tendency for investors to increase their share of euro assets in their portfolios.

As regards the ESCB, it will have a more favourable attitude towards the euro becoming an international currency than the Bundesbank had towards the Deutsche mark in the past. Duisenberg (1999) has stated that the euro system does not intend either to foster or to hinder the development of the euro as an international currency. It will take a neutral stance and leave that role to be determined by market forces. But, even if the ESCB wished to govern the extent of internationalization of the euro, it would probably not be able to do so. As argued above, it is the 'invisible hand' rather than the 'official hand' that determines the international use of currencies.

Well-developed financial markets

The most important issue is how quickly financial markets in Europe will integrate and thus how quickly they will gain in depth, breadth and transparency. Portes and Rey (1998) assume that the introduction of the euro will not lead to changes in volatility in these markets, implying that liquidity will drive developments in transaction costs. In addition, multiple equilibria are an important feature of the model of Portes and Rey. They present a number of alternative equilibria or scenarios, ranging from status quo via a so-called 'medium' euro scenario to a 'big' euro framework. In the latter, the euro replaces the dollar as vehicle in foreign exchange markets and becomes the international currency for financial asset transactions. In the 'medium' euro scenario, the euro replaces the dollar in financial asset markets but not as vehicle in foreign exchange markets. Portes and Rey conclude that a plausible scenario would be the one in which euro and dollar have more or less equal status (somewhere in between the medium and big euro scenarios). Initially, a status quo situation is likely to prevail, but a bigger role for the euro will occur rather quickly, namely in a period from five to ten years. Euro transaction costs would then fall below dollar transaction costs, provided that monetary authorities promote the internationalization of the euro and that financial market integration is completed within Europe, which would be all the more likely if the UK joins the euro area. This would also generate substantial welfare gains for Europe: a structural positive annual effect of 0.2 per cent of GDP.

As they themselves acknowledge, the results of Portes and Rey hinge on a number of crucial assumptions, such as the need for deep and transparent European financial markets, a significant role of the euro in official reserves and stimulation from the side of the ECB. It is worthwhile to elaborate more on the first issue, that is, the prospects for quick integration in European financial markets.

In a report written under the auspices of the European Commission (1999b) by a working group (in which experts from financial and official institutions participated) a number of concrete recommendations were formulated to increase the potential of one integrated European financial market (particularly the bond and equity market). Some of these recommendations have actually been implemented by the authorities, such as the redenomination of existing debt and continuity of price sources. Other recommendations by the working group were harmonized market rules and conventions and informal coordination of government debt issuing. In addition, other 'institutional' factors are relevant to creating an integrated capital market. Quite important, for instance, has been the decision by the ESCB to fully remunerate reserve requirements, which implies that no unnecessary burdens are placed on European financial institutions in the competition with financial institutions outside the euro area.

The ECB (1999c) has published an extensive study about the consequences of EMU on the European banking sector. The main finding of the study is that 'EMU is likely to act in the medium and long term as a catalyst to reinforce already prevailing trends in the EU banking system. In particular, EMU is expected to reinforce the pressure for the reduction of existing excess capacity, to put profitability under pressure and to lead to increased internationalisation and geographical diversification, also outside EMU, as well as to increased conglomeration and mergers and acquisitions'. What we have seen in practice is that in the run-up to EMU, markets have been adjusting very rapidly to the new environment – a process that continued unabated after 1 January 1999. Restructuring and merger and acquisition activities in the financial sector have become a common good. For the time being, however, the mergers and acquisitions are concentrated on wholesale banking and are mainly national affairs. The common market in retail financial services is still virtually non-existent. Due to national tax regulations, administrative procedures and the huge costs of market penetration, *inter alia*, it is hard to develop retail-banking activities in foreign countries.

Apart from this, there is also a downside risk to the rapid merger process. The report by the ECB contains an important warning, one that is also made by White (1998), namely that the restructuring process inherits a systemic risk in the sense that some banks may stay in the competitive fight too long, thereby taking excessively risky investment decisions. The key challenge for policy makers is thus to keep a very close eye on actual developments.

The official international use of currencies depends not just on transaction and intervention needs. Reserve-holding authorities' portfolio considerations are also important. In countries with a floating currency and sufficient reserves, the composition of reserve portfolios is determined by investment decisions and risk management. In this respect, a shift towards a greater share of the euro in total official reserves is probable. The euro is more attractive for portfolio considerations than the individual euro area currencies, because the liquidity of euro markets is higher. On the other hand, from considerations of risk diversification a single European currency is less attractive than separate euro area currencies, which could have a (probably smaller) opposite effect on the share of the euro.

Furthermore, it seems plausible that the euro will achieve a more prominent place in currency arrangements than has been the case for the Deutsche mark and the French franc. In economic terms, the mere size of the euro area could imply a greater incentive for outside countries to link their currency one way or the other to the euro. This will especially be the case with regard to Central and Eastern Europe and Africa (see Chapter 11 for a further examination of the role of the euro in currency arrangements). Poland, for instance, has announced that it will gradually move from a basket-peg (in which also the dollar features) towards a full peg to the euro. Apart from economic considerations, political motives might also form a reason for outsiders to link their currencies to the euro. The case of Cyprus is an example. To underscore its wish to join the European Union, the country decided to change its exchange rate regime from a peg to the pound sterling to a peg to the euro as of 1 January 1999.

Thus, a crucial factor for deep European financial markets is a change of attitude of lenders and borrowers. In this sense, it is useful to compare the financial structure in Europe with that in the other major economic powers. Table 7.6 presents a number of key financial market indicators.

Bond markets
In western economies, it is common for companies to finance their investment activities largely from internally generated funds (savings and reserves). Only around one-third of investment is financed from external sources; this goes for the United States, individual European countries and Japan (Berndsen, De Haan and Huisman, 1998). The differences between countries are related to the way external sources are tapped. As can be seen in Table 7.6, the financial systems in Europe and Japan are to a large extent bank-based, while in the United States market-based instruments dominate. The private sector goes to the banks and other financial institutions in Europe and to the market in the United States. Not only equity markets, but bond markets too are more mature in the United States than in the euro area.

In the US, the official authorities have issued huge amounts in the bond market, and the market for private debt is also sizeable. But securitization is

Table 7.6 Key financial data in the euro area, United States and Japan (end 1997, trillions of ecus, % of GDP in parentheses)

	Euro area		United States		Japan	
Bank deposits	4.7	(84)	4.0	(55)	3.7	(99)
Domestic credits	7.1	(129)	5.9	(82)	4.7	(127)
Domestic debt securities	5.0	(90)	11.4	(165)	4.0	(109)
of which private sector	1.9		4.7		1.2	
of which public sector	3.1		6.6		2.8	
Stock market capitalization	5.1	(66)	10.9	(139)	2.1	(50)

Source: ECB (1999d) and own estimates.

quickly becoming more and more important in Europe as well. A crucial force behind these developments is the growing importance that institutional investors attached to securities. In the past 15 years, the role of institutional investors has been growing enormously in the world financial landscape. In the OECD area, total assets held by institutional investors have increased from around 36 per cent of OECD GDP in 1981 to over 100 per cent in 1995 (Blommestein, 1998).[5] But, what is even more important, investment behaviour by institutional investors (and households) has changed significantly in recent years. Holdings of private placements by the government used to be the major category in the portfolio of Dutch institutional investors until the beginning of the 1990s. In less than ten years, portfolios have been radically diversified into equity and bond holdings which are now the major components.

Moreover, even though the bond market in the euro area is only approximately half the size of the US bond market (Table 7.6), from 1 January 1999 it has clearly gained in depth and liquidity. In comparison, the German bond market on its own, which accounts for around 40 per cent of the euro area market, was only a little more than one-fifth the size of the US bond market.

Important for the development of euro area bond markets is that the euro by itself has eliminated exchange rate risks. In fact, from May 1998 when the irrevocable bilateral conversion rates for the participating euro countries were pre-announced, we have seen a dramatic reduction in interest rate spread *vis-à-vis* Germany (ten-year bond yields), particularly for countries such as Spain and Italy. Remaining interest rate differentials show that the euro area bond market cannot be fully compared to the very liquid and uniform US Treasury bill market. Default risks, the availability of derivatives and taxation issues will continue to produce small differences in yields on bonds with the same maturity.

The outlook for the development of a private bond market is less clear-cut. When EMU started, a relatively liquid corporate bond market existed only in France.[6]

Equity markets

Portes and Rey (1998) discuss developments in bond markets but do not take equity markets into consideration (De Grauwe, 1998). Evidently, the consequences of EMU for equity markets are less clear-cut than for bond markets. The euro area equity market is considerably smaller than that in the United States (see Table 7.6). Moreover, there are still many differences in legal, accounting and tax regulations – such as taxation of securities' earnings and company earnings – in European countries.[7] Nevertheless, just as is the case in the banking sector, developments in equity markets proceed very quickly. Competition among stock exchanges in Europe is fierce. It is unlikely that all national stock exchanges in euro countries can survive on their own. The tone for strategic partnerships was set in July 1998 by the announcement that the Deutsche Börse AG and the London Stock Exchange were to set up an electronic trading system for the 300 largest European companies. At the beginning of May 1999, it was announced that the partnership would be extended to other continental European exchanges, among them those in Paris and Amsterdam. These are first indications of rapid adjustments in equity markets.

4. ESTIMATING THE INTERNATIONAL USE OF THE EURO

Portfolio management

There are a number of publications in which quantitative estimates have been made as to the prospective role of the euro in portfolio management (Bergsten, 1997; Persaud, 1997; Oort, 1998). Note that these estimates were made before it was known which countries would participate in EMU from the outset. Bergsten, who takes together private and official portfolios, assumes that every percentage point increase in a country's share of world GDP and trade produces a commensurate increase in its currency share. He calculates that the share of the euro in the world portfolio could increase to around 40 per cent if all EU countries joined EMU. This would imply a switch to the euro worth up to $1000 billion. Persaud estimates this switch to be around $600 billion. The results of research by Oort (1998) are comparable to those of Bergsten. Oort's equation points to an additional effect in favour of the euro share, however very small compared to the influence of size, namely as regards the openness of the economy (see Box 7.1). The euro area will be a relatively closed economy, which – as we saw in Section 2 – is favourable for economic and financial stability and thus for the international use of the euro.

Official reserves

As has been the case for portfolios, in several publications attempts have been made to quantify the future role of the euro in official reserves (Masson and Turtelboom, 1997; Persaud, 1997; Bergsten, 1997; Oort, 1998). Masson and Turtelboom describe the initial effects of the introduction of the euro on official reserves under the assumption that all countries would join. First, reserves within EMU denominated in European currencies by definition no longer form part of EMU reserves (and therefore of total world reserves). Second, official reserves within EMU are transformed into dollars and gold. Third, the authors estimate that some $105 billion of EMU reserves will be redundant. If we assume that these redundant reserves will be disposed of fully at the expense of dollar reserves, a dollar's share in total world official reserves of 62 per cent would result, and the share of the euro would turn out to be 16 per cent. It would still mean a small increase of the dollar's share, since total reserves would have fallen more.

Persaud (1997) not only reviews changes in EMU reserves comparable to Masson and Turtelboom, but on top of this predicts a portfolio adjustment by non-EMU countries. Dollar reserves would fall $310 billion and euro reserves would rise $105 billion, and their shares would turn out to be almost the same, about 40 per cent. Bergsten expects a shift in the world portfolio of official reserves between $100 and $300 billion. On the other hand, Alzola (1997) claims that other authors overreact. In his opinion, the relation of reserve policy with foreign trade is not so strong and central banks cannot easily dispose of reserves. Furthermore, Asian and Latin American countries, which hold a large share of world reserves, will keep their focus on the dollar for the time being, whereas Eastern European countries only hold a small share of world reserves.

Oort estimates a euro share in official reserves of up to a quarter. The estimated equation shows that not only economic size, but also – though to a much smaller extent – central bank independence is relevant here. Since the ECB will probably be more independent than the national central banks were on average, this provides for a small additional effect in favour of the euro share (see Box 7.1).

Will the euro go up or down?

As became clear above, there are many uncertainties as to the supply and demand effects of the introduction of the euro (money and assets), and thus as to the consequences for the euro's external value. In general, this issue has not been extensively discussed in economic literature. Where there has been some analysis, economists' views differ greatly. Portes and Rey (1998) are confident of a long-lasting increase in the demand for euro-denominated claims at a faster pace than the growth in euro liabilities. This is why they expect the euro to appreciate in real terms after EMU begins. On the other hand, McCauley (1997) does not expect the dollar to fall against the euro as a result of net portfolio shifts. Assuming a $30 billion supply shift from dollar into euro, he estimates that a 2 per cent drop in the dollar would be needed to restore portfolio balance, which is no more than the standard deviation of one week's movement in the dollar/mark rate. However, the assumed supply shift seems to be fairly small. Eikelboom, Schrijner and Wolswijk (1998) expect a net shift of $880 billion and estimate the euro to appreciate by 5–10 per cent.

Other economists – for instance, De Grauwe (1998) – have questioned the proposition that the increase in euro liabilities is likely to lag behind that in euro claims. Both liabilities and claims may just as well increase at the same pace, which implies that we simply do not know whether the euro will appreciate or depreciate.

5. CONCLUSIONS

In this chapter we have tried to answer the question to what extent the euro will be able to challenge the dollar as the major international currency. Thereby, we particularly focused on two aspects, the role of monetary policy and the development of financial markets.

First of all, it should be noted that the euro will not achieve stardom overnight. From the past we can learn that it is not easy to become the major international currency. It took the dollar a long time to take over from the pound sterling.

Having this in mind, a number of factors point to a rather optimistic perspective for the euro being able to challenge the dollar in the longer term: (i) the speedy integration of financial markets in Europe, particularly money and bond markets; (ii) the merger and restructuring process in the European banking sector; (iii) the considerable economic and financial size of the euro area; and (iv) the fact that monetary policy has undergone a fundamental change in most euro area countries, with a stronger focus on price stability and true independence of the central bank. Also, it is unlikely that the ECB will try to hinder the emergence of the euro as an international currency. On the other hand, one should note that although official stimulation may help to some extent, it is primarily the invisible hand rather than the official hand that determines the international use of currencies. Quantitative estimates show that the share of the euro could be highest in portfolio management at 40 per cent, whereas the euro share in the official reserves could rise to almost 25 per cent.

The international monetary system might thus develop into a bipolar system rather quickly. We should probably not tip the scale too much in favour of overoptimism about the future role of the euro. Capital markets in Europe will in the near future remain much more fragmented than the very deep and liquid American markets. A full integration of the European bond market is likely to occur only after the EU has become a full political union as well. For it was Mundell (1983) who reminded us that the top currency is provided by the top power.

NOTES

1. See for instance Portes and Rey (1998), McCauley and White (1997), Prati and Schinasi (1997), Bakker and Kapteyn (1997), Oort (1998), DeBandt (1998), White (1998), ECB (1999c) and European Commission (1997).
2. A basket peg is a currency peg not to just one currency but to a weighted composite of currencies. In a crawling peg regime the currency is adjusted quasi-automatically and mostly pre-announced in response to the inflation difference with the country the currency is pegged to. In the case of managed floating the central bank supports the rate through frequent interventions aimed at achieving an 'equilibrium level'.
3. See for instance Bergsten (1975), Mundell (1983), Laney (1988) and ECU Institute (1995).
4. The estimation method used was SUR (Seemingly Unrelated Regression). The countries examined were the United States, Germany, Japan, the United Kingdom, France, Switzerland and the Netherlands for the official foreign exchange reserves, and in addition Canada, Italy and Australia for the international bond issues. Besides the equations mentioned here, equations with other explanatory variables were estimated (such as nominal exchange rates and their variability, export share, issue of international bonds by country, capital account restrictions index), sometimes over sub-periods. See Oort (1998) for details.
5. Developments in the Netherlands were more pronounced: at the end of 1997, assets of Dutch institutional investors amounted to around 150 per cent of GDP.
6. Anecdotal information tells that bond issuance grew rapidly in the first quarter of 1999. The volume of corporate bonds issued rose almost sevenfold compared to the first quarter of 1998. In the Netherlands, activity by the private sector on bond markets has been increasing since the middle of the 1990s, in particular by the financial sector. This might set the stage for the development of a larger and deeper private bond market.
7. Note that there are still many differences in trading systems, due to historical and social-cultural aspects, government regulation and supervision on stock exchanges. Interestingly, however, over a decade a certain extent of convergence of trading systems in Europe has

taken place in reaction to the Big Bang in London in 1986 (Berndsen, De Haan and Huisman, 1998). Nowadays, trading systems on most stock exchanges are of a so-called hybrid nature: retail trade is served by order-driven systems and wholesale trade by quote-driven systems, the latter to adjust to the wishes of institutional investors, which have become an increasingly important party on equity markets.

PART THREE

Policy and Institutions

ES8
F12

8. Institutional Setting of the European System of Central Banks

Carel van den Berg, Reinder van Dijk and Broos van der Werff

In the first years after the Second World War France controlled and restricted Germany's coal and steel production in the French occupied zone to prevent a resurrection of Germany as a military power. When the Cold War developed between the United States and the Soviet Union, the United States began to see a stable West Germany as vital to its European and – by implication – its global interest. France had to change its policy. To counter the worries of the French industrial lobbies and its political elite, two visionary Frenchmen (Monnet and Schuman) proposed that France and Germany would enter talks to 'pool' or 'fuse' their markets for coal and steel. Germany welcomed the idea. The pool was to be regulated by an independent High Authority and other European countries were invited to join in. Indeed, the Benelux countries and Italy joined the effort and this led to the establishment of the European Coal and Steel Community in 1956.

Many of today's institutional characteristics of the European Community can be traced back to this first sectoral community. The Dutch government proposed to establish a committee of ministers that could give the High Authority orders by majority voting. In their view coal and steel interacted with the rest of the economy and this justified a role for the national governments. Monnet and Schuman agreed, provided the ministers took decisions on policies proposed by High Authority. The following institutional pattern emerged: · the initiative lay with the High Authority; decisions affecting member states would involve the Council of Ministers; accountability to parliaments would be vested in the Common Assembly and to the law in the Community's own Court of Justice (Dûchene, 1996). Since then institutional integration has grown in an evolutionary and gradual way.

A major step has recently been made by the transfer of monetary sovereignty to the European System of Central Banks (ESCB). This chapter describes its institutional characteristics and the relations of the ECB with other European institutions. We conclude with a comparison of the ESCB with the Federal Reserve System of the United States and with some thoughts about how the ESCB may develop in the future.

1. MAIN INSTITUTIONAL FEATURES OF THE ESCB

The European System of Central Banks comprises the ECB and the 15 national central banks (NCBs) of the Member States of the European Union.[1] Only the NCBs of the 11 Member States which have introduced the euro take part in the decision-making regarding the single monetary policy, while the other four NCBs continue to conduct their own monetary policy.[2] For the sake of easy reference, the term 'Eurosystem' is used to denote the system consisting of the ECB and the 11 NCBs of the Member States participating in EMU.[3] If and when all Member States participate in the euro area, the term 'Eurosystem' will become a synonym for the ESCB. The word 'system' refers to an institutional framework of a common set of rules by which both the ECB and NCBs are governed. This section describes the institutional setting of the ESCB (and the Eurosystem) by analysing its policy making process.[4] This process consists of a complex admixture of centralizing and decentralizing elements: policy decisions are taken at centralized level, are jointly prepared by the ECB and NCBs, and are mainly implemented at decentralized level by the NCBs (see Figure 8.1).

Decision making

The ESCB is governed by the two decision making bodies of the ECB, the Governing Council and the Executive Board.[5] The Executive Board comprises the President, Vice-President and four other members, all chosen among persons of recognized standing and professional experience in monetary or banking matters. It represents the supranational element in the structure of the ECB as its members are appointed (for a non-renewable period of eight years) 'by common accord' of the governments of the Member States.[6] The Executive Board is in charge of the day-to-day administration of the ECB and implements monetary policy in accordance with the guidelines and decisions laid down by the Governing Council and gives thereto the necessary instructions to the NCBs.[7] The daily execution of monetary policies takes place in response to market developments which implies that there is a continuous need for operational decisions from the Executive Board. The Governing Council is a mixed supranational and intergovernmental body consisting of the members of the Executive Board and the Governors of the NCBs participating in the EMU.[8] It is 'the supreme decision-making body on all matters relating to the tasks of the System'[9] in

Figure 8.1 Eurosystem policy making process

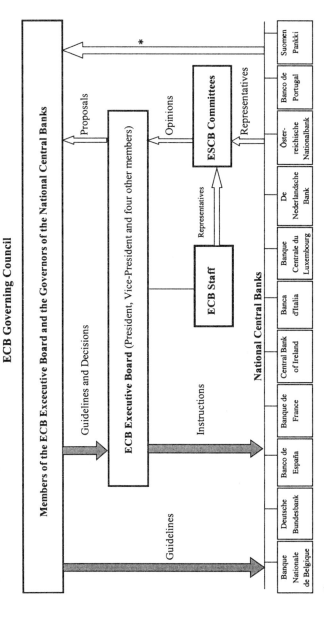

* Each NCB assists its own governor with the preparations for the meetings of the Governing Council

⇒ Decision-making / Policy Implementation

⇒ Policy Preparation

particular on strategic monetary policy issues, including those on intermediate monetary objectives and key interest rates.

The voting system is a reflection of the federal character of the Governing Council. Each member of the Governing Council has one vote and most decisions, including the ones on interest rates, are taken by simple majority.[10] It is, however, likely that in practice the members of the Governing Council will try to reach consensus for the decisions on interest rates.

The Governors of the NCBs are appointed for a period of not less than five years by their respective governments and are – like the Members of the Executive Board – independent and therefore not allowed to 'seek or take instructions from the Community institutions or bodies, from any government of a Member State or from any other body' (Article 108 EC Treaty). Though the background of the Governors certainly plays a role in their policy considerations, they participate in a personal capacity in the meetings of the Governing Council and are supposed to act in the interests of the Community as a whole. Personal independence of the members of the Executive Board is guaranteed by the fact that a member can only be retired compulsorily by the European Court of Justice if that member no longer fulfils the conditions required for the performance of his or her duties or has been found guilty of serious misconduct. This rules out the possibility of removal because of political reasons. The same strict criteria apply to the Governors of the NCBs. Furthermore, the Governing Council does not publish the detailed minutes of its meetings (including the votes of its individual members), thereby avoiding political pressure from the national governments on the individual members of the Governing Council.[11] However, the outcomes of the deliberations, that is, the decisions, are made public immediately at the press conference which follows meetings of the Governing Council.

Policy preparation

The NCBs and ECB both play a role in the process of policy preparation. The staff of the NCBs not only assist their own Governor with the preparations for the meetings of the Governing Council but also participate in the meetings of the ESCB Committees. There are 13 Committees covering all the different fields of activity of the ESCB, such as monetary policy, payment and settlement systems, supervision of credit institutions, and statistics.[12] These Committees provide expertise in their fields of competence, facilitate the decision making process of the ESCB and may prepare studies of specific topics when requested by the Governing Council or the Executive Board. Secretarial assistance and in most cases also a chairperson is provided by the ECB.[13] The Executive Board of the ECB is an important actor within the policy making process of the ESCB. Its members are the managing directors of the work units of the ECB and are responsible for the preparation of the meetings of the Governing Council. Furthermore, they function as an intermediary between the ESCB Committees and the Governing Council as the former are to report to the Governing Council via the Executive Board.

Policy implementation

Policy implementation takes mainly place at the national level by the NCBs in accordance with the principle of decentralization enshrined in Article 12.1, third paragraph, ESCB Statute: 'To the extent deemed possible and appropriate the ECB has recourse to the NCBs to carry out operations which form part of the tasks of the ESCB.'[14] Decentralized implementation is useful, given the knowledge NCBs have of the own national financial markets and local institutional circumstances. The Executive Board of the ECB coordinates policy implementation. The NCBs are therefore to act in accordance with the guidelines and instructions of the ECB[15] and may be summoned by the ECB to appear before the European Court of Justice in case of non-compliance.

2. TASKS OF THE ESCB

The most important function of central banks in general is the formulation and implementation of monetary policy. In addition central banks around the world perform a variety of related functions. Central banks are often fully or partly responsible for determining the exchange rate and managing the foreign reserves. Effective central bank independence requires that the central bank has a say in the choice of the exchange rate regime as exchange rate policy and monetary policy are closely linked at both the level of objectives and the operational level. Central banks play a role in managing the payment system and most of them are given responsibility for promoting the stability of the financial system. The prudential supervision of banks and other financial institutions and the service of lender of last resort are important functions in this field. Another classical central bank function is its role as bank of the government, that is, as fiscal agent of the government. The next section describes how central bank tasks and activities are divided between the ECB and NCBs. Three different categories of tasks can be distinguished. First, tasks which belong to the exclusive competence of the ESCB, such as monetary policy and the management of the official foreign reserves. Second, fields of tasks in which both the ESCB and the NCBs may play a role, such as supervision and payment systems. And finally, tasks which fall under the sole responsibility of the NCBs, such as the fiscal agency function.

Division of tasks and activities between the ECB and NCBs

Article 105(2) of the EC Treaty mentions four basic tasks of the ESCB, which concern monetary policy, foreign exchange operations, holding and management of the official foreign reserves, and the operation of payment systems. The primary task of the ESCB is 'to define and implement the monetary policy of the Community'. Monetary policy formulation belongs to the exclusive competence of the Governing Council and is conducted at decentralized level by the NCBs in accordance with the rules and proceedings adopted by the Governing Council and within this framework on the instruction of the Executive Board (Chapter 9 deals with monetary policy in more detail).

The second task is to conduct foreign exchange operations in accordance with Article 111 of the EC Treaty. This article relates to external monetary policy and gives responsibilities to the Ecofin Council, acting on the advice of the ECB, for either the conclusion of formal agreements or the adoption of general orientations for exchange rate policy. The division of competences between the Ecofin and ECB in this field will be outlined below, while the exchange rate policy issues will be discussed in more detail in Chapter 11.

The third task concerns the holding and management of the official foreign reserves of the participating Member States. Part of the official reserves has been transferred to the ECB and may be used for exchange rate and monetary policy operations. The NCBs in turn are allowed to perform transactions in the remaining reserves to fulfil their obligations towards international organizations such as the IMF. This refers to all types of banking transactions including borrowing and lending operations. All other transactions in these foreign reserve assets are – above a certain threshold – subject to approval by the ECB, not to make a judgement on the substance of the transaction, however, but only 'to ensure consistency with the exchange rate and monetary policies of the Community'.[16]

The fourth basic task is the promotion of the smooth operation of payment systems. An efficient payment system is a prerequisite for the establishment of a single money market. The task has been materialized through the establishment of the Trans-European Automated Real-time Gross-settlement Express Transfer (TARGET) system which provides the banking sector in the euro area with a European interbank payment system for (mainly large value) transactions in euros. TARGET is a completely decentralized system consisting of the 15 national interbank payment systems of the Member

States, and the Interlinking which links the different payment systems. The ECB Payment Mechanism is also part of TARGET and provides the ECB with a direct connection through which the ECB can make and receive TARGET payments.

Ancillary tasks

The EC Treaty and ESCB Statute mention four ancillary tasks. These tasks relate to the issue of banknotes and coins, prudential supervision, collection of statistical information and some advisory functions concerning European Community and national legislation.

The first ancillary task is the exclusive right of the ECB to authorize the issue of banknotes within the Community. This means that the issue of new banknotes, the standards applying to the re-issue of used banknotes, the withdrawal of banknotes, decisions on the number of notes put into circulation, and any other act which has a bearing on the circulation of banknotes is subject to prior approval of the ECB in order to avoid any divergence between the treatment of banknotes by the different NCBs (Smits, 1997, p. 206). Decisions on these matters are taken by the Governing Council. The actual act of bringing the banknotes into circulation will be carried out by the NCBs.[17]

The issue of coins does not belong to the competence of the ESCB and is a task of the Member States, though the volume of the coins to be issued is subject to approval by the ECB. Furthermore, the Ecofin Council has adopted in accordance with Article 106, second paragraph of the EC Treaty (after consulting the ECB) 'measures to harmonise the denomination and technical specifications of all coins intended for circulation to the extent necessary to permit their smooth circulation within the Community'.

The ECB and NCBs have a joint task in the field of prudential supervision of credit institutions. The ESCB is 'to contribute to the smooth conduct of policies pursued by the competent authorities relating to the prudential supervision of credit institutions and the stability of the financial system',[18] while the actual policy making for and performance of supervision remains a task of the Member States and is carried out by the NCB or by a separate agency.[19] Although the EC Treaty limits the competence of the ECB in the field of supervision to the contribution 'to the smooth conduct of policies', this may change in the future as the Ecofin Council is entitled to confer upon the ECB specific tasks concerning supervision.

The third ancillary task concerns statistical data collection. Without statistical data, the ECB would not be able to formulate and implement monetary policy. The ECB, assisted by the NCBs, is to collect the necessary statistical information and to contribute to the harmonization of statistical data collection. For these purposes the ECB is to work in close collaboration with – among others – Eurostat (the Statistical Office of the European Commission), the national statistical offices of the Member States, and international institutions such as the Bank for International Settlements and the International Monetary Fund. NCBs may also have the task – assigned by the national government – to collect statistical data for national purposes.

Finally, the ECB (not the ESCB) has some advisory functions. It must be consulted on any proposed Community act in its field of competence, and by national authorities regarding any draft legislative provision in its field of competence. The authorities of the Member States are to consult the ECB in particular on draft legislative provisions which are related to currency matters, means of payments, national central banks, collection, compilation and distribution of relevant statistics, payment and settlement systems and 'rules applicable to financial institutions insofar as they materially influence the stability of financial institutions and markets'.[20] The ECB may also submit opinions on matters in its field of competence on its own initiative.

Non-ESCB tasks

Except for the tasks and activities the NCBs fulfil as part of the ESCB, they may perform in correspondence with Article 14.4 of the ESCB Statute own tasks 'unless the Governing Council finds, by a majority of two thirds of the votes cast, that these interfere with the objective and tasks of the ESCB'. This clause confirms once more that the NCBs are an integral part of the ESCB and therefore subject to rules and procedures of the ESCB. Several examples of own NCB tasks have already been mentioned: the NCBs are responsible for their own national payment system, they may have the task of collecting statistical data for national purposes and they may also (if delegated by their government) issue coins. Other examples are the fiscal agency function, which most central banks fulfil on behalf of their government[21] and advising the government on financial-economic policy issues.

Lender of last resort (LOLR) function

Discussions have been going on in the Eurosystem about the question whether extending emergency liquidity assistance (ELA) should be seen as an 'own' NCB task in the sense of Article 14.4 ESCB Statute or as a task of the Eurosystem (Buiter, 1999; Van den Berg and Van Oorschot, 1999). Acting as lender of last resort could be defined as providing on an *ad hoc* basis liquidity to solvent but illiquid financial institutions or to the financial system as a whole. Liquidity to the financial system as a whole is decided upon by the centre, that is the ECB, and provided through the participation of all NCBs of the Eurosystem, either through (additional) regular tender operations, quick tenders (taking one hour or less between announcement and allotment) or bilateral transactions. Regular tenders are open to all banks, whereas a short-list of the most active banks is used for quick tenders and bilateral operations.[22] Furthermore, lending should always be based on adequate collateral (Article 18.2 of the ESCB Statute).

Supporting an individual bank is a more complicated operation. Overnight borrowing under the marginal lending facility (Lombard) against collateral is of course an option open to all banks with a liquidity shortage. However, a bank may also have a collateral shortage (in which case an urgent decision is necessary whether to accept less than adequate collateral), or the bank may need liquidity assistance over a longer period. For instance, the bank could be a foreign branch whose parent bank is located in a country going through a financial crisis or the bank may be part of a financial conglomerate having financial problems in other parts of the conglomerate. It is possible that credit lines of other banks to this bank are cut or shut down over a longer period. In principle, an NCB should not be allowed to engage in active direct lending to an individual bank. The purpose of such a rule is to protect the singleness of monetary policy throughout the euro area. In exceptional circumstances the ECB itself should be able to undertake a bilateral transaction with one or a few banks. The General Documentation on ESCB Monetary Policy Instruments and Procedures leaves open such a possibility.[23] The NCB that wishes ELA for one of its banks should file such a request with the ECB. The decision by the Governing Council could be arranged via a quick teleconference.

Defining emergency liquidity assistance not as a Eurosystem task but as an 'own' task of an NCB would probably result in a more transparent and faster procedure. The compromise that has been found is to leave aside the question whether ELA is an Article 14.4 (ESCB Statute) function, or not. ELA will be considered a responsibility of NCBs, while subject to the restriction that direct liquidity assistance above a certain threshold (defined as the overall size of the ELA operation envisaged by one or more NCBs for a given financial institution or a group of financial institutions) should, time permitting, be brought before the ECB Governing Council. The ELA can be rejected by the ECB Governing Council with a qualified majority, but only for undue interference with the monetary stance of the ESCB. However, rejection is very unlikely because the liquidity effect of even large ELA operations could probably be easily sterilized by other ESCB operations. More than that, instantaneous sterilization might not even be necessary in view of the enormous size of the euro money market. Anyway, ELA operations should always be reported to the ECB to allow the ECB to monitor the overall stability of the financial system of the euro area. Providing liquidity assistance is not the only option open to the ECB in case of financial problems. The ECB could also engineer a takeover of the bank, possibly with a loss for the shareholders of the problem bank in order to discourage imprudent behaviour by bank management (moral hazard).

3. INDEPENDENCE AND EXTERNAL RELATIONS

A basic feature of the ESCB is its independence as enshrined in Article 108 of the EC Treaty: 'When exercising the powers and carrying out the tasks and duties conferred upon them by this Treaty and the Statute of the ESCB, neither the ECB, nor a national central bank, nor any member of their decision-making bodies shall seek or take instructions from Community institutions or bodies, from any government of a Member State or from any other body.' The ECB and NCBs have both legal personality[24] so they can act separately from the other EU institutions and the Governments of the Member States. In order to prevent the undoing of institutional independence by political pressure on the individual members of the Governing Council, the members have been granted personal independence from their respective Governments of the Member States and from Community institutions (as explained in Section 1). [25]

The independence of the ECB does not, however, exclude an open dialogue with the political authorities of the Member States and the European Community. On the contrary, exchange of views is of utmost importance to ensure a coordinated approach to the economic and monetary policies of the Community and may also contribute to the accountability of the ESCB. Furthermore, on certain matters such as exchange rate arrangements, both the monetary authorities and the economic authorities (that is, the Ecofin Council) have a say, making the dialogue between both authorities even more opportune.

The dialogue between ECB and political authorities

Interaction between the ECB and other EU institutions takes place through mutual participation in several meetings. The meetings of the Governing Council of the ECB may be attended by the President of the Ecofin Council and a member of the Commission.[26] They do not have the right to vote though the President of the Ecofin may submit a motion for deliberation and has therefore the opportunity to influence the agenda of the Governing Council. Likewise, the President of the ECB shall be invited to participate in the meetings of the Ecofin Council when the Council is discussing 'matters relating to the objectives and tasks of the ESCB'.[27] The President is also regularly invited to meetings of the Euro-11, an informal forum composed of the ministers of finance of the Member States participating in EMU. An important function of the Euro-11 is to guard the Stability and Growth Pact[28] in order to avoid excessive national government budget deficits. (The Stability and Growth Pact is explained in more detail in Chapter 10.) The Euro-11 addresses furthermore issues such as the representation of the euro area in international fora and possible exchange rate arrangements. Decisions on these matters can, however, only be taken by the Ecofin Council because of the informal status of the Euro-11. Its meetings, which are not open to the public, usually precede the meetings of the Ecofin Council.

The Economic and Financial Committee (EFC) provides for a framework within which the dialogue between the economic and monetary authorities can be prepared and continued on the level of senior officials. The EFC was established at the start of the third phase of EMU and is the successor to the Monetary Committee. It consists of two officials of the Commission, two of the ECB, one official of the ministry of finance or economics[29] from each Member State and one representative from each NCB.[30] The EFC prepares the meetings of the Euro-11 and the Ecofin Council, is 'to keep under review the economic and financial situation of the Member States and of the Community', may be consulted in the procedure concerning the Exchange Rate Mechanism II (ERM-II)[31] and prepares the Ecofin Council's reviews of the development of the exchange rate of the euro'.[32]

The ECB is to submit an annual report on the activities of the ESCB and on monetary policy to the European Parliament, the Council and the Commission, and also to the European Council.[33] The President of the ECB is to present this report to the Council and to the European Parliament, 'which may hold a general debate on that basis'. Furthermore, the President of the ECB and the other members of the Executive Board can be heard by the European Parliament, at the request of Parliament or on the initiative of the ECB. Several Member States have also worked out this element of accountability on the national level. The Governors of the central banks in Belgium, the Netherlands, Spain, France, Ireland, Portugal can be asked to appear before Parliament in order to explain the monetary policy pursued by the ESCB.[34]

External representation

The representation of the ESCB at the international level has been determined in accordance with Article 111(4) of the EC Treaty and Article 6.1 of the ESCB Statute. Article 111(4) deals with positions the EU can take by a qualified majority at the international level as regards issues of particular relevance to EMU. In accordance with the same article, albeit now by a unanimous decision in the Council, the representation of the EU is decided with due regard for the allocation of powers laid down in Articles 99 and 105 of the EC Treaty. This means that the ESCB is to represent the EU for monetary policy issues. Article 6.1 of the ESCB Statute states that the ECB decides how the ESCB shall be represented in international fora. It has decided that the ECB President shall represent the ESCB in the most important international fora such as the G7, the BIS and the Interim Committee of the IMF. Furthermore, an observer from the ECB participates in selected meetings of the Executive Board of the IMF.

Division of competences between the European Commission, the Council of Ministers, the European Parliament and the ESCB

The institutional framework comprising the Commission, the Council of Ministers and the European Parliament has hardly changed since the first days of European integration. The Council, consisting of the national ministers, is the only body with the power to approve EU legislation. However, the Council does not have the right of initiative. This right, namely the right to table a legislative proposal, is reserved to the Commission, which consists of two appointees for each of the five largest Member States and one for the other Member States. Votes in the Council are weighted, more or less according to the size of the Member State, while votes within the Commission are not weighted. The powers of the European Parliament have been extended recently by the Treaty of Amsterdam but do not pertain to the monetary field.

Within this family of European bodies the ESCB has its own special place. With regard to the formulation and execution of its basic tasks, the ESCB has been designated to have exclusive competence. In three cases, the ESCB has been endowed with the right to initiate Community legislation.[35] The first case relates to the legal framework within which the ESCB may impose obligations on third parties, such as banks and reporting agencies. The second case concerns the possibility of amending some specific articles of the ESCB Statute following a light amendment procedure but still requiring the approval of the Council of Ministers.[36]

The third case in which the ECB has the right to initiate legislation relates to the conclusion of formal exchange rate arrangements. Exchange rate policy is dealt with in Article 111 of the EC Treaty, which states that the Council of Ministers may, acting unanimously on a recommendation from the ECB or from the Commission, conclude 'formal agreements' on an exchange rate system for the euro with the authorities of non-Community currencies. A 'formal agreement' is understood to refer to Bretton Woods types of agreement, entailing a central rate and intervention obligations at the margins of a fluctuation band. Decisions on adjustment or abandonment of the central rate require a qualified majority of the Council based on, again, either a recommendation from the ECB or from the Commission. In the field of exchange-rate policy the involvement of the Parliament is limited. They are either consulted (on the conclusion of formal agreements) or informed (after the central rate of the euro has been adjusted). In all reality it has to be said that formal exchange rates for the euro *vis-à-vis* the dollar or yen are an unlikely event to happen.

In the absence of a formal agreement the Council, acting by a qualified majority, may 'formulate general orientations for exchange-rate policy in relation to these currencies' (Article 111(2), EC Treaty). Such orientations can only be formulated on the basis of a recommendation from the ECB or the Commission. According to the Treaty these general orientations may not jeopardize the objective of price stability of the ESCB.

4. COMPARISON BETWEEN ESCB AND FED

It is interesting to compare the ESCB to the US Federal Reserve System (Fed), as both are federally organized central bank systems. Their set-up consists of a centre (the ECB, respectively the Board of Governors and their staff) and a number of 'regional' central banks (the 11 national central banks respectively and the 12 district reserve banks). This section compares the internal structure as well as the external position (independence and accountability) of both systems. First, a brief overview of the historical evolution of the Fed is given.

History of the Federal Reserve System

The Federal Reserve System was created in 1913 by act of the US Congress.[37] Its initial task was mainly to guarantee financial stability. It was seen as an answer to the frequent banking crises at the beginning of the century, some of which had provoked deep recessions. The federal structure involving 12 individual reserve banks and a centre (Board of Governors) was deliberately chosen as it prevented the financial establishment from getting too much influence over the system. The location of the Board in the political centre of Washington, D.C., and not in New York, served the same purpose.

The Fed's early years were marked by internal conflicts stemming from a lack of a clear monetary policy strategy as well as from an unclear division of competences between the Board of Governors and the individual reserve banks (Dykes and Whitehouse, 1989). These conflicts hampered an adequate monetary policy reaction to the Great Depression since the large number of bank failures during those years was seen to have aggravated the recession. In reaction Congress agreed on new laws (Banking Act 1933, Banking Act 1935) that shifted the balance of power to the centre. Actual Fed policy remained, however, for some time very much influenced by the administration and specifically by the need to accommodate the fiscal deficits resulting from the expansive New Deal policies and the participation in the Second World War. The Accord (1951) between the Fed and the Treasury for the first time clearly established the Fed's control over monetary policy. During the following decades Congress took more interest in the Fed and in monetary policy in particular. A recurring theme was the appeal for more transparency and accountability of the Fed's policy. This eventually led to the passing of the Full Employment and Balanced Growth Act (1978), which requires the Chairman of the Board to testify twice a year before Congress on monetary policy. These testimonies should make clear how the Fed's monetary policy supports the policies of the administration in terms of the stated goals of maximum employment, stable prices and moderate long-term interest rates. In 1980 the Depository Institutions Deregulation and Monetary Control Act was passed which requires the Federal Reserve Banks to ask for fees for their payment services offered to commercial banks, with the aim of stimulating competition in this field.

Internal organization

The ESCB has a more decentralized organization than the Fed. This can be illustrated by a number of factors such as the composition of the policy making body, the responsibility for monetary policy implementation and the distribution of staff between centre and national central banks.

First of all, the national central banks of the ESCB outnumber the centre in the Governing Council (11 national central bank governors to 6 Executive Board members). Future expansion of the euro area through the acceptance of more members will push the balance even further away from the centre. In the Federal Reserve System, the centre dominates the vote in the Federal Open Market Committee (7 Board members against 5 of the 12 Reserve Bank presidents; of the latter the president of the Reserve Bank of New York is a permanent member, while the others serve on a rotating basis). This difference seems to be mainly a matter of degree and it is uncertain whether it will be important in practice. Anyway, all members of the ECB Governing Council are supposed to act in the interest of the Community as a whole.

Second, the national central banks of the ESCB are fully engaged in the implementation of policy through the use of their local standing facilities and their participation in open market activities. Moreover, they are responsible

Figure 8.2 Size of staff of euro area NCBs in relation to population

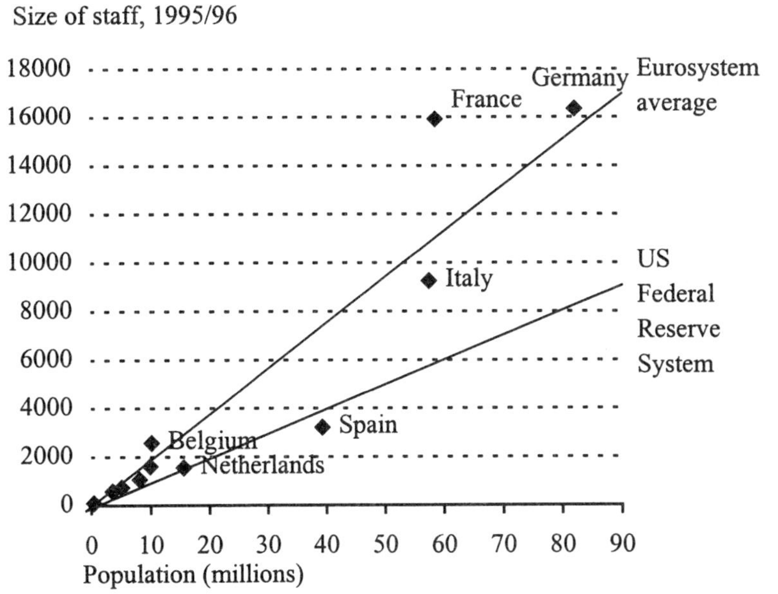

Size of staff, 1995/96

for the management of the international reserves. They are bound by guidelines set by the Governing Council of the ECB. This contrasts with the Fed where some specialization by the Reserve Banks has been achieved. All open market operations are carried out by the New York Fed, which is also responsible for the management of reserves and the implementation of foreign exchange interventions. Furthermore, several reserve banks have specialized in different aspects of payment systems support. These differences can be explained historically and especially by the differing structures of financial markets in the US, which are nation-wide, and those in Europe, which are organized along national lines.

Third, the different structures of both systems are reflected to some extent in the numbers of employees and their distribution across both systems. The ESCB, which covers an economy comparable to that of the US, employs nearly twice as many staff (53,700) as the Fed (25,800). The average staff:population ratio for the ESCB is 180 per million as against 90 for the Fed. Scaled by their respective populations the staffing of individual national central banks of the ESCB displays a wide variation (Figure 8.2). The Bundesbank and the Bank of France are at the upper end of the spectrum, while the Bank of Spain and the Netherlands Bank are at the lower end – the last two with regard to relative size being roughly comparable with the Fed. These differences can partly be accounted for by non-system tasks of, especially, the Bundesbank and the Bank of France.[38] The higher average staffing of the ESCB compared to the Fed could partly be ascribed to specialization gains earned by the Fed. The division of staff between the centre and the regions is for the ESCB much more uneven than for the Fed: the percentage of total staff employed in the centre amounts to 1 per cent for the ESCB while the corresponding figure is nearly 7 per cent for the Fed. This difference remains large even when one allows for the number of staff in the area of supervision – which is a function performed by the Fed but not by the ECB. This leads some observers (Begg *et al.*, 1998) to the conclusion that the ECB staff should be expanded in order to develop a truly European perspective within the system.

Fourth, the ECB has no role in the selection of national central bank governors, which is a prerogative of the governments of the individual member states. In contrast, the Board of Governors of the Federal Reserve System has to give its approval to nominations of reserve bank presidents.

Finally, in contrast to the Federal Reserve Banks the national central banks of the ESCB only share their seignorage, that is, the income resulting from the issue of euro banknotes. They do not share their operating costs, nor are they subject to budgetary approval by the ECB. The responsibility for cost control ultimately is a national affair since the profits of the national central banks are paid out to the governments. Within the Fed cost control is organized federally, with a major role for the Board of Governors, which is in turn subject to scrutiny by the Congress through the General Accounting Office. None the less, the Fed is self-financing and not subject to the budgetary appropriation process.

Independence and accountability

The primary objective of the ESCB is to maintain price stability. Without prejudice to the objective of price stability, it is to support the general economic policies in the Community with a view to contributing to the achievement of the objectives of the Community as laid down in Article 2 of the EU Treaty (Article 2 ESCB Statute). The Fed seems to be less independent and more accountable to the government as its primary objective is much broader than maintaining price stability. The Fed is legally required to direct its policy towards achieving the primary macroeconomic objectives as spelled out in the Full Employment and Balanced Growth Act (1978), Section 2(b). These objectives include amongst others full employment, balanced growth, adequate productivity growth and reasonable price stability. The Fed should coordinate its policy with that of the President and the Congress and it should set explicit short-term and medium-term goals in order to attain these objectives. In choosing its intermediate and operational policy targets the Fed is highly autonomous.

As regards the accountability to parliament and government authorities the position of the ECB is markedly different from the Fed's. The ECB president regularly appears in the European Parliament and in the meetings of the Euro-11 and the Ecofin in order to explain monetary policy and to respond to questions. Likewise, the national central bank governors may explain policy decisions in their national parliaments. The accountability of the Fed towards Congress has a strong legal basis and is much more pronounced. This logically follows from the broader mission (multiple objectives) of the Fed, which implies that the Fed has to make trade-offs between the various objectives of general government policy. The main channel for exercising its accountability is the semi-annual 'Humphrey-Hawkins' testimony[39] given by the Fed chairman before the US Congress. Congress has repeatedly demonstrated in the past that it wants to influence monetary policy and that it has the capacity to do so by threatening to amend the legal position of the Fed. The difference in accountability of both systems is also reflected in the nomination procedure for members of the ECB Executive Board and those of the Federal Reserve Board of Governors. Unlike the European Parliament, which has no right to reject the governments' nominees, the US Senate has a real say through its right to refuse to confirm the President's nominees.

5. THE ESCB IN THE FUTURE

Is it possible to predict in which direction the structure and tasks of the ESCB could develop during the coming decades? One assumption is that the same centralizing forces that acted upon the structure of the Fed will also shape the future ESCB. The experience of the Fed suggests that every financial crisis increases the pressure to centralize power in the centre. Of course, one could argue that in the ESCB decision making is already completely centralized (Governing Council of the ECB) with the notable exception of the role of lender of last resort. Mismanagement of a banking crisis involving more than one country could lead to calls to entrust decision making power in the area of emergency liquidity assistance, including its implementation, to the ECB.

Another issue is that centralization, or at least concentration of activities, will further cost-efficiency and is therefore likely to happen. However, two caveats apply. First, in the US the Fed is under the scrutiny of the General Accounting Office, which increases the cost-awareness of the Federal Reserve System. In Europe the European Court of Auditors only examines the operational efficiency of the management of the ECB, and not that of the NCBs.[40] The NCBs are under the scrutiny of their Supervisory Councils and, in some cases, a Board of Auditors. The pressure to reduce costs by concentrating operational tasks (in the ECB or in one of the NCBs) is therefore weaker than in the US. The ESCB Statute is even quite explicit in advocating implementation in a decentralized way. Article 12.1 of the Statute stipulates that 'to the extent deemed possible and appropriate . . . the ECB shall have recourse to the national central banks to carry out operations which form part of the tasks of the ESCB'. One could argue that the possible creation of pan-European banks will act as a force to centralize execution of monetary policy in one or a few places. However, at this moment the Eurosystem does not allow remote access to monetary credit, that is, each euro area bank can apply for and receive ESCB liquidity only at its own central bank. This does not distort the level playing field because these central banks apply uniform conditions.[41] A second caveat is that when the Fed was established money market activities (including foreign reserve management) were already largely concentrated in one place, that is New York. The ESCB, on the other hand, has been created by merging mature central banks, all with their own expertise and facilities. One has therefore to be careful in drawing parallels between the Fed and the ESCB in this respect.

A third relevant factor is the accession of the out-Member States to EMU and the accession of a number of East European countries to the EU and later to EMU. This will increase the problem of coordination between all the parts of the ESCB. The solution to this problem lies in further centralization. One could even wonder whether the size of the Governing Council could grow limitlessly, because this would dwarf the voting rights of the six Executive Board Members.[42]

At a more general level two forces should be mentioned which militate against a rapid concentration of central bank activities in the euro area. First, information technology allows banks to operate from different locations. Developments in information technology make decentralized implementation of monetary policy a viable option. Second, unlike in the US, central bank boundaries in the euro area coincide with national borders.[43] This implies that handing over operational functions to the ECB or another NCB will be felt more rapidly as loss of national identity.

APPENDIX 8.A. NUMBERING OF EC TREATY ARTICLES

The Treaty of Amsterdam introduced a new numbering of the EC Treaty Articles. All Article numbers in this book refer to this new numbering. The table below links the 'old' and the 'new' Article numbers.

Table 8.A1 New and old numbering of EC Treaty Articles

Old number	New number	Subject
Title VI	Title VII	Economic and monetary policy
Chapter 1		Economic policy
Article 102 A	Article 98	Objectives economic policy
Article 103	Article 99	Global guidelines
Article 103 A	Article 100	Financial assistance in case of economic difficulties
Article 104	Article 101	No monetary financing
Article 104 A	Article 102	Privileged access
Article 104 B	Article 103	No bail out clause
Article 104 C	Article 104	Excessive deficits
Chapter 2		Monetary policy
Article 105	Article 105	Price stability
Article 105 A	Article 106	Issue of banknotes and coins
Article 106	Article 107	ECB/ESCB
Article 107	Article 108	ESCB independence
Article 108	Article 109	Compatibility national legislation
Article 108 A	Article 110	Legal powers ECB
Article 109	Article 111	Exchange rate policy
Chapter 3		Institutional provisions
Article 109 A	Article 112	Executive board and general council
Article 109 B	Article 113	Mutual participation in meetings
Article 109 C	Article 114	EFC
Article 109 D	Article 115	Proposals and recommendations

Table 8.A1 New and old numbering of EC Treaty Articles (continued)

Old number	New number	Subject
Chapter 4		Transitional provisions
Article 109 E	Article 116	
Article 109 F	Article 117	
Article 109 G	Article 118	
Article 109 H	Article 119	
Article 109 I	Article 120	
Article 109 J	Article 121	
Article 109 K	Article 122	
Article 109 L	Article 123	
Article 109 M	Article 124	
Title VI A*	Title VIII	Employment
Article 109 N*	Article 125	
Article 109 O*	Article 126	
Article 109 P*	Article 127	
Article 109 Q*	Article 128	
Article 109 R*	Article 129	
Article 109 S*	Article 130	

Note: * New, as in the Treaty of Amsterdam.

NOTES

1. Article 2 ESCB Statute. At the start of EMU the Member States of the European Union were Belgium, Denmark, Germany, Greece, Spain, France, Ireland, Italy, Luxembourg, the Netherlands, Austria, Portugal, Finland, the United Kingdom and Sweden.
2. Denmark, Greece, the United Kingdom and Sweden have not (yet) introduced the euro.
3. The EC Treaty and the ESCB Statute do not make a formal distinction between the ESCB and the Eurosystem. The term 'Eurosystem' has been introduced by the Governing Council of the ECB.
4. The main sources of legislation of the ESCB are the EC Treaty, the ESCB Statute and the ECB Rules of Procedure. In particular the Articles 8, 10, 11, 12, 14 ESCB Statute and Articles 9 and 10 ECB Rules of Procedure are relevant for this section.
5. As long as there are Member States with derogation, there will be a General Council functioning as the third decision-making body of the ECB. It comprises the President and Vice-President of the ECB, the Governors of the NCBs (including the NCBs of the Member States with a derogation) and the other members of the Executive Board participating without the right to vote. It performs tasks which the ECB took over from the

European Monetary Institute and which, owing to the derogation of one or more Member States, still have to be performed in the third stage. The General Council also contributes to particular activities of the ESCB, such as the ESCB's advisory functions, the collection of statistical information, and the necessary preparations for irrevocably fixing the exchange rates against the euro of the currencies of the Members States with a derogation (Articles 45, 46 and 47 ESCB Statute).

6.   The appointment takes place at the level of the Heads of State or Government, on recommendation from the Ecofin Council after it has consulted the European Parliament and the Governing Council (Article 11.2 ESCB Statute).

7.   In addition, the Executive Board may have powers delegated to it where the Governing Council so decides (Article 12.1, second paragraph, ESCB Statute).

8.   In the literature the effectiveness of the Governing Council is doubted. Begg *et al.* (1998) characterizes the Governing Council of the ECB as a weak centre as it comprises 11 powerful governors of national central banks and only 6 members from the Executive Board. Buiter (1999) points out that if all current EU members join EMU in due course, there will be 21 members. He thinks that the one-country-one-vote principle will have to be given up, as the current group of 17 is already too large for a serious and productive exchange of views, discussion and group decision taking.

9.   As stated by the Committee of Governors in the Commentary to its Draft for the ESCB Statute (*Europe*, Document No. 1669/1670, 8 December 1990, p. 22) cited in Smits (1997, p. 95, footnote 350).

10. The President has the casting vote in the event of a tie (Article 10.2 ESCB Statute). Weighted voting in combination with a qualified majority rule applies to decisions on the policies for issues such as the subscription by NCBs to ECB capital, the allocation of monetary income received by central banks, profits and losses of the ECB and the transfer of foreign reserve assets to the ECB. In these cases, the votes of the Governors of the NCBs are weighted on the basis of their shares in the subscribed capital of the ECB while the members of the Executive Board are excluded from voting. Finally, recommendations on the amendment of the Statute of the ESCB require a unanimous decision by the Governing Council (Articles 10.3 and 41.2 ESCB Statute).

11. The Governing Council argues that the ESCB Statute forbids publication of the individual voting records of its members. Article 10.4 ESCB Statute states that 'The proceedings of the meetings shall be confidential. The Governing Council may decide to make the outcome of its deliberations public'. It is, however, doubtful whether this implies that the individual voting records may not be published. Buiter (1999, p. 10) thinks it does not, provided the individual votes are defined to be part of the *outcome* of the deliberations, rather than as part of the proceedings. Anyway, there are some arguments in favour of publishing the voting behaviour (Buiter, 1999; Begg *et al.* 1998). In other countries (e.g. the US, the UK and Japan) central banks do publish the minutes including the individual voting records.

12. The 13 ESCB Committees are the following: the Accounting and Monetary Income Committee, the Banking Supervision Committee, the Banknote Committee, the Budget Committee, the External Communications Committee, the Information Technology Committee, the Internal Auditors Committee, the International Relations Committee, the Legal Committee, the Market Operations Committee, the Monetary Policy Committee, the Payment and Settlements Systems Committee and the Statistics Committee. In addition to these committees, there are several working groups.

13. In the case of three committees, the chairperson is not provided by the ECB but by one of the NCBs.

14. This principle should be regarded as a 'practical working arrangement which puts emphasis on local, instead of central performance of Community tasks' (Smits, 1997, p. 112). It should not be confused with the principle of subsidiarity as enshrined in Article 5, second paragraph, EC Treaty. Neither can it be considered an application thereof. The principle of subsidiarity applies only in areas that do not fall within the exclusive competence of the European Community. It is therefore not applicable to the tasks of the ESCB, as these tasks are part of the exclusive competences attributed to the Community.

15. For this Section see Articles 5, 16, 23, 30, 31 and 35.6 ESCB Statute and Articles 105(4) and 106(2) EC Treaty.
16. Article 31.2 ESCB Statute. In correspondence with Article 31.3 ESCB Statute, the Governing Council has issued guidelines in order to facilitate such operations.
17. Although the ECB may according to Article 106(1) EC Treaty also issue banknotes, the issue of banknotes is likely to happen only at decentralized level by the NCBs.
18. Article 105(5) EC Treaty and Article 3.3 ESCB Statute. For an extensive analysis of this task, see Smits (1997, pp. 319–363).
19. See Kapteijn, Verloren van Themaat and Gormley (1998, p. 1004): 'Although the Committee of Governors of Central Banks has proposed that prudential supervision be included among the ESCB's principal tasks, the drafters of the Treaty of the European Union declined to follow this advice, as it could result in complications in those Member States in which supervision is entrusted to another authority.' Within the EU, only in Italy and the Netherlands does supervision fall under the exclusive competence of the central banks.
20. Council Decision 98/415/EC of 29 June 1998 on the consultation of the European Central Bank by national authorities regarding draft legislative provisions, Official Journal 1998 L 189/42.
21. The fiscal agency function is also mentioned explicitly in Article 21.2 ESCB Statute.
22. Defined as any procedure where the Eurosystem conducts a transaction with one or a few targeted counterparts in the Member States without tender.
23. In exceptional circumstances the Governing Council of the ECB may decide that the ECB undertakes a fine-tuning operation. Fine-tuning operations are executed (normally by quick tenders or bilateral procedures) on an *ad hoc* basis with the aim of managing the liquidity situation in the market and of steering interest rates, in particular in order to smooth effects on interest rates caused by unexpected liquidity fluctuations in the market (General Documentation on ESCB Monetary Policy Instruments and Procedures).
24. Article 107(2) EC Treaty.
25. For an extensive analysis of the independence of the ESCB, see Smits (1997, pp. 152–69).
26. The same holds for the meetings of the General Council (Article 113(1) EC Treaty). It should be noted, however, that at the meeting of the General Council the President of the Ecofin is not allowed to submit a motion.
27. Article 113(2) EC Treaty.
28. European Council Resolution of 17 June 1997 on the Stability and Growth Pact, Official Journal 1997, No. C236/1.
29. An official from the ministry attending the Ecofin Council (in most Member States the ministry of finance, in some others the ministry of economics) is appointed to participate in the EFC meetings.
30. All members may be accompanied by an alternate. See the Council Decision of 31 December 1998 adopting the Statutes of the Economic and Financial Committee, Official Journal 1999 L 5/71 and the Council Decision of 21 December 1998 on the detailed provisions concerning the composition of the Economic and Financial Committee, Official Journal 1999, L358/109.
31. European Council Resolution of 16 June 1997 on the establishment of an exchange-rate mechanism in the third stage of economic and monetary union, Official Journal 1997, No. C236/5.
32. Article 114, second paragraph, EC Treaty.
33. Article 113, third paragraph, EC Treaty; repeated in Article 15.3 ESCB Statute.
34. According to the respective legislation of the mentioned Member St ates.
35. This right of initiative in these cases is shared with the Commission; in fact if the ECB takes the initiative, the Commission will only be consulted and vice versa. In a number of other cases the Council of Ministers can only adopt legislation after having consulted the ECB.
36. Articles 41 and 42 ESCB Statute.
37. For a complete overview of the history of the Federal Reserve System, see Friedman and Schwartz (1963).

38. An example of such a non-system task for both the Bundesbank and the Bank of France is determination of the creditworthiness of companies.
39. Full Employment and Balanced Growth Act (1978), section 108.
40. Article 27 ESCB Statute.
41. However, remote access to intraday credit is allowed as this falls under the freedom of payments.
42. According to Buiter (1999) the Council is in its present size already too large from the point of view of efficient decision making. See note 8 of this chapter.
43. In the US, district borders cut in many cases right through a State. Furthermore, there are 50 States and only 12 Federal Reserve districts.

(Euspt)

ES2 E31
F42 F36

179 - 200

9. The Monetary Policy Strategy of the Eurosystem

Jan Marc Berk, Aerdt Houben and Jan Kakes

Central banks around the world face a complex task when conducting monetary policy. Although most of them have a reasonably clear view of their primary goal of price stability, and although they all have powerful instruments to achieve this goal, there is considerable uncertainty as to how exactly to employ these instruments. Since the seminal work of Friedman (1961) it is well-known that there is a considerable and varying time lag between the actions of a central bank in adjusting its policy instruments and the effects on the policy objective. Because of these lags, the monetary policy maker must take a forward-looking approach in the decision making process. Central elements in this approach include a forecast of the final goal over some time horizon, and a view on the transmission mechanism between the adjustment in the policy instrument and the policy goal. For a central bank to achieve its ultimate objective, it would be desirable to know exactly how monetary policy affects inflation and real output. In practice, however, such knowledge is far from perfect.

The inherent scarcity of unambiguous information on which to base monetary policy decisions (Berk, 1998a) makes it important that the central bank has a well-understood monetary policy strategy, that is, it should clearly state what its intentions are and how it envisages realizing these intentions. A clear monetary policy strategy provides a coherent framework for internal policy deliberations. It moreover constitutes a powerful instrument to communicate the current policy orientation to the general public, which in turn can help to stabilize inflation expectations. In addition, strategic goals provide benchmarks by which the central bank can be made accountable for its actions.

This chapter discusses the monetary policy strategy employed by the Eurosystem. In the next section, we first discuss some conceptual issues, including the alternative monetary policy strategies that were considered by the Eurosystem. Section 2 then sketches the environment of the euro area at the start of monetary union and discusses its implications for the choice of strategy. The strategy that the Eurosystem actually adopted is set out in Section 3 and subjected to a broad assessment in Section 4. The fifth section briefly discusses what we can expect from this monetary policy strategy, against the background of the Eurosystem's objectives as specified in the Maastricht Treaty. Section 6 concludes.

1. CONCEPTUAL ISSUES

As spelt out in Article 105(1) of the Treaty of Maastricht, the primary objective of the European System of Central Banks is to maintain price stability. There are two issues regarding this mandate. First, why should price stability be a policy objective? And, second, why should price stability be the prime objective of an independent central bank? On the first issue, aiming monetary policy at price stability does not mean that price stability is a final objective of economic policy, since it does not directly influence the welfare of individuals or society, as the volume of output and aggregate employment do. Rather, price stability is conducive to realizing these latter variables, as it creates a stable macroeconomic environment and thereby establishes a necessary precondition for sustained economic growth. In short, price stability is a means to an end rather than an end in itself. As a result, the economic and social benefits of price stability are not straightforward to identify. None the less, they are substantial. Box 9.1 sets out the main reasons for pursuing price stability.

On the second issue, price stability is naturally associated with monetary policy, since it is generally accepted that inflation is a monetary phenomenon in the long run. In this respect, monetary authorities throughout the world are now moving to adopt medium- to long-run price stability as their primary goal. The chief reason for making price stability the prime goal of monetary policy as conducted by an independent central bank is the inflationary bias inherent in monetary policy. This notion has its roots in the 'time inconsistency' literature, as developed by Kydland and Prescott (1977). The thrust of this argument is that a monetary policy maker who pursues price stability as well as employment growth could end up with a higher inflation outcome, and with no better employment outcome, than one who is solely focused on price stability. In order to achieve the goal of price stability, the Eurosystem has at its disposal a broad set of instruments, including reserve requirements, standing facilities (the marginal lending facility and the deposit facility) and open market operations; see EMI (1997a) for details. However, the effects of these policy instruments on economic activity and inflation are

Box 9.1 Why pursue price stability?

Price stability has manifest advantages. First of all, it helps shape a stability-oriented macroeconomic context. Empirical evidence (Hess and Morris, 1996; Edey, 1994) shows that price developments are more predictable when the inflation rate is low and that price stability thus enhances the predictability of the macroeconomic environment. A situation of broadly stable prices also allows households and firms to base their economic decisions on more reliable information, as they find it easier to distinguish movements in relative prices from movements in the general price index. Both of these aspects ultimately lead to a more efficient allocation of resources.

A second benefit to be derived from a stable price environment is that borrowers are not required to pay a premium to cover the risk of an unexpected rise in the general price level. In consequence, real interest rates will be lower, thereby encouraging agents to commit more resources to productive activities.

A third benefit of price stability is that it avoids the risk of borrowers being confronted with a rising real value of (nominally fixed) financial debts, which occurs in the event of an unexpected and sustained price decline. A rising real debt burden may have substantive negative effects on real economic activity, as this amplifies financial fragility (for households, enterprises, governments and banks) and as borrowers are normally more engaged in productive activities than lenders.

Fourth, high inflation or persistent deflation is costly for society even when it is perfectly anticipated. The widespread need to take price level changes into account in every kind of nominal contract implies that extensive resources are diverted from alternative and more productive uses. These are the well-known menu costs and 'shoe leather costs' of inflation. The former are borne by sellers who must continuously update price lists; the latter by households who will spend needless time and effort in order to economise on liquid balances. Moreover, if the tax system is not completely indexed to changes in the price index, inflation in the end has real distribution effects, which, in practice, entails an automatic increase in the tax burden.

Fifth, price stability is beneficial for the political cohesion of society, because inflation or deflation implies an arbitrary redistribution of wealth, which tends to hit the weakest members of society the hardest, as they maintain a higher proportion of their economic resources in liquid assets and as they have less instruments at their disposal to cover price risks.

---

separated both by time (the lags are long) and by behavioural processes (the lags are variable). By the latter we mean that, although monetary policy actions exert an important influence, economic activity and inflation are ultimately determined by the behaviour of various economic agents. Given the fact that human behaviour is, to a certain extent, unpredictable, the effects of policy actions are uncertain. A coherent way by which the monetary policy maker can take the consequences of (unavoidable) unexpected developments into account is by using intermediate targets. These are variables that are determined by the behaviour of both private sector agents and policy makers. Instead of directly focusing on realizing the ultimate target of price stability, the policy maker first determines the value of the intermediate target that would be consistent with price stability, and subsequently acts to achieve this projected target value. Apart from intermediate targets, the policy maker may also use so-called information variables. These variables can be defined as having information value for prospective price or output developments, without however being an object of control (as is the case with intermediate variables). Information variables may include variables that, in another context, may be viewed as an intermediate target. For example, the growth rate of the money stock can be viewed as an indicator of the potential strength of demand pressures in the economy, but it may also serve as an intermediate policy target.

The task facing policy makers is then to choose particular intermediate targets and information variables and to develop procedures for their use such that the economy is most likely to attain and preserve price stability. The way in which the policy maker resolves these issues constitutes the monetary policy strategy. The strategy then manifests itself in monetary policy decisions – that is, in decisions on the choice and intertemporal variation in policy instruments aimed at achieving the projected outcome for the intermediate target variable.

Possible strategies

In the remainder of this chapter we will, for expositional reasons, identify a policy strategy by the choice of intermediate target.[1] On this choice, a voluminous literature has developed. Based on current central bank practices and taking into account theoretical considerations, five possible strategies have been considered by the Eurosystem: money targeting, inflation targeting, exchange rate targeting, interest rate targeting, and nominal income targeting (EMI, 1997b). Of these five possible strategies, two were finally nominated by the EMI for consideration by the Eurosystem: money targeting and inflation targeting. At the same time, the possibility of combining the chief elements of these two strategies was also left open. For a short digression on the three options that were dismissed, see Box 9.2.

   The option of money targeting is based on the three important assumptions that money growth is predictably related to inflation, precedes inflation, and is broadly controlled by the central bank. If these assumptions hold, the central bank can achieve its ultimate goal of medium-term price stability by keeping the actual rate of money growth at, or close to, a trend rate that corresponds with stable prices and potential output growth, and that takes account of structural changes in money velocity. Deviations between the two rates will, under this strategy, elicit policy reactions. Money targeting has attractive features. For one thing, by focusing on a variable (money growth) that is typically considered a central bank matter, this strategy may enhance the independence of the central bank and thereby reduce the inflationary bias in monetary policy. Moreover, since information on money growth is publicly available, a money targeting strategy is relatively easy to monitor by the public at large. A special advantage for the Eurosystem is the explicit focus that money targeting places on euro-area-wide developments, since national monetary aggregates lose their meaning in a monetary union. By emphasizing the supranational character of monetary policy, this euro-area-wide focus may therefore contribute to a more European interpretation of monetary policy. The main disadvantages of money targeting lie in the validity of its presumptions: if money growth and future inflation do not follow a stable pattern and if the central bank is not able to effectively control money growth, money targeting is doomed to run into difficulties.

   An inflation targeting strategy aims at directly steering the final target variable, the inflation rate. Since monetary policy affects the inflation rate only with a lag, monetary policy actions under this strategy are based on a comparison between the targeted inflation rate (that is, the rate of inflation deemed consistent with the price stability objective) and the relevant inflation forecast. The latter variable incorporates all information on the future inflation rate including, but not limited to, money growth. This

---

Box 9.2 Alternative monetary policy strategies considered by the Eurosystem

The overriding objective of the Eurosystem's monetary policy strategy is to maintain price stability in the euro area. For this reason, an exchange rate targeting strategy was not considered appropriate since, for an area as large and as closed as the euro area, an externally oriented strategy may be inconsistent with domestic price stability. This is because extra euro area trade only has a relatively small impact on the euro economy, implying that economic developments in the euro area may easily diverge from those in the country or group of countries to which the intermediate exchange rate target would be linked. Put differently, the risk of conflicts between the internal and external price stability objectives would be substantial.

An alternative would be to use an interest rate as an intermediate target. This was not considered a feasible strategy since it presupposes that the central bank is able to identify the equilibrium real interest rate consistent with price stability. In practice, however, this knowledge is subject to major uncertainties. Moreover, pursuing an interest rate target may elicit market testing and thereby fuel financial market volatility. A third alternative strategy would be to use the growth rate of nominal income as an intermediate target. This, however, was also deemed infeasible. While such a strategy would provide a clear nominal framework, it has the serious drawback that nominal income is hardly controlled by the central bank. Moreover, such a strategy is relatively vulnerable to data revisions and incorrectly suggests that the Eurosystem would be indifferent to the price development within the overall nominal income development.

---

broad-based approach is an important advantage of inflation targeting. Moreover, this strategy stresses the responsibility of the central bank to fulfil its price stability objective. And, by relating policy actions to prospective price developments rather than to an abstract concept of money, inflation targeting highlights an outcome that the public is likely to be especially concerned about. Disadvantages of this strategy include the fact that the inflation forecast is not an unambiguous variable, which makes the strategy difficult to monitor by the general public, thereby making policy less transparent. This difficulty is compounded by the fact that the quality of the inflation forecast can only be judged after a considerable time lag. Besides this, the heavy focus on reaching a specific inflation outcome creates the risk that, notably in the case of supply side shocks, short-term price stability is bought at the expense of excessive output variability.

It should be stressed, however, that there is a substantial degree of similarity in the actual implementation of monetary policy under either strategy, even if they differ in the weight attached to monetary aggregates. In particular, both approaches are based on the same final objective (price stability) and both are explicitly forward-looking. Moreover, in practice, both strategies employ a wide range of indicators to assess the appropriateness of the monetary policy stance. This is explicitly the case for inflation targeting, but also applies to money targeting since central banks pursuing this strategy have typically interpreted their targets in a pragmatic and flexible manner.[2]

2. THE ECONOMIC LANDSCAPE AT THE START OF EMU

Any decision regarding monetary policy strategy has to take account of the environment in which policy is to be implemented. This is because inflation is ultimately determined by decisions of economic agents that are shaped by a myriad of structural, institutional and behavioural factors. In this respect, the monetary policy makers of the Eurosystem are confronted by unusually large uncertainties. This may be partly attributed to the structural changes taking place in the euro economy, and especially in the financial sector. Put differently, the economic landscape of EMU has not yet been accurately mapped out. For instance, there is ample evidence that the banking system, both within and outside the euro area, is currently going through a period of substantial change (ECB, 1999c; Groeneveld, 1999). Heightened competition, integrating capital markets and advancing information technology are all forces contributing to financial innovation, disintermediation and excess capacity in the banking sector. The move to monetary union may be expected to accelerate these changes through several channels.

First, the introduction of the euro will reduce financial transaction costs and increase the liquidity of financial markets in the euro area. And, to the extent that the euro becomes an important international currency, the demand for euro-denominated assets for transaction purposes and as a store of value is bound to rise. The launch of the euro may thus prompt significant portfolio reallocation by residents and non-residents alike.

Second, the financial system of the euro area is directly affected by the adoption of a common framework for monetary policy operations. In particular, the introduction of fully remunerated reserve requirements impacts the cost structure of the banking system and thus, ultimately, also private portfolio decisions. The strength of this impact will differ across countries depending on the specific operational framework before the start of monetary union. For example, in some countries (such as Germany, Spain and France) the introduction of full remuneration of reserve requirements may increase the tendency to pay interest on bank deposits at close to market rates, while in other countries (such as Belgium) these requirements may constrain the flexibility of banks' credit activities.

Third, the regime shift associated with monetary union may itself enhance the credibility of monetary policy in participating countries with weak monetary policy track records. This can lead to shifts in demand for financial assets as inflation risk premia decline and expectations regarding future monetary policy adjust. Although inflation expectations and long-term interest rates have reached historically low levels, it may be assumed that the process of portfolio adjustment to the new situation still has some way to go.

The uncertainty surrounding future developments is relatively large in other economic sectors as well. Indeed, although fiscal, structural and income policies remain decentralized, the environment facing national policy makers has also changed dramatically. Examples of such changes include the rules laid down in the Stability and Growth Pact and the irrevocable loss of monetary and exchange rate policies to address country-specific shocks. Moreover, wage and price setters in private markets are bound to change their behaviour. In particular, the greater price transparency prompted by EMU may be expected to increase competitive pressures and wage discipline in the traded goods sector.

All of these factors, and others, may lead to structural breaks in economic behaviour during the initial phase of monetary union that are difficult to forecast with any precision. What is more, they are difficult to monitor, and even to identify in hindsight, because fully harmonized and reliable statistical data are still a scarce commodity in the euro area. Although temporary in nature, these statistical limitations constrain the scope for analysing euro area trends on the basis of historical patterns, even abstracting from the likely structural breaks in underlying economic behaviour.

Implications for the choice of monetary policy strategy

Uncertainty has important implications for the choice of strategy. Consider first money targeting. In this strategy, a stable money demand function is a necessary condition to judge whether a specific range for money growth is compatible with price stability. Although empirical studies have regularly found evidence in favour of the existence of a stable long-run demand function for money in the EU (Browne, Fagan and Henry, 1997), the changes in financial markets are likely – at least temporarily – to exert a negative influence on the stability of money demand. Moreover, the stability that has been found in backward-looking studies may only be a statistical artefact reflecting the law of large numbers, since aggregation will tend to diversify national sources of instability and thus to dampen their effects (Arnold, 1994). Time will tell.

In addition, the financial market integration and innovation that accompanies EMU may give rise to new liquid financial products whose growth is less tightly controlled by the central bank, particularly in the short run. In this context, a number of studies (Cabrero *et al.*, 1998; Vlaar and Schuberth, 1999) estimate that the controllability of money growth is likely to be significantly weaker in the euro area than in Germany in the recent past. This is attributed to the relatively large amount of short-term deposits earning no or very little interest in Germany. In consequence, a monetary tightening has a strong effect on money growth in Germany, while it has a weak or even perverse effect in other countries, as liquid deposits remunerated at close to market rates become more attractive when monetary policy is tightened. These issues of stability and controllability imply that a strategy of money targeting would be rather risky.

To a large extent, inflation targeting faces similar problems. Specifically, the uncertainties associated with the regime switch reduce the reliability of inflation forecasts, which play a key role in this strategy. This is because such forecasts are invariably based on estimates of past relationships between economic and financial variables – relationships that may shift following the advent of monetary union. Although, given inertia, the underlying structural changes may be slow, their overall effect on economic relationships is likely to be large and difficult to predict. This will especially hold for changes in financial markets. For instance, a more competitive banking sector that eases credit constraints on consumers will change the interest and income sensitivity of consumption, making it problematic to gauge the impact of monetary policy using historical data.

The task of making economic forecasts for the euro area is likely to be further complicated by changes in how economic agents form their expectations. In line with the path-breaking work of Lucas (1976), a regime change such as EMU is bound to prompt adjustments in private sector expectations, and thus in private sector behaviour (Berk and Van Bergeijk, 1999). In sum, the manifold changes in the euro economy have implications for the monetary policy strategy of the Eurosystem that extend beyond the stability of money demand.

3. THE MONETARY POLICY STRATEGY

Against the background of the predetermined institutional setting as well as of the prevailing uncertainties, the Eurosystem has chosen a monetary policy strategy consisting of three key elements (ECB, 1999a). First, the overriding objective of monetary policy – price stability – has been precisely defined. Second, money has been assigned a privileged role in the monetary policy decision making process. And, third, the strategic framework explicitly incorporates a broad-based assessment of prospective inflationary pressures. These central elements are elaborated on below.

The definition of price stability

The Eurosystem has opted to further clarify its mandate by precisely specifying what price stability means. Such a clear-cut objective helps avoid any controversy over the monetary policy orientation, while also contributing to a firm anchoring of inflation expectations. At the same time, it offers an objectively measurable and readily monitorable yardstick for central bank accountability. In this context, price stability has been defined as 'a year-on-year increase in the Harmonized Index of Consumer Prices (HICP) for the euro area of below 2 per cent'. Moreover, this definition has been determined as a medium-term objective.

This definition signals important characteristics of the monetary policy orientation of the Eurosystem. By explicitly referring to the development of the harmonized consumer price index for the euro area, the Eurosystem has indicated that it will calibrate its policies on the basis of monetary, economic and financial developments in the euro area as a whole. In principle, monetary policy will therefore not react to idiosyncratic regional or national developments. By adding that price stability is to be maintained over the medium term, the Eurosystem has underscored the forward-looking nature of its policy-setting. This specification also acknowledges the existence of short-term price movements that are outside the direct control of monetary policy or that monetary policy may consciously wish to accommodate. For instance, the monetary authorities may elect not to offset the first round effects of oil price shocks or fiscal measures (such as adjustments in consumer taxes). As such effects will then only have a temporary impact on inflation, the central bank may avoid destabilizing the real economy while maintaining price stability over the medium term. Finally, by defining price stability in terms of price increases, sustained declines in the harmonized consumer index for the euro area have been made inconsistent with price stability. By implication, and as also emphasized by ECB president

Duisenberg, the Eurosystem has committed itself to combat not only inflation, but also deflation.

The reference value for money

Money has been assigned a central role in the Eurosystem's strategy for maintaining price stability (ECB, 1999b). This reflects the view that inflation is ultimately a monetary phenomenon and that money growth is a precursor of price developments. Given broadly stable money demand, actual money growth then provides a compass for monetary policy decisions, in contrast for example to actual inflation, which is largely determined by monetary policy actions implemented some six to eight quarters earlier. In this light, the Eurosystem announced a first reference value for money growth of 4½ per cent per year. This reference value relates to the broad aggregate M3, which is expected to be more stable because it internalizes substitution effects between different liquid assets (Box 9.3). In order also to filter out incidental and seasonal influences, performance under the reference value is to be measured on the basis of the average year-on-year money growth over a three-month period. Furthermore, with the aim of enhancing transparency, the Eurosystem has published the components from which the reference value has been derived.

Specifically, the reference value has been constructed on the basis of the norm for price stability (a year-on-year HICP increase of below 2 per cent), the trend growth of real output (projected at 2–2½ per cent per year) and the trend decline in money velocity (estimated at ½–1 per cent per year). Thus, the chosen reference value corresponds to the minimum of the ranges when the inflation norm is assumed at 2 per cent and to the maximum when it is set at 1 per cent.

The specification of a reference value for money as a strategic gauge provides further insights into the monetary policy orientation of the euro area. On the one hand, the announcement of a reference value for money indicates that monetary developments will play a prominent role in the considerations driving monetary policy – in line with the tradition of the Bundesbank. On the other hand, the money growth norm has been defined as a reference value and not as a target. This is intended to convey the message that deviations under the reference value will not mechanically lead to policy reactions, but in normal circumstances will signal risks to price stability. The role of money growth as a privileged indicator, rather than an intermediate target, is further expressed by the specification of the reference value as a single number and not a range. Thus, the emphasis is not on whether the norm is actually met, but rather on the information provided by significant and sustained deviations from the reference value.

Box 9.3 The new monetary aggregates for the euro area

An appropriate measure of money is indispensable in monetary union. To this end, European Union member countries in 1992 agreed on a partial harmonization of monetary statistics, which led, inter alia, to the well-known concept of 'harmonized' broad money, M3H. In order to eliminate the remaining differences in scope and definition and to prepare fully comparable statistics for EMU, monetary statistics have been compiled according to uniform requirements since September 1997. Back data approximating these uniform requirements are available from the beginning of 1980.

There are, broadly speaking, two main differences regarding the scope of the 'old' and 'new' monetary statistics. The first concerns the definition of a homogeneous money-issuing sector. To this end, the Monetary Financial Institutions (MFI) sector has been uniformly defined as comprising all resident institutions that take deposits from the public, or issue liabilities which are close substitutes for deposits, and that grant credit. This sector includes not only the 'traditional' credit institutions as defined in Community law, but also inter alia central banks and collective investment institutions with highly liquid liabilities (such as money market funds).[3] The second main difference pertains to the geographical concept used in the definition of the money-holding sector. This concept encompasses all balances held by euro area residents with MFIs located anywhere in the euro area. In consequence, the money aggregates of the euro area now include cross-border holdings that were previously not covered in the national aggregates.

The monetary aggregates of the euro area thus comprise monetary liabilities of MFIs and the central government (Post Office, Treasury) vis-à-vis non-MFI euro area residents, excluding the central government. As regards the definition of the new monetary aggregates, M1 includes currency in circulation and overnight deposits; M2 includes M1 plus deposits with an agreed maturity up to two years and deposits redeemable at notice up to three months; and M3 includes M2 as well as repurchase agreements, money market shares/units, money market paper and debt securities with an original maturity up to two years held by euro area residents.

Other information variables

In view of the uncertainties – especially during the initial phase of monetary union – about the stability and controllability of euro money demand, steering monetary policy tightly on the basis of money growth would be an unduly risky enterprise. This has prompted the Eurosystem to indicate that it will base policy decisions not only on the assessment of money growth relative to the reference value, but also on a host of other indicators for future inflation in the euro area. Examples of these indicators are the euro exchange rate (only to the extent that it influences the domestic price level), labour costs, the output gap and commodity prices, as well as model-based inflation forecasts and implicit price and interest rate expectations incorporated in financial market variables. While money growth may provide a reliable policy compass over the medium term (assuming the demand for euro indeed proves to be sufficiently stable and controllable), such a wide-ranging assessment increases insight into price developments over the shorter term. As a figure of speech, money growth may be seen as the Eurosystem's nominal anchor, moored in the bedrock of the price stability definition, and the other indicators are the considerations that determine the length and slack of the anchor cable.

4. APPRAISING THE MONETARY POLICY STRATEGY

An appraisal of the Eurosystem's monetary policy strategy may in the first instance be conducted on the basis of the standard pre-announced by the European Monetary Institute (EMI, 1997a,b). In particular, six criteria were identified for the selection of the monetary policy strategy, of which the first – effectiveness – essentially encompasses the others. The remaining five criteria relate to whether the strategy contributes to the transparency, medium term orientation, continuity and accountability of monetary policy making, and whether it is consistent with the given independence of the monetary authorities. These criteria may be considered crucial to the establishment of a credible monetary policy that stabilizes inflation expectations and thereby facilitates the maintenance of price stability.

The selected strategy seems amply to meet this standard.[4] The criterion of transparency is observed in so far as the quantitative price stability definition unequivocally establishes what the Eurosystem's end goal is. By providing an explicitly derived reference value for money growth and by simultaneously acknowledging the role of other information variables, the Eurosystem has also indicated how it will set out to achieve that end goal. This latter role admittedly introduces an unspecified degree of eclecticism, but that too is transparency: not making monetary policy making look any easier than it actually is. The medium-term orientation has been explicitly incorporated in the price stability definition. Moreover, this orientation is reflected in the trend computation of the real growth and velocity assumptions underlying the reference value for money. And the continuity of the monetary policy strategy may be inferred from each of the three key elements. In particular, the price stability definition tallies with the normative price stability assumption (usually 2 per cent) that the Bundesbank has incorporated into its money targets since 1985, with the price stability definition that the EU central banks agreed upon in 1990 ('a level of inflation close to zero, . . . i.e. a maximum of 2 per cent in the medium run'; see Raymond, 1990), and with the price stability objectives of the Banque de France and the Banca d'Italia in the 1990s (announced in terms of price increases of up to 2 per cent during the coming year). The reference value for money growth is similarly rooted in European monetary tradition. Specifically, the emphasis on money developments and the explicit derivation of the reference value stems from the monetary policy strategy that the Bundesbank has pursued with considerable success during the past two-and-a-half decades. At the same time, the selection of a point reference rather than a range dovetails with the objective that the Banque de France, the Banca d'Italia and the Banco de España have set for money growth in recent years. And the explicit use of information variables other than money reflects the custom of those euro area countries that have previously pursued inflation targets (Finland and Spain). Thus, a large degree of continuity has been preserved with regard to the monetary policy orientation of many EMU participants. The exception is, of course, provided by the countries that had previously targeted the exchange rate, which evidently constitutes an inappropriate strategy for the relatively closed euro system. As regards the fifth criterion, establishing accountability, both the price stability definition and the reference value for money growth provide distinct yardsticks against which the performance of the monetary authority may be assessed. Finally, the chosen strategy is consistent with the independent status of the Eurosystem, to the extent that the prime element – the price stability definition – corresponds with the prime objective on which the Eurosystem's policy independence is legally founded. At a more subtle level, the reference value for money further underpins this independence in so far as it focuses attention on a variable that is predominantly influenced by the monetary policy makers themselves.

From a broader perspective, the Eurosystem's strategy choice may be appraised by drawing a comparison with the key elements of the monetary policy strategy of other major central banks (Houben, 1999). On the basis of such an international comparison, the Eurosystem's strategy gives the impression of being relatively solid (Table 9.1). In terms of institutional structure, the Eurosystem is one of the most, if not the most, independent central banks in the world (De Haan, 1997; Bini Smaghi, 1998). Moreover, this independence is expressly linked to an unequivocal overriding end objective of price stability. This is a combination that outside the EU can solely be found in Japan (following the recent changes in central bank legislation). But the Eurosystem is the only monetary authority that has complemented this institutional independence and clarity of mandate with a clear-cut and objectively measurable definition of what price stability really means. In addition, although the major uncertainties during the transition to monetary union have prevented the announcement of an intermediate policy target, the Eurosystem has sought to enhance the transparency of its decision-making by establishing a well-founded reference value for money growth as a privileged policy indicator. In all, the strategy choice thus gives every reason to expect price stability in the euro area to be maintained.

5. ROOM FOR OTHER OBJECTIVES?

We now turn to the question whether there is any scope to pursue additional objectives next to the primary goal of price stability. In this context, the Maastricht Treaty explicitly states that, without prejudice to the overriding goal of price stability, monetary policy should support the general economic policy objectives of the European Community. These are formulated in Article 2 of the Treaty establishing the European Community as follows:

> The Community shall have as its task . . . to promote throughout the Community a harmonious and balanced development of economic activities, sustainable and non-inflationary growth respecting the environment, a high degree of convergence of economic performance, a high level of employment and of social protection, the raising of the standard of living and quality of life, and economic and social cohesion and solidarity among Member States.

Obviously, these objectives are very broad and thus subject to various interpretations. In general, however, fostering economic activity may be seen as a central objective in Article 2. As price stability establishes a necessary precondition for sustained economic growth (see Section 1), it can be seen that the Eurosystem, by achieving price stability, indirectly contributes to the achievement of the central objective in Article 2. A related issue is the question of whether a monetary policy geared to price stability should also expressly aim to stabilize output growth. In particular, there may be short-term price movements that should be accommodated in order to avoid buying short-term price stability at the cost of increased output variability. Crucial in

Table 9.1 Key elements of the monetary policy strategy of several central banks

	Eurosystem	Deutsche Bundesbank[1]	US Federal Reserve	Bank of Japan	Bank of England	Swiss National Bank
Political independence legally established?	Yes	Yes	Yes	Yes	No (inflation target set by the Treasury)	Yes
Unequivocal primary end objective?	Yes (price stability)	Yes (maintain value of the currency)	No (price stability and employment)	Yes (price stability)	Yes (price stability)	No (national interest, interpreted as price stability)
Price stability objective clearly defined?	Yes (HICP price increase below 2% per annum over the medium term)	No (implicit: money growth target based on 2% inflation per annum)	No	No	Yes (2½% RPIX inflation per annum)[2]	No
Intermediate policy target?	No	Yes (1998: M3 growth 3-6%)	No	No	No (implicit: forecast inflation 2.5% per annum)	Yes (base money growth 1% per annum)
Privileged policy indicator?	Yes (4½% reference value for money growth 3-month average, year-on-year)	No	Yes (indicative ranges for money growth, M2; 1-5%, M3; 2-6%; and for debt: 3-7%)	Yes (official money growth projection 1999: M2+CDs 4%)	No	No

Notes: [1] Prior to 1999. [2] RPIX = CPI excluding mortgage payments.

194

this respect is whether demand or supply factors dominate the development of prices and real activity (Poole, 1970; Papademos and Modigliani, 1990).

In so far as developments are driven by demand shocks, the objectives of stabilizing prices and output run in parallel. Hence, in this situation, a monetary policy strategy that aims at price stability automatically dampens output fluctuations. In a way, this is reflected in the Eurosystem's reference value for money growth, which has been established using estimates for trend output and trend velocity. In so far as the development of broad money growth (and of complementary indicators of inflation) is likely to lie above the reference value during an upswing in domestic demand and below it during a downswing, this automatically introduces a countercyclical element in the monetary policy orientation.

The situation is quite different, however, when the economy faces supply shocks. In that case, prices and output are negatively correlated, and monetary policy geared at short-run price stability could therefore adversely affect a stable growth path of real activity.[5] Examples of such supply disturbances are technological innovations and energy price shocks. These should lead to changes in relative prices to the extent that these shocks have a structural character. When such a shock occurs, a monetary policy aimed at directly countering any upward price movement may cause serious welfare losses, given the existence of downward nominal rigidities. Similarly, a monetary policy aimed at immediately offsetting downward price effects may spark an inflationary momentum in economic sectors that are not directly influenced by the supply shock.

The monetary policy strategy of the Eurosystem in our view leaves some room to foster a stable growth of economic activity without prejudice to the principal objective of price stability. This conjecture is based on two observations. First, price stability is implicitly defined as a range. Second, price stability has been determined as a medium-term objective, implying that a temporary movement outside this range may still be considered consistent with medium-term price stability. The Eurosystem could deploy this room for manoeuvre, for example in the event of supply shocks that reflect structural changes and that exert temporary pressure on the inflation rate. This flexibility would entail accommodating the immediate price effects of such shocks, allowing a timely adjustment of relative prices to the changed economic environment. Of course, monetary policy must then counter any second-round price effects to avoid wage–price spirals that would compromise price stability over the medium term.

Can the response of monetary policy makers to short-term developments in real activity and prices, as described above, be observed in practice? In this regard, a number of recent studies (Taylor, 1993; Clarida, Galí and Gertler, 1998; Peersman and Smets, 1998) have established that several

Box 9.4 The Taylor rule

Taylor (1993) proposed a simple policy rule that describes monetary
policy in many countries surprisingly well. According to this so-called
feedback rule, monetary policy is tightened when output is above
potential or inflation is above target, while it is loosened when output is
below potential or inflation is below target. The Taylor rule is commonly
expressed as follows:

$$i_t = r^* + \pi_t + \gamma_1 (y_t - y^*) + \gamma_2 (\pi_t - \pi^*)$$

where i_t is the nominal short-term interest rate, r^* is the neutral real
short-term interest rate, y_t is output, π_t is inflation, y^* is the natural output
level and π^* is the inflation target. Obviously, the parameters γ_1 and γ_2
are supposed to have positive values, indicating the aversion of monetary
authorities to deviations of inflation from its target and to output gaps.
Furthermore, it is plausible to assume that γ_2 is greater than one.
Otherwise, if γ_2 is less than one, the real short-term interest rate ($i_t - \pi_t$)
would decrease when inflation rises, which may be expected to fuel
inflation, thereby further lowering the real short-term interest rate,
eventually triggering an inflation spiral. Taylor used weights of 0.5 and
1.5, respectively, for the parameters γ_1 and γ_2. In a number of studies
(Clarida, Galí and Gertler, 1998; Peersman and Smets, 1998),
econometric estimates are used to determine these weights, whereby the
outcomes have been broadly similar to those used by Taylor.

In order to get some idea of the relevance for the euro area, Figure 9.1
plots interest rates calculated using the Taylor rule for the euro area and
for Germany.[6] For the parameters γ_1 and γ_2 a range is used instead of a
single value, in order to take into account uncertainty about the weights.
The solid lines depict the actual three-month interest rates, while the
shaded area indicates a range for the Taylor interest rate which captures
all combinations between the coefficients γ_1 and γ_2 in which γ_1 varies
between 0.25 and 0.75 and γ_2 between 1.25 and 1.75. This range
conforms well with parameter estimates found in econometric studies of
the Taylor rule.[7] The figure shows that, most of the time, actual short-
term interest rates follow a similar pattern to that set by the Taylor rule.

central banks follow a so-called 'Taylor rule', according to which the short-term interest rate is essentially explained by deviations from an inflation objective and by the size of the output gap. Interestingly, these studies point out that this rule adequately describes the behaviour of central banks with very different monetary policy strategies, including the Federal Reserve, the Bundesbank and the Bank of England. These results beg the question whether the Taylor rule is a useful benchmark for the ECB. Against this background, Figure 9.1 plots the actual short-term interest rate and the Taylor interest rate, that is the interest rate implied by the Taylor rule, for the euro area over the past two decades. Of course, this hypothetical rate should be interpreted with caution since it is applied to a weighted average of – at times very different – monetary policies. To circumvent this problem, we also focused on the Bundesbank, which can to some extent be considered the predecessor of the Eurosystem. As can be seen from both graphs in Figure 9.1, the Taylor interest rate closely follows the development in the short-term interest rates over most of the sample, although there are also periods with significant deviations. For instance, the period around 1986 shows a marked difference, which can be explained by the low (in some countries even negative) inflation rates due to a collapse of the oil market. This deviation from the Taylor rule is consistent with the idea that monetary policy in the short run accommodates price changes caused by supply shocks. In the early 1990s, short-term interest rates in the euro area were significantly higher than predicted by the rule, while in Germany the interest rate remained close to the Taylor benchmark. This can be explained by the fact that the Bundesbank raised the interest rates to combat inflation, which had increased in the wake of German unification. Although the economic conditions in most of Europe did not call for a monetary tightening, other countries had to follow Germany's lead on account of their exchange rate commitment within the ERM.

This empirical exercise is of course subject to several caveats. The relevance of the Lucas (1976) critique deserves emphasis in this respect. Although Figure 9.1 indicates a fairly close fit of actual and Taylor interest rates for the euro area over the period 1980–98, there is no reason to presume that this fit will necessarily carry over to EMU. This is because the parameters used in the calculation of the Taylor interest rate will probably change as a consequence of EMU. In particular, the preferences of the national central banks over the past decades, notably regarding inflation, are not necessarily the same as those of the Eurosystem. Furthermore, the interest rate policy of most national central banks was largely determined by their exchange rate target, which provided less scope to respond to specific national developments in the output gap and inflation. Nevertheless, the exercise illustrates that actual central bank behaviour is not characterized by

*Figure 9.1 Short-term interest rates and corresponding Taylor
            rates, 1980-98 (%)*

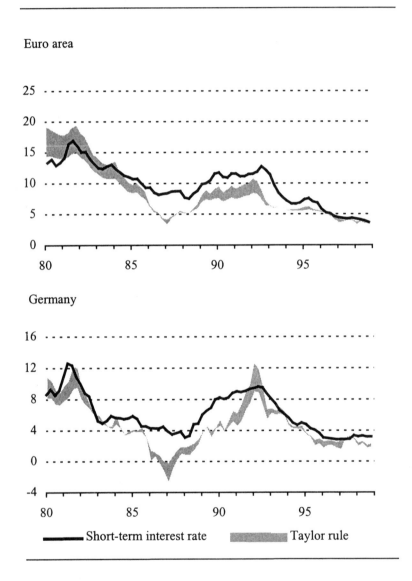

Euro area

Germany

Short-term interest rate   Taylor rule

a mechanical focus on inflation, but also pays attention to considerations
related to economic activity.

6. CONCLUDING REMARKS

Monetary policy decisions are always taken in a context of uncertainty. This is related to the difficulty of assessing the current state of the economy and to the time lag between the use of policy instruments and their effects. In this latter respect, uncertainty can be reduced by enhancing the consistency of monetary policy making and the stability of policy expectations. That is where the role of a monetary policy strategy comes in. A monetary policy strategy spells out what a central bank is aiming for and how it seeks to pursue that aim. This helps create a coherent framework for internal policy deliberations and provides a structure for external communication on monetary policy issues. These elements are interrelated, because the communicability of the strategy depends primarily on whether it is actually used in the internal decision making process. In other words, the central bank should not only say what it is doing, but should also do what it is saying.

The strategy adopted by the Eurosystem does justice to the specific circumstances facing the monetary policy makers at the start of EMU. On the one hand, the unusually large uncertainties associated with the regime shift require somewhat greater policy flexibility. On the other hand, these uncertainties underscore the need to anchor inflation expectations and to give structure to internal and external monetary policy debate. In this light, the Eurosystem has announced a clear-cut, objectively measurable commitment to price stability in the euro area. At the same time, it has indicated that it will base its decisions towards that goal on a pragmatic assessment of money growth relative to a reference value and on a wide range of other indicators for prospective price movements in the euro area. In our view, this strategic framework not only complies with the key criteria formulated by the European Monetary Institute, but also compares favourably with the current practices in the central banking community.

The strategy employed by the Eurosystem should ultimately be judged on whether it delivers the objectives of monetary policy as laid down in the Treaty on European Union. This implies that the policy actions of the Eurosystem should foster economic activity to the extent compatible with the overriding goal of price stability. The strategy promotes this in various ways. First and foremost, maintaining price stability establishes a necessary condition for sustained economic growth. Second, by establishing a central reference value for money growth based on trend developments in output and velocity, the strategy incorporates an element of countercyclical monetary policy. Third, by defining price stability as a positive inflation rate not exceeding 2 per cent and by specifying this as a medium-term objective, some leeway has been created to gear monetary policy to reducing output variability. Of course, this is nothing new: we provide a simple illustration that the actual monetary policy behaviour of the central banks of the Eurosystem during 1980–98 paid due attention to both inflation and output.

In the final analysis, judicious policy depends on the wisdom and will of the decision makers. A coherent strategy is not a panacea and provides no assurance that the specified objectives will be met. But a solid strategy does enhance policy consistency and continuity. On this score, the Eurosystem's strategy bodes well for sustained price stability in the euro area.

NOTES

1. This is strictly speaking not correct. The most obvious counterexample is the so-called eclectic policy strategy followed by the Federal Reserve System in the United States. This strategy is characterized by the absence of intermediate targets and the use of a variety of information variables, with different weights placed on different variables depending on the circumstances. In part, this reflects the hybrid statutory mandate of the Federal Reserve, with price stability and employment specified as equal objectives.
2. By way of illustration, the most ardent of money targeters, the Bundesbank, has met its target in less than half of the years since it introduced money targeting. Moreover, there is empirical evidence that the Bundesbank hardly reacts to changes in (forecasted) money growth and that, in terms of actual policy implementation, it may better be described as an inflation targeter; see Bernanke and Mihov (1997). Moreover, the US experience during the 1979–82 Volcker period illustrates that 'pure' money targeting leads to pronounced interest rate volatility and, for practical purposes, may be viewed as unworkable.
3. For a detailed description and definition, see the *Money and Banking Statistics Sector Manual-Guidance for the Statistical Classification of Customers*, published by the EMI in 1998, as well as the *Money and Banking Statistics Compilation Guide* (EMI, 1998).
4. This is not to say that the strategy of the Eurosystem did not receive any criticism. For example, the decisions not to adopt an explicit policy target, not to publish inflation forecasts, not to reveal voting patterns and to delay publication of the minutes of meetings of the Governing Council for 30 years are perceived by some as indications of insufficient openness, transparency and accountability (for instance, Buiter, 1999; *The Economist*, 1998). In the view of critics, this perceived lack of transparency is likely to amplify the uncertainties surrounding monetary policy in the initial years of EMU. However, against these criticisms it may be argued that, especially in view of the initial uncertainties, the Eurosystem should not overstate the accuracy with which it can steer developments in money or inflation, that openness on voting patterns would make the Council members more susceptible to nationally oriented pressures, and that the extensive monthly introductory statements following Governing Council meetings (which are placed on the Internet) fulfil much the same role as the publication of minutes would.
5. For empirical evidence on the correlation between prices and output, see Van Els (1995).
6. The Taylor interest rates have been calculated using the sample averages of the real interest rate for r^* and assuming an inflation target of 2 per cent. The output gap has been calculated with quarterly GDP data, using the Hodrick-Prescott filter based on a sample that was extended by the European Commission's forecasts for real activity and inflation in order to reduce the endpoint problem (Giorno *et al.*, 1995).
7. For the German output gap coefficient, Clarida, Galí and Gertler (1998), Peersman and Smets (1998) and Begg *et al.* (1998) report estimates of, respectively, 0.25, 0.28 and 0.34. For the inflation gap coefficient, these studies find, respectively, 1.31, 1.30 and 1.07. Peersman and Smets also estimate a Taylor rule for the euro area, using aggregated data over the period 1990–98. They find parameters of 0.52 and 1.46 for the output gap coefficient and inflation gap coefficient respectively, which are close to the values that were originally used by Taylor (1993).

10. The Pact for Stability and Growth

Hans Brits and Marc de Vor

There are good reasons, mostly of a political economy nature, to have arrangements for fiscal policy in a monetary union that is not a political union. In the Delors Report (1989, pp. 23–25) it is stated that:

> an economic and monetary union could only operate on the basis of mutually consistent and sound behaviour by governments and other economic agents in all member countries. In particular, uncoordinated and divergent national monetary policies would undermine monetary stability and generate imbalances in the real and financial sectors of the Community. . . . In the budgetary field, binding rules are required that would: firstly, impose effective upper limits on budget deficits of individual member countries of the Community, . . . secondly, exclude access to direct central bank credit and other forms of monetary financing, . . . thirdly, limit recourse to external borrowing in non-Community currencies. Moreover, the arrangements in the budgetary field should enable the Community to conduct a coherent mix of fiscal and monetary policies.

The institutional framework that is now in place to a large extent reflects the opinion of this central bankers dominated committee. Member States have committed themselves to a budgetary position 'close to balance or in surplus'. This chapter outlines and analyses the fiscal policy rules of the EU game. The Maastricht Treaty obligations for the government budgets and the Pact for Stability and Growth that was concluded at the Amsterdam summit are described in the first section of this chapter. The economic rationale of the Pact, in light of the challenges that are posed to decentralized fiscal policy in a monetary union, is discussed in the second section. The third section reviews the first year's experience with the functioning of the Stability and Growth Pact. It is shown to be not completely satisfactory, in particular because a rather minimalistic interpretation of the 'close to balance' commitment is followed. In the fourth section we develop an alternative, quantified, approach which would require Member States to aim for more ambitious budgetary targets, in order to cope with budgetary fluctuations, high debt ratios and the costs associated with ageing populations.

1. THE INSTITUTIONAL FRAMEWORK[1]

The Maastricht rules

In the negotiations for the Maastricht Treaty, fiscal policy was one of the most intensely debated subjects.[2] Five articles in the EC Treaty together form the framework for fiscal policy as an instrument of macroeconomic policy.[3] Article 99 deals with policy coordination and surveillance. Article 101 forbids monetary financing of the deficit. Article 102 disallows privileged access to credit by governments. Article 103 stipulates a 'no bail out' clause, forbidding governments to bail out a country that faces financial problems. Finally, Article 104 requires Member States to avoid excessive deficits, with an attached protocol that quantifies criteria for the Member States' general government deficit and debt.

The Treaty provisions have the same emphasis as the Delors Report had. Though leaving room for further initiatives, the main purpose seems to be to prevent 'gross errors' (mentioned in Article 104) that could unduly burden the common monetary policy and thereby jeopardize the stability of the monetary union. In essence, decisions on budgetary policies remain a national competence, but bounded by certain rules. In earlier days, the Werner Report (1970) had gone much further by calling for Community-level decision-making on essential elements of budgetary policies.

The main vehicle for policy coordination based on Article 99 is formed by the so-called Broad Guidelines. The Guidelines are discussed by the European Council and ultimately adopted by the Council acting by a qualified majority. In the area of fiscal policy, both general and country-specific guidelines are given. Its legal form is a recommendation, which means it is not binding. If economic policies of a Member State are found to be inconsistent with the broad guidelines, the Council can make a specific recommendation to the Member State concerned.

The specific purpose of Article 104 is to prevent excessive government deficits in Member States. As a rule, a government deficit can be considered 'excessive' if either the deficit exceeds a reference value, specified as 3 per cent of GDP in an attached protocol, or the debt ratio exceeds a reference value, specified as 60 per cent of GDP. If an excessive deficit in a Member States persists, this may lead to binding decisions by the Council to spur a Member State to correct the situation, and to sanctions if a Member State fails to comply. The sanction mechanism in Article 104 became operational only after the so-called Third Stage of EMU had started on 1 January 1999. But before that date, when the EU had entered the Second Stage on 1 January 1994, the obligation to avoid an excessive deficit was already into force and actually the ultimate 'sanction' did apply: Member States not fulfilling this requirement could not enter Economic and Monetary Union (see Chapter 3).

Waigel calls for a stability pact

After the Maastricht Treaty had come into force, the discussion on the role of fiscal policy in a monetary union continued unabated, both in the academic world and amongst policy makers. In the fall of 1995 the German Minister of Finance, Waigel, launched the initiative to come to a 'stability pact' containing three elements: a medium-term target for government deficits of 1 per cent of GDP, automatic sanctions if there was an excessive deficit and a 'stability council' as a decision-making body.

At first, the initiative met with considerable scepticism. The proposal clearly went beyond the Maastricht rules, and knowing how difficult it had been to craft the delicate compromise that had found its place in the Maastricht Treaty, it was feared that this whole discussion would be reopened. But after agreeing that the existing rules would not be changed, but just supplemented within the Treaty provisions, the discussions became more constructive, leading to an agreement on the basic nature of such a pact during the informal Ecofin meeting held in April 1996 in Verona. In particular, it was agreed that governments should aim for budgetary positions 'close to balance or in surplus' in the medium term. Agreement on the contents and form of the stability pact was reached at the end of that year at the Dublin summit, and finally the pact was formally adopted at the Amsterdam summit in June 1997 under the new name 'Pact on Stability and Growth'. The name change was a gesture towards the new socialist French government. A more substantial concession to French demands was a separate resolution, outside the Stability and Growth Pact, on employment and growth.

The Amsterdam rules

The Stability and Growth Pact formally consists of two Council regulations and a resolution of the Amsterdam European Council.

The first Council Regulation (No. 1466/97) strengthens the surveillance and monitoring of budgetary policies based on Article 99 of the Treaty. It requires the members of the euro area to submit stability programmes; the *outs* continue to submit convergence programmes. The stability programmes should contain the medium-term objective for the budgetary position of close to balance or in surplus, and the adjustment path towards this objective, the main assumptions on relevant economic developments, a description of measures being taken or proposed to achieve the objectives of the programme, and a sensitivity analysis. The programmes are made public and must be updated annually. Based on assessments by the Commission and the Economic and Financial Committee,[4] the Council examines the programmes, and delivers an opinion in which it may invite a Member State to strengthen its programme. The Council monitors the implementation of the programmes, and if a significant divergence is identified, it may issue an 'early warning' to a Member State, in the form of a recommendation under Article 99(4) of the Treaty. Although this regulation finds its basis in the 'coordination article' 99, the main emphasis is on the provision of additional safeguards to prevent the 'gross errors' referred to in Article 104. An illustration of this point is that the Council is asked to examine whether the key element of the stability programmes, the medium-term objective, 'provides for a safety margin to ensure the avoidance of an excessive deficit' (Article 9 of Regulation 1466). Excessive deficits are just mentioned in Article 104. The only 'coordination elements' in Regulation 1466 are that the Council examines whether the contents of the stability programme facilitates the closer coordination of economic policies and whether the economic policies are consistent with the Broad Guidelines.

The provisions of Article 104 are further strengthened by the second Council Regulation (No. 1467/97), which speeds up and clarifies the excessive deficit procedure. Its function is to enhance the credibility of the sanction mechanism in Article 104, by making the procedure as predefined and explicit as possible within the limits of the Treaty. Provisions that could serve as 'escape clauses' are given definitions that prevent misuse. The concept mentioned in Article 104 that an 'exceptional and temporary' overrun of the reference value for the deficit is not considered excessive has been restricted to apply only when the overrun stems from an unusual event outside the control of the Member State concerned or when it results from a severe economic downturn, the latter being defined as an annual decline of real GDP of at least 2 per cent. Moreover, in both cases budgetary forecasts by the Commission must indicate a fall of the deficit below the reference value at the end of the unusual event or severe downturn. The various steps to be taken in the excessive deficit procedure by the Commission, the Economic and Financial Committee and the Council are specified in such a way that if a Member State does not undertake corrective action, the ultimate decision to impose sanctions is taken within ten months of the reporting of a deficit deemed to be excessive. At first, the sanction consists of the obligation to make a non-interest-bearing deposit of between 0.2 and 0.5 per cent of GDP, depending on the size of the excess. After two years, if the Member State still has not corrected the excessive deficit, the deposit is converted into a fine. To underline the political commitment to the Stability and Growth Pact, the Amsterdam European Council complemented the Council Regulations with a resolution. In this resolution, the European Council 'solemnly invites all parties, namely the Member States, the Council of the European Union and the Commission of the European Communities, to implement the Treaty and the Stability and Growth Pact in a strict and timely manner.' In particular, the (not legally binding) resolution invites the Council always to impose sanctions if an excessive deficit is not corrected, and urges always to require non-interest-bearing deposits and convert them into fines after two years. The (binding) regulation itself requires these measures 'as a rule', because a completely automatic sanction procedure would go beyond the Maastricht Treaty, requiring a change of the Treaty provisions with regard to EMU, which was ruled out from the start.

Follow-up of Amsterdam

The Stability and Growth Pact sets budgetary rules for the Third Stage of EMU, which started on 1 January 1999. In the run-up to the decision that was taken at the beginning of May 1998 on which countries would adopt the euro, it was felt that some additional effort was necessary to enhance confidence in the budgetary authorities and strengthen the credibility of the medium-term budgetary consolidation goal in the Pact. After all, there was a danger of budgetary slippage because the decision on EMU participation was based on 1997 performances, and the Pact would only kick in later. The markets and the public might need some additional reassurance. Therefore, on the initiative of – again – the German Minister of Finance Waigel, the Ecofin Council on 1 May 1998 issued a declaration (known as the 'Waigel declaration') in which the ministers committed themselves to use better economic conditions to reinforce budgetary consolidation, to undertake greater efforts the higher the debt to GDP ratio was, and to submit stability programmes before the end of the year (instead of 1 March 1999 as required by Council Regulation 1466).

During 1998, the Monetary Committee fleshed out the specification of the stability programmes. Its final *Opinion on the Content and Format of Stability and Convergence Programmes* was endorsed by the Ecofin Council of 12 October 1998. The key issue was how to interpret the phrase 'a medium-term objective for the budgetary position of close to balance or in surplus'. As declared by the Council in its Resolution of 17 June 1997: 'adherence to the objective of sound budgetary positions close to balance or in surplus will allow all Member States to deal with normal cyclical fluctuations while keeping the government deficit within the reference value of 3% of GDP'. From this it was concluded by the Monetary Committee that in the assessment of the medium-term objectives and their fulfilment, account had to be taken of the cyclical position. To this end, the Commission's Services' cyclical adjustment method was considered a useful approach. In setting the appropriate medium-term objective, other considerations were also regarded as of major importance, such as the need to take account of other sources of variability and uncertainty in budgets, the need to ensure a rapid decline in high debt ratios and the need to cater for the costs associated with population ageing. The Committee believed that the medium-term objective should be achieved no later than by the end of 2002.

2. ECONOMIC RATIONALE OF THE PACT[5]

Fiscal rules in the monetary union

A potential problem in EMU is that fiscal policy could jeopardize the ECB's primary objective of maintaining price stability. Large deficits are likely to increase inflationary expectations. Also, they could undermine confidence, resulting in pressure on the euro and higher risk premia. Furthermore, high debt ratios make countries vulnerable to increases in interest rates: heavily indebted countries may readily fall in a negative spiral of rising interest payments, rising deficits and rising debt (Berndsen, 1997). The fiscal policies of individual Member States will have repercussions for the monetary union as a whole, particularly when the no-bail-out clause that the EC Treaty provides for does not turn out to be entirely credible. For example, if a country runs a large deficit in EMU, the long-term interest rate of *all* participating countries will be influenced, whereas before EMU the exchange rate could have mitigated the effect on the interest rates in other countries.

One can imagine that the ECB could experience pressure to ease monetary policy in order to alleviate financing problems of countries that face large deficits. Of course, the ECB is a very independent central bank, but it still has to build up a reputation and this will be easier to accomplish in an environment where Member States have no reason for putting pressure on monetary policy. In essence, this is a political economy argument for adopting the fiscal rules described in the previous section. The future will tell to what extent these rules are indeed effective. At this point, a prudent strategy with respect to the decentralized fiscal policies may be beneficial, particularly because public finances of several Member States do not seem to be on a solid footing yet.

Asymmetric shocks

An important issue frequently discussed in the context of monetary union deals with the so-called asymmetric shocks (Artis, 1999). These shocks have a different impact on separate countries, such as a sudden change in energy prices (for example in 1974 and 1979), a surge in domestic spending (such as after the German reunification) or a disturbance of trade (such as in Finland as a result of the collapse of the Soviet Union). In a monetary union, a participating country cannot use monetary or exchange rate policy to offset the effects of these country-specific shocks. A country has to determine whether it is likely to suffer from these asymmetric shocks in order to assess the 'costs' of being part of a currency area. The past does not, however, necessarily give a reliable picture of the future. At this moment it is not clear what the magnitude or the frequency of asymmetric shocks will be in the EMU era: the establishment of EMU is in itself a regime shift (Van Bergeijk, 1999). On the one hand, it can be argued that asymmetric disturbances will be more limited in the future, because the stability oriented macroeconomic policies reduce the likelihood of policy induced shocks. Also, European monetary integration could lead to an intensification of intra-industry trade, resulting in greater cross-country symmetry. On the other hand, it can be argued that in the long run EMU will set in motion a regional specialization process similar to the United States, making asymmetric (sector-specific) shocks more likely. Clearly, this issue is not yet resolved, but it seems that asymmetric shocks cannot be discarded in the future. Given the fact that there is no central federal fiscal authority commanding a European budget, EMU could face a potential stabilization problem.

Automatic stabilizers

How does the Pact cope with this? The starting point of the Pact is that Member States set their medium-term budgetary targets close to balance or in surplus. This means that the budget should be balanced on average over the business cycle: during an economic upswing surpluses have to be realized in order to compensate for the deficits that will emerge during economic downturns. In other words, fiscal policy should be organized in such a way that the so-called automatic stabilizers, both on the revenue and the expenditure side, can do their job. Hence, when the economy is above its trend path, the 'growth dividend' should not be used to conduct a procyclical fiscal policy, but should result in budget surpluses. Conversely, in the face of economic adversity, for example caused by an asymmetric shock, a country should not have to resort immediately to a tighter – and in the short run potentially detrimental – fiscal policy, but should be in the position to allow the budgetary position to deteriorate. The working of the automatic stabilizers should be restricted to the extent that the deficit does not exceed the 3 per cent of GDP ceiling, except in the case of an (exceptionally) severe recession.

A policy of balanced budget over the business cycle has another important advantage: it will lead to a rapid decline of high debt ratios, making it easier to cope with the future costs associated with the ageing of the populations, such as public pensions and healthcare costs. By reducing the government debt, the burden that under the present social security arrangements is shifted onto future generations will also be alleviated, as is shown by the so-called Generational Accounting studies, surveyed by Kotlikoff (1998).

Fiscal insurance schemes

The Pact thus relies on automatic stabilization on the national level, not on a European budget that can be used to stabilize the effects of asymmetric shocks. Given the strong pressure of some Member States, such as Germany and the Netherlands, to reduce their contribution to the central EU budget, this does not seem to be the time to find a solution for asymmetric shocks on the European level. But the automatic fiscal stabilizers alone will not always be able to stabilize the economy. Von Hagen (1999) has recently surveyed the studies dealing with the possibilities of so-called 'insurance schemes', which are specifically designed to channel income from countries enjoying a positive asymmetric shock to countries suffering a negative one. Designing such mechanisms is difficult because, like all kinds of insurance, fiscal insurance among EMU members would be surrounded by moral hazard problems. The effectiveness of market mechanisms for adjustment could for example be undermined. Also, these schemes are likely to interfere with redistributive tendencies across Member States. Assuming that poor states have relatively high income volatility in EMU, it can be shown that a fiscal insurance scheme would entail redistribution from these poor states to the rich ones. Redistribution is of course a separate issue from stabilization, but in this form it is likely to be politically difficult to accept. Von Hagen cites various pieces of empirical evidence to suggest that the size of fiscal insurance in the US and other monetary unions like Canada is rather small (the budget absorbs at best up to 10–20 per cent of asymmetric shocks). Moreover, Sleijpen (1999) shows that in the United States stabilization is largely carried out through the federal budget and that this can also be accomplished by the mechanism of automatic stabilization in the budgets of the EMU members. All in all, it can be concluded that both from empirical and theoretical investigations it follows that fiscal insurance schemes do not seem to provide an attractive means to stabilize economic developments in EMU.

Coordination of fiscal policies?

This leaves us with a situation where – despite the working of the automatic stabilizers – the policy mix of fiscal and (centralized) monetary policy may be considered inappropriate in EMU. For example, although EMU did not yet exist, monetary policy was too easy during most of 1998 for several small and fastgrowing Member States. In the future, monetary policy may also be too tight for some countries. In the event of an unbalanced policy mix one could call for a 'fiscal supplement', which, ideally, should be coordinated on the European level, but the Pact is not concerned with that. Without coordination Member States may take a wait-and-see attitude, hoping to free ride on other countries' stabilization policies. Particularly when it comes to stimulating the economy, individual countries may be afraid of the sanctions that prevail under the Pact if the deficit exceeds the 3 per cent ceiling and may therefore refrain from taking a fiscal initiative. Coordination of fiscal policies may – in theory at least – result in better economic outcomes, but this would entail much more political integration in Europe though (for example, a far more efficient decision-making process), a situation that is still far away.

Apart from the coordination issue one may raise the old question as to whether and to what extent EMU countries (or any country) should consider discretionary fiscal policies (Knot, 1996). It is broadly understood that active fiscal policies are surrounded by several problems: there is uncertainty with respect to the 'correct' economic model, there is a risk of procyclical policies as a result of slow parliamentary approval and implementation, and frequent changes in taxes and public spending may cause supplyside inefficiencies. Active fiscal policy does therefore not seem to be the obvious way to stabilize the economy.

Other adjustment mechanisms

There are several other adjustment mechanisms that may supplement the fiscal stabilizers. The labour market for example provides stabilization in the form of wage flexibility and/or labour mobility. It is well-known that Europe does not do a very good job on this score, but since EMU makes relative prices more transparent, one may expect wage flexibility to improve in the future. More competitive product markets can also play an important role in dampening the effects of economic disturbances. The completion of the Single Market will contribute to the integration of product markets in Europe, although this may take some time (European Commission, 1997). Capital markets, finally, also mitigate shocks, since they enable investors to hold or attract financial assets from many regions. Financial markets are still fragmented in Europe, but as a result of EMU and the introduction of the euro these markets may become much more integrated in the (near) future, allowing therefore for some stabilization of economic developments (see Chapter 7). Particularly, this financial integration process will increase the possibilities for 'self-insurance', since capital markets are expected to remain open at limited extra costs for countries in distress, even though of course the rules of the Pact are a restriction.

3. THE STABILITY AND GROWTH PACT IN PRACTICE[6]

The first round of stability programmes

Most countries succeeded in presenting their stability programmes before the end-December 1998 deadline of the 'Waigel declaration' and all of them before the original deadline of 1 March 1999. Table 10.1 gives an overview of the budgetary targets in the programmes, the growth assumptions underlying the projections and the so-called structural deficits as calculated by the Commission.

The Member States have committed themselves to achieve the medium-term target of close to balance or in surplus by 2002 at the latest. Yet, as is also noted in the European Central Bank's 1998 *Annual Report* (ECB, 1999e), a majority of the Member States aim at deficits of around 1 per cent or even higher at the end of their current programmes. Only Ireland and Luxembourg had budgetary positions that can be considered close to balance or in surplus in 1998, before the start of the Third Stage.

The structural, or to be more precise cyclically adjusted, deficits give a yardstick to measure whether a Member State has a sufficiently wide safety margin under the 3 per cent deficit ceiling in order to deal with normal cyclical fluctuations. In order to make this judgement it has to be determined how large normal cyclical fluctuations of the budget deficit are. The Commission has developed country-specific benchmarks that are considered to be consistent with the Pact (Table 10.2). The calculations are based on current estimates for the cyclical sensitivity of the budget in each individual Member State and on (several assumptions regarding) the maximum negative output gap likely to occur in EMU. The method results in two extreme cases per country as the bounds of the range of budgetary positions that would allow Member States to let automatic stabilizers operate. The mid-point of this range is called the benchmark. Clearly, when the sensitivity of the budget

Table 10.1 Overview of stability programmes (% of GDP)

	GDP growth (%)			Government balance			Structural balance		
	98 (1)	99 (2)	00/02 (3)	98 (4)	99 (5)	02 (6)	98 (7)	99 (8)	02 (9)
Belgium	2.9	2.4	2.3	-1.6	-1.3	-0.3	-1.6	-1.4	-0.5
Germany	3.0	2.0	2.5	-2.5	-2.0	-1.0	-1.9	-1.7	-1.0
Spain	3.8	3.8	3.3	-1.9	-1.6	0.1	-1.5	-1.7	-0.1
France	3.1	2.4	2.5	-2.9	-2.3	-1.2	n.a.	-2.3	-1.4
Ireland	9.5	6.7	6.1 [a]	1.7	1.7	1.6 [b]	0.0	0.1	0.3 [b]
Italy	1.8	2.5	2.8 [a]	-2.6	-2.0	-1.0 [b]	-1.9	-1.5	-1.1 [b]
Luxembourg	5.7	3.4	3.7	2.1	1.1	1.7	n.a.	n.a.	n.a.
Netherlands	4.0	2¼	2¼	-1.3	-1.3	-1.1	-1.8	-1.6	n.a.
Austria	3.3	2.8	2.3	-2.2	-2.0	-1.4	-2.2	-2.2	-1.4
Portugal	4.2	3.5	3.2	-2.3	-2.0	-0.8	-2.3	-2.1	-0.9
Finland	5.5	4.0	2.6	1.1	2.4	2.3	-0.5	0.5	1.8

Notes:
[a] 2000/01.
[b] 2001.

to the cycle is high (low) and the economy shows a high (low) degree of volatility, more (less) stringent benchmarks for the government deficit are obtained in order to create enough room for automatic stabilizers to operate. In general, Table 10.2 illustrates that balanced budgetary positions would provide Member States with ample room to deal with 'normal' cyclical fluctuations while keeping the deficit below 3 per cent of GDP. Finland should clearly aim for a surplus.

Ecofin assessment

In the period from October 1998 to March 1999 the Ecofin Council issued opinions on the stability programmes submitted by the Member States, based on assessments by the Commission that were discussed in the Economic and Financial Committee. According to Article 5 of Council Regulation 1466, the Council has to focus on an examination of the medium-term budget objective, the economic assumptions and the measures taken to achieve the

Table 10.2 Benchmark figures for Member States' budgetary position
consistent with the Pact

	Sensitivity of the budget balance to the cycle	Benchmark budgetary positions (% of GDP)
Belgium	0.6	-1.0
Germany	0.5	-1.1
Spain	0.6	-0.4
France	0.5	-1.5
Ireland	0.5	-0.9
Italy	0.5	-1.2
Luxembourg	0.6	0.0
Netherlands	0.8	-0.1
Austria	0.5	-1.3
Portugal	0.5	-0.6
Finland	0.7	1.3

Source: European Commission.

objective. In most Member States, the safety margin as calculated by the Commission has been the dominating force in setting the medium-term target. Other considerations, such as mentioned in the *Opinion on the Content and Format* (other sources of variability, high debt ratios, costs of ageing) play a less explicit role in most programmes and the Ecofin assessment. In judging the medium-term targets, the Council has not been particularly consistent.

There are five countries that have a significant extra safety margin above the room needed to cope with normal cyclical fluctuations (compare columns (6) and (9) of Table 10.1 with the last column of Table 10.2).[7] Of this group, only in the case of the country with the smallest margin, Spain, has Ecofin recognized that an additional safety margin exists. In the opinions on three other countries, it is merely stated that the targets are 'sufficient' (Belgium and Ireland) or 'adequate' (Luxembourg) to be in conformity with the Stability and Growth Pact. The fifth country with an additional safety margin, and moreover the largest projected surplus in the medium term, Finland, was told that the target was sufficient to provide a safety margin against breaching the 3 per cent deficit threshold as a result of normal fluctuations, but that only 'in this sense' was the programme in line with the requirements of the Pact, and that in view of the future effects of population ageing a further improvement of government finances was needed. Three countries have a very small additional safety margin: Italy, France and Germany. Of all these countries, it is said that the target would allow automatic stabilizers to work 'without any large risk' of exceeding the 3 per cent of GDP reference value and that 'in this sense' the programme is in line with the provisions of the Pact. These countries also are recommended to aim for a lower deficit, because of high debt (Italy), budgetary uncertainties (France) or just because (Germany). Moreover, Italy gets a severe (dis)qualification in the beginning of the opinion, noting that the objectives in the programme only 'go in the direction' of meeting the requirements of the Stability and Growth Pact. This qualification seems to be based more on a disbelief in the underlying assumptions than on an assessment of the objectives as such. This scepticism turned out to be justified only a few months later, when Italy in the Ecofin discussion on the Broad Guidelines announced that the 1999 and 2000 targets would be out of reach due to the worsened economic situation.

Austria and Portugal just fall short of providing sufficient room to cope with cyclical fluctuations on the basis of the Commission benchmarks. Strangely enough, they do not get more severe treatment than the previous group. In the case of Austria, it is said that the target would be sufficient to allow automatic stabilizers to work without risk of breaching the 3 per cent, that is, the 'any large' qualification is not used. On the other hand, the Austrian budgetary strategy is called 'risk-prone' and a more ambitious deficit target is said to have been appropriate for a list of reasons. Portugal does get the 'at any large risk' qualification, but despite having a target that is 0.2–0.3 per cent of GDP above the Commission benchmark gets away with only very weak advice ('could be advocated') to aim for a wider safety margin.

Finally, the budget deficit of the Netherlands is projected to be around 1 per cent of GDP in 2002, which is way off the Commission's benchmark. However, the Council acknowledges that this is based on a cautious scenario with 2¼ per cent annual economic growth. According to the opinion, the so-called middle scenario, based on a growth rate of 2¾ per cent, would bring the deficit close to balance. It is stated that the underlying budgetary position provides 'some' safety margin to prevent the deficit from breaching the 3 per cent threshold. A statement whether this in any sense meets the requirements of the Pact is (wisely?) left out.

As regards the economic assumptions underlying the programmes, the Ecofin Council is generally satisfied. The scenarios are considered 'attainable' (Ireland), 'plausible' (Portugal, Luxembourg), 'realistic' (Austria, Spain, Germany, France), even 'prudent' (Belgium, Finland) or 'cautious' (Netherlands). In the cases of Germany and Portugal there is specific mention of downside risks. Italy however is criticized that its macroeconomic framework seems 'clearly too optimistic'. According to reports in the press, the Commission suggested that the Council asked for an updated programme. This was not followed by the Council.

The Council is also supposed to examine whether the measures taken or proposed are sufficient to achieve the targeted adjustment path towards the medium-term budgetary objective. This issue is hardly mentioned in the opinions. Only in the case of Italy is it noted that additional corrective measures could be required to reach the objective.

All in all, the Ecofin opinions are only mildly critical. Although in most opinions remarks are made that suggest that the Council thought the programme should have been stronger, the Council does not invite any Member State to adjust its programme accordingly. The opinions tend to be less specific than the recommendations made under Article 104 at the time when most Member States had an excessive deficit. One could hold the view that this is justified because there are no longer 'gross errors', and that this is what all these procedures in essence are all about. On the other hand, the Stability and Growth Pact was very explicitly presented as a strengthening of the surveillance of the Member States' budgetary policies.[8] In the light of the contents of the opinions and the relatively short amounts of time that the Council apparently devotes to the discussion of the programmes, one could question whether the Pact lives up to its intentions.

4. A QUANTIFIED ASSESSMENT OF THE MEDIUM-TERM TARGETS[9]

What is close to balance?

A crucial issue in the assessment of stability programmes is the interpretation of the medium-term target 'close to balance or in surplus'. Having a budgetary position close to balance or in surplus provides for a safety margin to ensure the avoidance of an excessive deficit. It is important to note that the reverse implication is not valid: having a deficit close to balance or in surplus provides a sufficient safety margin, but having a safety margin, for example, sufficient to deal with cyclical factors does not necessarily mean that the budgetary position is close to balance. Some countries, especially France and Austria, are less sensitive to cyclical influences on the budget, according to the Commission's calculations. Just looking at the Commission's benchmark would imply a medium-term target of 1.5 per cent of GDP for France and 1.3 per cent of GDP for Austria, which seems hard to interpret as 'close to balance'.

How large should the safety margin be? In the discussions on the design of the Pact, it was concluded that the size of the margin could differ per country. Consequently, consideration (14) of Council Regulation 1466 states that the Council 'should take into account the relevant cyclical and structural characteristics of the economy of each Member State'. Cyclical factors are further singled out in consideration (4) and in the Resolution of the European Council: 'Adherence to the objective of sound budgetary positions close to balance or in surplus will allow all Member States to deal with normal cyclical fluctuations while keeping the government deficit within the reference value of 3% of GDP'. In the assessment by the Council as prepared by the Commission and the Economic and Financial Committee, only these cyclical factors have been quantified to evaluate the safety margin. The safety margin needed to cope with cyclical factors then is taken as a kind of minimum position, and subsequently other factors are dealt with, but in a qualitative and less systematic way.

As mentioned, other factors are specified in the *Opinion on the Content and Format*: other sources of variability and uncertainty in budgets, the need to ensure a rapid decline in high debt ratios, and the costs associated with population ageing. These other factors can in principle also be quantified, as is shown below. Of course, it has to be recognized that this exercise involves arbitrary choices and can only be the starting point of a thorough assessment of budgetary positions. On the other hand, the Commission's calculation of benchmarks on cyclical influences has arbitrary elements as well, and has perhaps become too much the central yardstick just because it is specific and quantified.

Other sources of variability and uncertainty in budgets

Apart from cyclical factors, there are many other sources of variability and uncertainty in budgets. Movements in interest rates usually do not have a clear relation with the business cycle and may have substantial budgetary effects, especially in countries with large government debt at short maturities. Revenues from state companies can fluctuate. Coping with a crisis in the banking sector may need public money. Consequences of policy measures, such as tax reforms, are hard to predict. Bad weather may bring unexpected costs. The behaviour of local governments, which in some countries form a substantial part of total government, is not completely under the control of the central budgetary authority. To assess these kinds of factors, it is necessary to look closely at country-specific circumstances. To get an overall quantified measure, we apply a statistical approach. After eliminating the cyclical component in the budget deficits, the variance of the remainder (corrected for trend movements[10]) is a measure of other budgetary uncertainties. In general, they tend to be somewhat smaller than cyclical factors and on average larger for countries where cyclical variability is high as well. In combining cyclical factors and other sources of variability, care has to be taken of the correlation between the two.[11]

The need to ensure a rapid decline in high debt ratios

The Maastricht Treaty sets a maximum reference value of 60 per cent of GDP for the Member States' government gross debt. As long as debt ratios are above this value, a judgement has to be made whether the ratio is 'sufficiently diminishing and approaching the reference value at a satisfactory pace'. As is pointed out in Chapter 3, the Ecofin Council has used this escape clause in a rather liberal way. On the other hand, the 'Waigel declaration' adopted by this same Council contains the statement that: 'The higher the debt-to-GDP ratios of participating Member States, the greater must be their effort to reduce them rapidly.' A measure for the speed of the debt reduction was developed by the European Monetary Institute in its Convergence Report submitted to the Council as advice on the decision on participation in EMU. On the basis of assumptions on trend growth (in conformity with Commission estimates) and inflation (2 per cent), and assuming a constant deficit after the medium-term target has been reached, it can be calculated how long it will take before the debt ratio comes below the reference value. Applying a norm to this time span, for example, 10 years, gives a desired value for the medium-term target. For the countries with high debt ratios, Belgium and Italy, this approach points to the need for more ambitious medium-term targets than currently envisaged in their stability programmes.[12]

The need to cater for the costs associated with population ageing

The population of most industrialized countries is ageing at an increasing speed. According to demographic projections, this process will reach a peak in the first half of the twenty-first century. An ageing population implies a considerable burden on the public finances of a country, because pension payments and health expenditures in particular are age-related.[13] A Commission's Services report by Franco and Munzi (1997) contains projections of the increase in age-related public expenditures in a number of European countries. Heeringa (1999) extends the projections to some countries missing from the Commission report. To derive budgetary targets from these projections, one needs to interpret the phrase 'to cater for the costs associated with population ageing'. Here, it is taken to mean that budgetary targets are set such that the increase in age-related expenditures is just about

Table 10.3 Assessment of budgetary targets (% of GDP)

	Target implied by:			
	Cyclical factors and other variability	Debt ratio	Ageing	Actual target
Belgium	-0.3	**1.2**	0.1	-0.3
Germany	-0.7		**1.3**	-1.0
Spain	**-0.3**		-0.4	0.1
France	-0.8		**2.1**	-1.2
Ireland	**0.2**		-1.2	1.6
Italy	-0.8	**1.6**	0.2	-1.0
Luxembourg	**1.1**		n.a.	1.3
Netherlands	-0.5		**0.7**	-1.1
Austria	-0.8		**3.4**	-1.4
Portugal	0.8		**3.5**	-0.8
Finland	**2.5**		1.9	2.3

Source: Based on Heeringa (1999).

met by the simultaneous decrease in interest expenditures stemming from declining debt ratios. In this way there is no need for further cuts in other expenditures or increases in government revenues to cope with the costs of ageing, once the medium-term target has been reached. As in the case of high government debt, countries which expect a high increase in age-related expenditures (which actually can be considered a kind of 'hidden debt') need more ambitious deficit targets than the safety margins based on cyclical fluctuations and other sources of variability would imply.

Overall assessment

Table 10.3 summarizes the quantification of the three 'other' factors. The highest value (that is, the largest surplus or smallest deficit) in columns (1) to (3) of Table 10.3, indicated in bold, gives the desired target according to our approach. For all countries but Spain, the desired target is a surplus. The medium-term targets adopted by Ireland, Luxembourg and Spain are still sufficient to meet the higher standards. Belgium and Finland, which received a nod of approval from the Ecofin, fail to clear the new hurdles: Belgium should have done more to get its debt ratio down faster;[14] Finland needs an even larger surplus to cope with its high budgetary variability. The other six were not completely up the mark anyhow, and this conclusion is strengthened by the quantification of the different factors. In particular, the need to cater for the costs of ageing calls for substantial surpluses in most of these countries. In Italy, as in Belgium, it is the high debt ratio that requires a stronger effort. Of course, the analysis is subject to important qualifications. As regards the consequences of ageing, Member States still have time to take measures that might reduce the budgetary burden. The reduction of debt ratios in some countries can be speeded up by the privatization of state companies. However, the bottom line is that most Member States have submitted stability programmes that only fulfil a very minimalistic interpretation of the Stability and Growth Pact. This means in all likelihood that further budgetary consolidation will be necessary after the completion of the current programmes.

5. CONCLUSION

The rules laid down in the Treaty and the Stability and Growth Pact contain all the elements needed to keep budgetary positions under control whilst at the same time leaving enough flexibility to let fiscal policy play its role as shock absorber and stabilization instrument. However, most Member States have yet to reach a budgetary position that indeed allows this flexibility. Most of them entered EMU with government deficits only just below the 3 per cent ceiling. Even more important, the first round of stability programmes shows a lack of ambition to move towards budgetary positions that really can be called 'close to balance or in surplus'. If Member States, in conformity with the spirit and letter of the Stability and Growth Pact, aim to achieve safety margins for cyclical and other budgetary fluctuations while bringing down high debt ratios quickly and catering for the budgetary costs associated with population ageing, far more ambitious medium-term fiscal targets are necessary.

NOTES

1. A comprehensive treatment of the institutional setting can be found in Amtenbrink, De Haan and Sleijpen (1997) and ECB (1999f).
2. A flavour of this discussion is given in Szász (1999).
3. Tax policy (Title V of the Treaty) is considered an internal market issue and falls outside the scope of this book.
4. The Economic and Financial Committee is the successor to the Monetary Committee as from 1 January 1999.
5. Houben (1997) covers part of the issues in this section. For a game-theoretic framework of monetary and fiscal interactions within EMU, see Bolt (1999).

6. ECB (1999f) gives a description and assessment of the first year's experience from the point of view of the ECB.
7. Strictly speaking, only the comparison with column (9), the cyclically adjusted deficit, is relevant for assessing the size of the safety margin. However, since both the position in the cycle in the medium run and the calculation of cyclically-adjusted deficits in general have a large margin of uncertainty, the assessment has also taken into account the actual deficit targets, which moreover are the targets the Member States have stated in their stability programmes.
8. The *Opinion on the Content and Format of Stability and Convergence Programmes* states that: 'The Commission's and the Council's role is considerably enhanced relative to the "old" convergence programmes.'
9. This section draws on Heeringa (1999).
10. The trend in the cyclically adjusted deficits is eliminated by using a Hodrick-Prescott filter, which is also used by the Commission in its calculation of the cyclical component.
11. The cyclical component is determined on the basis of Commission calculations. The standard deviation of the combined factors is determined by the formula:
    $\sigma_{a+b} = \sqrt{(\sigma_a^2 + \sigma_b^2 + 2cov_{a,b})}$. The result is used to calculate a 95 per cent confidence interval.
12. It must be noted that Belgium's current budgetary strategy of keeping the primary surplus constant at 6 per cent of GDP leads to a continuing improvement in the actual deficit, and therefore to a more rapid decline in the debt ratio than our calculation suggests.
13. For an overview of the macroeconomic and financial implications of ageing populations, see Group of Ten (1998).
14. However, see note 8.

(ς,ηµ) F31
F33
F36

11. Exchange Rate Policy of the Euro Area

Cindy van Oorschot, Focco Vijselaar and Coen Voormeulen

From the perspective of the euro area, it is not self-evident that the exchange rate is a matter of concern. The euro area is a large, relatively closed economy, in contrast with the individual Member States. The replacement of 11 national currencies by the euro means lower turnover and less excitement in foreign exchange markets. But one goal of EMU was intended to be the elimination of exchange rate risk within the euro area.

Although the exchange rate matters less than it did in the past, it still deserves attention. First, because it is an important indicator of inflation prospects (through its impact on import prices) and therefore for the monetary policy strategy of the ESCB. Second, exchange rates could become seriously misaligned, thereby distorting economic activity and hampering the efficient allocation of financial resources. Although these effects will be limited due to the low degree of openness of the euro area, they cannot be ignored. Third, exchange rates could show excessive volatility, thereby impairing the efficiency and stability of the financial system.

'The' exchange rate does not exist, as there are many exchange rates that will differ in their significance to the euro area economy. For analytical purposes, we distinguish three geographical levels of exchange rate policy in this chapter: the global level (euro against dollar and yen), the regional level (euro against the currencies of geographically close non-EU countries) and the European Union level (euro against the currencies of EU countries outside EMU, the so-called *outs*).

This chapter starts by defining the constraints on the exchange rate policy of the ECB from a legal and economic point of view. Next, the three geographical levels of exchange rate policy will be discussed. At the global level, the relationships between the euro, dollar and yen are symmetric in the sense that neither currency is the anchor currency, while at the regional and

European Union level the euro will be the anchor. The central question at the global level, discussed in Section 2, is which exchange rate policy would be best for the ECB against the yen and the dollar in particular. At the regional level, the euro could serve as a nominal anchor for countries that wish to stabilize their economy or that wish to converge to the euro area economy in order to become EU or EMU participants. Section 3 examines which kind of exchange rate regime might be most desirable in this context. Section 4 takes a closer look at exchange rate policy within the EU. This so-called ERM-II, the successor to ERM-I, is investigated for its set-up, features and importance.

1. LEGAL AND ECONOMIC CONTEXT

Institutional framework

Article 3a of the Treaty on European Union[1] determines that the activities of the Community include the definition of a single exchange rate policy. The article also states that the primary objective of the exchange rate policy will be to maintain price stability. Article 3a thus sets the tone for any exchange rate policy of the euro area against non-EU countries: any policy that hampers the goal of price stability is not permitted.

Article 109 clarifies the distribution of responsibilities with regard to exchange rate policy of the euro between the Ecofin Council (Ministers of Finance and Economics) and the Governing Council of the ECB. From this Article, it is clear that the Ecofin Council has competence with regard to the formulation of exchange rate policy. According to Article 109(1), the Ecofin Council can decide with unanimity on formal arrangements between, for example, the euro, dollar and yen. In the absence of such an exchange rate system, the Ecofin Council can according to Article 109(2) formulate – with a qualified majority – general orientations of the exchange rate policy of the euro area. Both formal agreements and general orientations should be without prejudice to the objective of price stability. And in both cases the Ecofin Council should at least consult the ECB.

Article 109 should be read in conjunction with Article 105. From Article 105(2) it becomes clear that the ESCB is responsible for the day-to-day implementation of exchange rate policy. Foreign exchange interventions are thus an instrument for which the ESCB has exclusive competence.

The European Council of Luxembourg (December 1997) discussed the division of responsibilities as described in the Treaty. The European Council concluded that the Ecofin Council may formulate general orientations for exchange rate policy in exceptional circumstances only, such as in the case of a clear misalignment. These general orientations should always respect the independence of the ESCB and be consistent with its primary objective, that is, to maintain price stability. The European Council did not formulate any conclusions on formal agreements.

Economic framework

Central banks can choose either an internal or external orientation with regard to their monetary policy strategy. This choice is related to the choice between monetary policy autonomy and exchange rate stability. The integration of financial markets has made this choice more explicit. This can be shown by the incompatible monetary triangle in Figure 11.1 (Wellink and Knot, 1996)

Figure 11.1 The incompatible monetary triangle

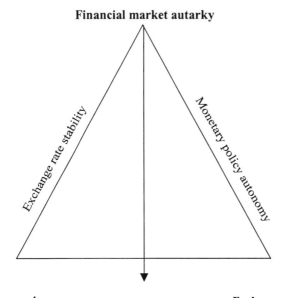

This triangle shows the inconsistency between the objectives (i) financial market integration, (ii) exchange rate stability and (iii) monetary policy autonomy. These objectives are presented along the sides of the triangle; each side represents the complete fulfilment of a particular objective. The larger the distance to a side of the triangle, the less important the corresponding objective is considered by the authorities. When a country positions itself at one of the corners, it chooses to achieve fully two objectives while completely giving up on the third. Countries which prefer a less extreme position locate themselves somewhere inside the triangle, which implies a less than complete fulfilment of all three objectives. Due to the liberalization of capital movements over the past two decades, all OECD countries have reached the base of the triangle. The downward arrow in Figure 11.1 indicates this trend.

Regarding the global level (euro against the dollar and yen), the ESCB is thus faced with only two extreme positions: exchange rate float and monetary union. Given the primary goal of price stability, the ESCB has only one choice left: a free float. A free float is the only way to avoid any external constraints on domestic policy autonomy in a world with liberalized capital movements. The ESCB will thus be situated in the right-hand corner of the triangle. Regarding the regional level (euro against the currencies of geographically close non-EU countries), non-EU countries that aim to converge with the euro area in order to become EU or EMU participants will opt for a fixed exchange rate against the euro. They will be situated in the left-hand corner of the triangle, where there is no monetary autonomy.

2. EXCHANGE RATE POLICY IN A TRIPOLAR WORLD

The industrialized world consists of three major economic blocs. The exchange rate developments between the three blocs therefore almost naturally attract a lot of interest in financial markets. Euro-dollar trading has, from the start, established itself as the most active and liquid segment in the foreign exchange market.

Apart from its inflationary consequences, the major concern with exchange rates is that they may become misaligned. As Figure 11.2 illustrates, this is not a wholly theoretical situation. Between 1987 and 1999, the exchange rate between the dollar and the Deutschmark (as proxy for the euro) did not show irregularities. It even stayed within a band of ±15 per cent around the average exchange rate, incidentally the same band that applied in ERM-I. As long as the US and Germany followed responsible macro-economic policies (low inflation, fiscal discipline), nothing really strange happened to the exchange rate. By contrast, the dollar became a greatly overvalued currency in the middle of the 1980s due to a policy mix of high fiscal deficits and high interest rates. Broadly speaking, two partly overlapping options exist (besides responsible macroeconomic policies) to counter misalignment: (i) target zones and (ii) foreign exchange market interventions.

Figure 11.2 The dollar-mark exchange rate

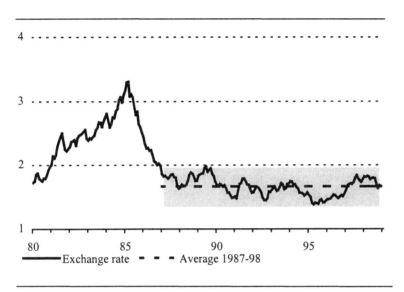

Target zones

Target zones can exist in several forms. Characterizing features of a target zone are the width of the band, the frequency of adjustments of the zones, the degree of commitment and the degree of public knowledge of the zone (Frenkel and Goldstein, 1986). On the basis of these characteristics, two extremes can be distinguished: a hard target zone and a soft one. A hard target zone is characterized by a formal arrangement explicitly directed at keeping the exchange rate within a narrow band, with intervention obligations at the upper and lower limit. The soft version relates to a more informal agreement where the exchange rate is allowed to vary in a wide and easily adjustable band, without any intervention obligations at the limit.

Advocates of target zones claim that where a system of flexible exchange rates fails to produce stability in exchange rate relationships, target zones may succeed. In a direct way via interventions, but also through consultations on macroeconomic policies whenever the exchange rate reaches the agreed limits. Target zones could thus contribute to the coordination and disciplining of domestic policies, like ERM-I did in Europe.

However, although the concept of target zones can be defined in theory, practice could be harder. In practice, hard target zones imply obligatory interventions in the foreign exchange market. For the euro area, this might pose a problem, as the Treaty determines that exchange rate policy should primarily be directed at the goal of price stability. As argued below, non-sterilized interventions almost automatically threaten this. As a result, the exchange rate cannot be but the outcome of monetary policy, instead of its objective.

Furthermore, exchange rate stabilization requires agreement on the level of equilibrium exchange rates between all competent authorities involved. Moreover, there should be a clear commitment to adapt economic policies in case the exchange rate moves too far away from this level. In the case of dollar/euro stabilization, for instance, this would require consensus between the ECB, the Federal Reserve Board, the Ecofin Council and the US Treasury Department. Financial markets are of course well aware of these difficulties. They might act on it by testing the limits of the agreed fluctuation band and speculate against the policy makers' commitment. Speculation will thus be encouraged, instead of diminished. Thus even soft target zones can trigger turbulence and second-guessing of financial markets and may be, in themselves, a source of instability.

Foreign exchange interventions

Where target zones are more or less standing arrangements, coordination of policies is, in general, more short-lived. It can take the form of one-off light measures or, in a more ambitious variant, be directed at a certain goal over a somewhat longer time-horizon. With respect to coordination, the 1985 Plaza agreement offers a good example from which to draw a few lessons from (Box 11.1).

Coordination usually means joint interventions and interventions by speech. Non-sterilized interventions provide an effective instrument (though probably not very efficient compared to the direct use of the interest rate) to change exchange rates. However, in practical terms, this will be no option for the ECB. Non-sterilized interventions imply interest rate changes, but the interest rate instrument is already reserved for achieving the primary goal of price stability. And as Tinbergen (1956) explained, two goals cannot be reached simultaneously by using only one instrument.

By contrast, sterilized interventions are not very effective according to a host of empirical papers (Frankel and Dominguez, 1993; Catte et al., 1994; Weber, 1994). It can be readily understood why. In order to influence the exchange rate, a central bank has to alter the balance of demand and supply for foreign exchange. However, compared to the huge turnover in the foreign

Box 11.1 The Plaza agreement and its lessons

At the Plaza agreement on 22 September 1985, the Group of Five (US, Japan, UK, Germany and France) met in New York due to concern over the overvalued dollar. The communiqué stated that, at that time, 'some further orderly appreciation of the main non-dollar currencies is desirable' and that the G5 'stand ready to cooperate more closely to encourage this, when doing so would be helpful'.

Two important issues in disagreement between the G5 were the desired degree of depreciation of the dollar and the contribution of each country to the necessary interventions. A dollar depreciation in the range of 10–12 per cent which was mentioned in a 'non-paper' prepared by the G5 Deputies, could not be agreed upon by Germany and the UK. None the less, the Plaza agreement was successful in bringing down the dollar. The contribution of each country to the interventions, however, became a source of contention afterwards. In the view of the US, Japan had done its share, but Germany had not. Germany defended itself by stating that it could not intervene heavily as the Deutschmark had reached the upper limit in the ERM.

From the literature on the Plaza agreement, it becomes clear that the agreement did not come overnight. Some lessons can be drawn from the overall process (Funabashi, 1988). First of all, for coordination of policies to be successful, all parties should be of the opinion that coordination will yield better results than doing nothing. The European countries lacked enthusiasm for the Plaza agreement, as they thought that the overvalued dollar was a problem of the US and Japan. Furthermore, though the G5 members discussed the inconsistencies in each other's policies, they were not prepared to let external objectives overrule their domestic goals (like Germany with the ERM). It is unlikely that this view has changed. Second, it appeared that the intervention strategy figured out at Plaza was successful due to its unexpected character. This calls for restraint on the use of interventions in managing exchange rate relationships. Third, the Plaza agreement showed that reaching an agreement on a target or a range for the 'right' exchange rate is very difficult. Finally, even if the parties involved manage to decide on the exact size of under- or overvaluation, the division of the costs (the amount of interventions made by each party) can become a serious source of disagreement.

exchange markets, in 1998 as high as $1500 billion per day (gross figure), the amount of money central banks can use is rather limited.

However, noise trading may allow the central bank to have some leverage in the foreign exchange market. If a transaction is observed to take place, it provides information to other market makers. This fact alone may cause them to modify their own bids and offers. The identity of the person making the transaction may also convey information. So depending on the way in which a transaction is carried out, the information revealed will be different. The effect of sterilized intervention on the exchange rate may be transitory by itself, but noise trading activities induced by the transitory effect of intervention may help amplify and prolong the effect of intervention.

To be successful, however, the central bank should not only have very up-to-date market intelligence and be familiar with noise traders' reaction functions under alternative scenarios, but it should also be capable of taking very timely action (that is, catching market sentiment or catching speculators off balance). The central bank may also use speeches and press conferences to express its views on relevant fundamentals, thereby hoping to change traders' attitudes – which may be self-fulfilling – and thus support the interventions.

Rare interventions will be more effective than regular interventions because interventions that are anticipated will not affect the exchange rate. Moreover, a central bank which lacks autonomy in the field of exchange rate policy is more likely to be forced by the ministry of finance to engage in highly visible foreign exchange intervention, since politicians will want to show that they are really concerned with the competitiveness of domestic exporters (Almekinders, 1995). Independence of the central bank will reduce political pressures and therefore reduce the intervention bias (the amount of interventions that will be expected by the markets). Almekinders (1995) proposes that the more independent the central bank, the smaller and the more consistent the intervention efforts.

In sum, foreign exchange interventions can be an effective instrument whenever the exchange rate 'walks away' from fundamental equilibrium. The effectiveness of interventions will be enhanced through highly visible interventions (that is, reported interventions and/or support from speeches). Moreover, as expected exchange rate interventions are less effective than unexpected ones (compare the discussion on the Plaza agreement), interventions should be used infrequently and with the appropriate timing. As a result, joint sterilized interventions have to remain exceptional and have to be arranged on an *ad hoc* basis.

No neglect but monitoring

The exchange rate policy of the euro area with respect to the dollar and the yen can be characterized neither by activism nor by neglect. In our opinion, it will be characterised by two words: monitoring and self-restraint. Monitoring in the sense of following the development of the exchange rate for its influence on the inflation rate in the euro area. Self-restraint in the sense that only in very special circumstances, such as a clear misalignment or excessive volatility, might certain forms of foreign exchange rate intervention occur.

3. REGIONAL ROLE FOR THE EURO

The euro is currently used in a number of exchange rate arrangements of non-EU countries. The arrangements vary from currency boards via fixed exchange rate pegs to crawling pegs within trading bands (Table 11.1).

Table 11.1 Current exchange rate regimes involving the euro

Country	Exchange rate regime	Peg against
Bosnia Herzegovina	currency board	euro
Bulgaria	currency board	euro
Estonia	currency board	euro
CFA-zone	fixed peg	euro
Cap Verde	fixed peg	euro
Cyprus	peg with band	euro
Iceland	peg with band	basket incl. euro (76%)
Malta	peg with band	basket incl. euro (67%)
Macedonia	*de facto* peg	euro
Croatia	*de facto* band	euro
Hungary	pre-announced crawling band	euro (70%) US dollar (30%)
Chile	crawling peg	basket incl. euro (24%)
Israel	crawling peg	basket incl. euro (29%)
Poland	crawling peg	basket incl. euro (40%)
Turkey	crawling peg	basket incl. euro

Note: Exchange rate pegs against SDR are disregarded.
Source: IMF.

An exchange rate commitment normally reflects close economic ties. At present, Chile is the only country pegging – in part – to the euro which is not geographically or historically close to the EU. It is conceivable that the rationale for pegging to the euro grows with its role as an international means of payment and reserve currency (see Chapter 7). From an institutional point of view, it is important to note that all current arrangements are unilateral, with the exception of those with the CFA zone (*Communauté Financière Africaine*) and Cap Verde.

Targeting of exchange rates may help achieve desired objectives in the areas of inflation, real activity or the balance of payments (Latter, 1996). Macroeconomic performance is improved mostly in the area of inflation, due to both lower money growth (discipline effect) and lower velocity (credibility effect) (Gosh *et al.*, 1997). There seems to exist a close association between price stabilization and the resumption of growth in transition countries (Hernández-Catá, 1997). A stable exchange rate *vis-à-vis* a strong currency may, therefore, stimulate growth by curbing inflation.

This section takes a closer look at the CFA zone and the Central and Eastern European countries (CEECs). The exchange rate arrangement between France and the CFA countries dates back to 1948. It presents an example of successful monetary stabilization on an inflation-prone continent. Its importance stems from its size: the CFA zone comprises about 20 per cent of African GDP (Lensink, 1996, p. 81). As regards the CEECs, it is a stated intention of many of these countries to become members of the EU and eventually EMU. Therefore, the central question posed here is which kind of exchange rate regime might be the most desirable to achieve EU membership.

CFA zone

The CFA zone has a long-standing currency arrangement with France, built on close historical ties. From 1948 to 1999, the West African monetary union (UEMOA), the Central African monetary union (CEMAC) and the Comores maintained a fixed exchange rate *vis-à-vis* the French franc.[2] Since the start of EMU the African francs are coupled to the euro. The currencies were devalued only once. In early 1994, the UEMOA and CEMAC francs were devalued by 50 per cent, the Comorian franc by 33 per cent. The agreements must be seen against the background of the substantial economic cooperation aid provided by France, although no formal linkage exists.

Both monetary unions plus the Comores have their own central bank (and currency). The French fiscal authorities guarantee the convertibility of the CFA francs. The central banks have an operation account with the French Treasury in which they hold 65 per cent of their foreign reserves. The member states have an open international capital market amongst themselves. In order to maintain the credibility of the peg, the central banks draw up credit programmes for all CFA member states. The central banks are required by their statutes to cover their sight liabilities for 20 per cent by foreign exchange. Fiscal policy is constrained by limiting the amount the government can borrow from the central bank.

The arrangement has helped the CFA countries to maintain a high degree of monetary stability compared to other developing countries (6.3 per cent inflation in the years since 1980 against 21.9 per cent for other African countries). However, this success came at the cost of a highly appreciated real exchange rate, which is seen as one of the main causes of the recession in the CFA zone in the late 1980s and early 1990s (Klau, 1998). The question whether the peg has been to the advantage or disadvantage of CFA countries remains open to debate. The CFA countries cannot react to a deterioration of their competitive position caused by external shocks. A major disadvantage in this respect is the fact that many of the CFA zone export goods are invoiced in US dollar. Moreover, their economic structure – and development level – is quite different from that of the euro area. In other words, it is evident that the CFA countries and the euro area collectively do not form an optimal currency area. The use of the euro has in that respect no economic rationale, but purely a historical one.

As regards the institutional setting, it is important to note that since 1 January 1999, the European Community has exclusive competence for monetary and exchange rate matters in EMU. The CFA zone arrangement therefore had to be revised. It was considered that the arrangement would not have any material effect on the conduct of the single monetary and exchange rate policy of the euro area. The Banque de France has no obligation to guarantee the convertibility of the CFA franc. The financial implications for France are small. The Council therefore decided that the present arrangements could continue.[3] Under public international law they are considered agreements between France and the African countries concerned. However, in the event of changes of the parity between the French franc and the CFA and Comorian francs, France must inform the Economic and Financial Committee in advance. All changes which go beyond technical changes and which constitute changes of the nature or scope of these agreements will have to be approved by the Council of Ministers, for example, changes with respect to the composition of member countries or the principle of free convertibility. The ECB should be consulted in such cases.

Central and Eastern European countries

Many Central and Eastern European countries wish to become members of the EU and eventually EMU. The CEECs may use their choice of exchange rate regime as a policy signal concerning convergence and integration. There are three ways in which an exchange rate regime may matter in this respect. First, to the extent that the regime chosen results in a stable (or predictable) exchange rate, it may stimulate international trade with and direct investments from EU countries. Economic ties will thus be intensified. Moreover, as international trade and direct foreign investments are important for economic growth, it may help welfare convergence. Second, pegging to the euro means that the benchmark for inflation will be the inflation rate of the euro area. This is a rather direct way to nominal convergence. Third, depending on the precise exchange rate regime chosen, an arrangement may help institutional convergence, for example, with regard to the choice of monetary policy instruments.

The options for an exchange rate regime vary from a free float (that is, no arrangement) to a fixed peg or even a currency board. The arrangement that constitutes the best alternative for a given country is first of all an issue of whether the economic structure of the economy resembles that of the euro area to a sufficient extent. Second, if that is the case, it is a trade-off between flexibility and credibility. The more flexible the chosen regime, the less discipline will emerge from it and vice versa. This is a matter of judgement more than of theory. The different exchange rate regimes are reviewed below.

A first alternative is to have no exchange rate regime, that is, to have a free float. The main advantage of a free float is that the country is able to cope with asymmetric shocks through exchange rate movements. Policy makers have maximum discretion. This might be an advantage in some circumstances. However, it might be a disadvantage as well. In order to qualify for EU membership – and certainly for EMU membership – countries must show sustainable economic convergence with EU countries respectively EMU countries. This implies that economic policy makers have to gear their policies towards those of the EU or the euro area – as the mountain will not come to Mohammed. Consequently, it might be advisable to tie one's hands to the extent possible in order not to be tempted to refrain from good policies when bad weather comes along.

Reducing flexibility (and gaining credibility) can be achieved by adopting a crawling or fixed peg. Under a crawling peg regime, the exchange rate is devalued regularly along a (predetermined) schedule by a (predetermined) percentage. This regime has the advantage that credibility can be gained through exchange rate predictability, while at the same time it is recognized that inflation differences will not disappear instantly after pegging to an anchor currency. A crawling peg, by its regular devaluations, prevents the currency from becoming unduly overvalued. The expected domestic inflation rate will be the sum of the regular devaluations and the inflation rate in the anchor economy. In this respect, the strength of the system is also its weakness: as long as regular devaluations take place, inflation rates will continue to be higher than the benchmark inflation. There will be no full nominal convergence. Eventually, a crawling peg has to be changed to a fixed peg in order to reach full nominal convergence.

A fixed peg regime, however, will almost certainly result in an overvaluation of the national currency if it is implemented at a time when inflation differences with the anchor country are still considerable. At present, a fixed peg would probably be too rigid for most candidate member states. Their inflation rate has indeed come down over the last few years (from on average 129.4 per cent in 1990 to 9.3 per cent in 1998), but still remains high compared to the euro area average (1.7 per cent in 1998). A fixed peg would not allow for any adjustment to this inflation differential. The currencies involved will soon be overvalued, with detrimental effects on real growth. Currency crises will almost certainly be provoked as the commitment of the monetary authorities to hold on to the peg will be tested.

A currency board could overcome this problem. A currency board is a monetary institute which stands ready to exchange unlimited amounts of a foreign currency for national currency and vice versa against a fixed exchange rate. The currency board has to have a sufficiently high amount of reserves. In practice this implies that it will have a 100 per cent backing of liabilities. A strict precondition for currency boards is that they do not lend in the national currency. Lending would be detrimental to credibility as it undermines the backing of the liabilities. The banking sector can finance itself in the international money markets, especially in the money market of the backing currency. Free capital convertibility will therefore be almost a prerequisite for a successful currency board. It may be clear that a currency board curbs the freedom of policy makers in such a way that they are forced to follow proper policies. Macroeconomic convergence will thus be achieved. However, institutional convergence will not be achieved. A currency board is no real central bank. If countries want to join ERM-II or ultimately EMU they have to gain experience with central banking because, for example, monetary policy in EMU is implemented on a decentralized basis. Also the domestic banking system should become acquainted with a situation without the 'roughness' of the currency board. Moreover, policy makers should learn to discipline themselves in an ever more tempting world.

As to the outlook for CEECs, it cannot be expected that the EU will be involved in any exchange rate regime with them as long as they are not EU member states. The case of Sweden is a precedent in this respect as its request in 1992 for participation in ERM-I – thus before Sweden joined the EU – was denied. From an economic point of view, CEECs are at present not part of an optimal currency area with the EU, although some of them are getting close. The levels of inflation in most of the countries still require considerable depreciations to avoid serious overvaluation of their currencies. Membership of any exchange rate regime with fixed bands is, therefore, not a realistic option. The CEECs first have to reach such a level of inflation convergence that they can stabilize exchange rate developments in time, that is, before intervention margins of 15 per cent are reached. After joining the EU, the CEECs should not automatically join ERM-II. It would be best to wait until a fair part of inflation convergence is achieved, for example, by using a gradually declining crawling peg or other alternatives that allow for a sufficient degree of flexibility. Portugal may set an example in this respect. When Portugal successfully joined ERM-I in 1992, its inflation rate had already been on a downward trend for years.

4. THE NEW EXCHANGE RATE MECHANISM: ERM-II

The Exchange Rate Mechanism number 2 (ERM-II) is the natural successor to ERM-I. ERM-II was created against the background of a more general wish to coordinate economic policies in the EU. The single market had to be underpinned by a harmonious development of monetary, exchange rate and budgetary policies. Harmonious budgetary policies were translated into the Stability and Growth Pact (see Chapter 10). Harmonious monetary policies are automatically ensured, although only for EMU members. The goal of considering exchange rate policy as a matter of common concern is explicitly stated in Article 109m of the Treaty. 'Neglect' of the exchange rate is considered inappropriate.

Discussions about the establishment of ERM-II took place in 1995 and 1996 in both Brussels and Frankfurt. In the early stages of discussions, mainly the potential out countries (including later-ins Italy, Spain and Portugal) strove for an agreement on ERM-II. They were afraid of becoming confronted with a depreciating (own) currency, which would damage confidence and thereby push up domestic inflation and/or interest rate levels. A further consideration was that currency speculation could cause ins and outs to drift apart. Once an out, it would be increasingly difficult to get in afterwards. On the other side of the spectrum was Germany. Having the Deutschmark as the *de facto* anchor currency in Europe, Germany was the only country within Europe where policies were only slightly affected by exchange rate considerations. Consequently, the Germans, at least initially, did not feel much enthusiasm for an ERM-II arrangement.

France used to be the countervailing power in Europe, acting as the regular opponent of Germany whenever exchange rate issues came about. In doing so, France gradually changed its position. In ERM-I, France had to ensure that the interests of currencies under downward pressure (against the German mark) were protected. Now, France was in another ballpark. Being a definitive in country, it had to consider the new French currency, that is the euro, as its own currency. Consequently, during the discussions, France gradually floated from defending the interests of the outs to defending those of the ins. For the ins, the main interest in the new exchange rate mechanism was that ERM-II could prevent the outs from gaining an unfair competitive advantage through depreciation, thereby possibly damaging growth and trade prospects in the euro area. Eventually, ERM-II was agreed upon in June 1997. This section takes a closer look at ERM-II by discussing its institutional features and set-up as well as assessing its importance.

Legal set-up and principles

ERM-II is laid down in a resolution of the European Council concluded in Amsterdam in June 1997[4] and a central bank agreement, worked out by the then European Monetary Institute (EMI). It was agreed that membership of ERM-II would be voluntary, although out countries which have a satisfactory degree of economic convergence 'can be expected' to join the mechanism.

The main principles of the new mechanism were already spelt out in the report *Monetary and Exchange Rate Cooperation between Euro Area and Other EU Countries* written by the EMI for the European Council in Dublin.[5]. That report, in turn, built on the agreement reached in Florence by the European Council (June 1996) and the informal Ecofin meeting in Dublin in September 1996. The main principles are:

1. Exchange rate developments are of common interest (Article 109m).
2. Misalignments and excessive nominal volatility should be prevented.
3. Exchange rate policy cooperation cannot be a substitute for stability-oriented domestic policies.
4. For the ECB, price stability always comes first. This obviously constrains the use of the interest rate and/or interventions by the ECB.
5. Not all countries are the same: flexibility is required.
6. Outs are supposed to be pre-ins; not the other way around, implying that the euro would become the pillar of the system.

From these principles, the main characteristics (including the differences with ERM-I) were derived. The most noticeable features are discussed below.

Hubs and spokes and fluctuation margins

ERM-I was constructed as a symmetric arrangement because its parity grid meant that every currency held a central rate against every other currency: every country was equal. By contrast, ERM-II is constructed as an asymmetric arrangement. The euro is the pillar of the system (the hub) while the other currencies are only spokes. In ERM-II, it is made clear that Europe has changed: the out currency must 'converge' towards the euro, not the other way around.

Like under ERM-I, the width of the normal fluctuation band has been set at ±15 per cent around the central rates. A narrower band was not considered wise, as the crises within ERM-I in 1992 and 1993 had showed that market forces could hardly be countered by central banks, once speculation becomes severe. The narrower the bands, the larger the chance that speculation will arise – *ceteris paribus*. This decision therefore reflects the fact that, since the establishment of ERM-I, the liberalization and internationalization of capital flows substantially shifted the balance of power from central banks to market participants.

Nevertheless, countries can agree with the ECB to establish narrower bands within the mechanism. In this way, countries can demonstrate to the markets their determination to stay close to the euro, possibly in the future their own currency, once they are converged to a substantial degree with the euro area. Denmark, in particular, stressed the inclusion of these narrow bands. Denmark had a special position: its derogation status had nothing to do with its economic convergence process. In fact, Denmark would have been a certain in, had not the Danish people shown reluctance to enter the currency union in a referendum in 1992 (see Chapter 2). Denmark did not want to give up its stable external environment and finally entered ERM-II with a fluctuation band of ±2¼ per cent, the normal margins in ERM-I before the crises of 1992–93.

Decision making procedures

The UK's entry into ERM-I in October 1990 taught Europeans a lesson. The parity of the pound sterling was not only based on economic common sense, but also on political grounds. In fact, the UK chose its own central rate, announcing it publicly even before it had been agreed upon by the Ecofin Council. The parity did not last very long, as Chancellor of the Exchequer Lamont had to announce the withdrawal of sterling from ERM-I in 1992. The lesson for ERM-II was to ensure that decisions concerning the parity were taken care of in a common procedure. In the same vein, it was agreed that the appropriateness of central rates could be challenged by all participants, including the ECB. Realignments can, therefore, be more easily ensured than in ERM-I, where only the country itself normally started a realignment procedure.

If countries aim for a narrower fluctuation band, they can take the initiative. They have to agree upon a formal narrow band with the ministers of the ins and the ECB. The central bank governors of the ins are not involved. The ministers of other out countries can take part in the procedure, but are not entitled to vote. The latter feature is to ensure that other outs are not in a position to hamper the convergence process of other Member States in any way.

The resolution only mentions formal narrow bands (Article 2.4 of the resolution), not informal ones. Yet, the EMI report in the Annex of the Dublin conclusions (EMI, 1996) does mention informal bands and states that 'all other closer arrangements of a more informal nature would be agreed upon by the ECB and the central bank of the non-euro area Member State concerned'. Nowhere is it spelt out what a formal arrangement is and what an informal one would be. This is a typical grey area issue, where the competence of ministers and central banks is not very clear and has to be established in practice.

Intervention obligations

Intervention obligations must, on the one hand, find a balance between making clear to markets that the parities are strongly defended and, on the other hand, preventing the primary objective of the ESCB, that is, price stability, from being hampered. ERM-II achieves this balance in the following ways:

1. The bands are wide, making the possibility of interventions occuring relatively small. However, if the limits of the fluctuation bands are reached, interventions are obligatory and unlimited. They can be financed through a Very Short Term Financing Mechanism (VSTFM) with features comparable to ERM-I. In order to emphasize the fact that out currencies have to converge towards the euro, any possible costs attached to interventions must be borne by the outs, that is as long as the euro is the strong currency. The out central bank has to buy back its own currency from the ECB. If the currency collapsed under the pressure of the markets and the central rate were devalued, the out central bank would still have to reimburse the ECB.

2. It was explicitly stated in the Resolution of the European Council 'when currencies come under pressure, to combine appropriate policy responses, including interest rate measures with coordinated

intervention.' In other words: intervention has to be accompanied by interest rate action, which will make interventions much more effective.

3.   Intra-marginal interventions are possible. Unilateral interventions are subject to a prior approval procedure similar to the one established under ERM-I. Bilateral intra-marginal interventions are possible by mutual agreement. So if the ECB does not want to intervene, it does not have to.

4.   Probably the most important feature for the ECB is its right to suspend interventions when it considers that the continuation of interventions is not in accordance with its primary objective of price stability. This so-called 'safeguard clause' resembles a similar agreement between the Bundesbank and the German Federal government in ERM-I. It can be done if and when the primary objective – price stability – is endangered. Furthermore, the EMI Annex to the Dublin conclusions states that in considering suspension of interventions, the ECB will also take into consideration 'the credible functioning of the new exchange rate mechanism'. This was accepted by the ministers and became part of the presidency conclusions of Amsterdam (see Chapter 2). The main reason behind this is that the ECB should not defend a parity that is clearly misaligned. Such a defence could endanger its credibility.

Assessment

If a broader look is taken at ERM-II, it must be concluded that the euro area and the ECB have, in fact, few obligations towards the out currencies. ERM-II is a safety net, but an out country would be well-advised to rely upon it only with adequate care: the fall is long before the rescue comes in, the out country itself pays for the rescue operation, and the rescuer can stop the operation once it is concluded that the operation is too dangerous. It is better to consider ERM-II as a commitment by the out to voluntarily put constraints on its own domestic policies. Only when it stands firm and takes strong measures can it benefit from the help of the ECB. This seems logical, considering that the success of ERM-I was also its disciplining effect on domestic monetary and economic policies in countries whose currency came under downward pressure. Furthermore, it can be seen as a learning process: once in monetary union, countries lose the exchange rate instrument, so they inevitably have to adjust other policy instruments if their competitive position comes under pressure. Thinking about one's domestic policy mix in that way is useful, even before joining the euro area. Learning it the hard way in the euro area is not only a risky experiment for the country concerned, but could also possibly undermine the stability of the single currency itself. That is a risk the ins were apparently not prepared to take.

At the moment, ERM-II might be less important than the efforts put into it may seem to suggest. First, because only time can tell what the difference will be in practice between free floating and an exchange rate system where currencies are allowed to move to a considerable extent. Second, because it remains to be seen whether participation in the system will actually be a precondition for joining the currency union (see Chapter 3). From the discussions in Frankfurt and Brussels, it became clear that the UK and Sweden were quite keen on the removal of any such suggestion. If it turns out not to be a precondition, ERM-II may lose its incentive role to discipline domestic policies. Third, initially it was thought that a fair number of countries would participate in the system, but it turned out to be only two. Greece is in ERM-II in the envisaged way. Denmark is in ERM-II with a narrow band of ±2¼ per cent. The other outs, the UK and Sweden, decided not to join, whereas far more countries managed to take part in the currency union itself than was imagined beforehand. Looking into the future however, the importance of ERM-II might increase considerably when countries join the European Union and want to prepare themselves for EMU participation.

5. CONCLUDING REMARKS

The options with regard to the exchange rate policy of the euro against the dollar and the yen are restricted in a legal and economic sense. The overriding goal of the ECB of price stability, as set by the Treaty on European Union, limits the possibilities for foreign exchange interventions. Furthermore, as shown by the eternal triangle, the absence of capital restrictions and independence in monetary policy make a fixed exchange rate regime impossible – if it were preferred. In practice, the exchange rate policy of the euro will be characterized neither by activism nor by neglect. It should be characterized by two words: monitoring and self-restraint. Monitoring, as the ECB considers the exchange rate to be an important indicator of future inflation; self-restraint, as interventions can only be effective if executed on rare occasions.

Besides its relevance as an indicator for monetary policy of the ESCB, the euro could play an important role as nominal anchor for countries willing to achieve macroeconomic stabilization or convergence with the euro area. It is, however, important that countries which peg their currencies to the euro leave sufficient room for flexibility. The CFA zone has experienced a serious recession as the CFA francs became severely overvalued over the years – although the peg in itself has helped to stabilize inflation. As the inflation rates in the CEECs are still considerably higher than in the euro area, these countries should not strive for fixed exchange rate pegs. Nevertheless, some form of pegging – as opposed to a free float – might help to achieve nominal convergence. However, as for example the experience of Portugal shows, the convergence process will take a considerable period of time.

ERM-II is a safety net for those out countries that want to peg their currencies to the euro. However, the out country should rely upon it only with adequate care: normal margins around the central rates are wide (±15 per cent), the out itself pays for any rescue operation, and the ECB is ultimately not obliged to intervene. ERM-II should therefore be considered foremost as a means of expressing the commitment by the out to voluntarily put restrictions on its own domestic policies. It can therefore be seen as either a substitute for joining (Denmark) or as a part of the preparation process for EMU (Greece).

NOTES

1. All references are to Articles of the EC Treaty.
2. The UEMOA member states are: Benin, Burkina Faso, Côte d'Ivoire, Mali, Niger, Senegal and Togo. The CEMAC member states are: Cameroon, Central African Republic, Chad, the Republic of Congo, Equatorial Guinea and Gabon.
3. A similar agreement exists between Portugal and Cap Verde. The Cap Verde escudo is coupled to the euro. Its convertibility is ensured by a limited credit facility provided by the Portuguese government. The same conditions for provision of information to the EFC and approval by the Council apply as in the CFA zone arrangement.
4. Amsterdam European Council, 16 and 17 June 1997, *Presidency Conclusions.*
5. Dublin European Council, 13 and 14 December 1996, *Presidency Conclusions*, Annex 2 to Annex 1.

References

Abraham, K.G. and J.C. Haltiwanger (1995), 'Real wages and the business cycle', *Journal of Economic Literature*, **33**, 1215–1264.

Alberola E. and T. Tyrväinen (1998), 'Is there scope for inflation differentials in EMU?', Discussion Paper 15/98, Helsinki: Bank of Finland.

Alesina, A. (1989), 'Politics and business cycles in industrial democracies', *Economic Policy*, **85**, 55–98.

Alesina, A., E. Spolaore and R. Wacziarg (1997), 'Economic integration and political disintegration', NBER Working Paper 6163, Cambridge, MA: National Bureau of Economic Research.

Alesina, A. and R. Wacziarg (1999), 'Is Europe going too far?', NBER Working Paper 6883, Cambridge, MA: National Bureau of Economic Research.

Almekinders, G.J. (1995), *Foreign Exchange Interventions: Theory and Evidence,* Aldershot, UK and Brookfield, US: Edward Elgar.

Alogoskoufis, G., R. Portes and H. Rey (1997), 'The emergence of the euro as an international currency', CEPR Discussion Paper 1741, London: Centre for Economic Policy Research.

Alzola, J.L. (1997), 'EMU and the euro: Euro won't trigger drop of dollar', *Economic & Market Analysis* (16 May 1997), Salomon Brothers.

Amtenbrink, F., J. de Haan and O.C.H.M. Sleijpen (1997), 'Stability and Growth Pact: Placebo or panacea' (I) and (II), *European Business Law Review*, **8** (9 and 10), 202–210 and 233–238.

Arnold, I.J.M. (1994), 'The myth of a stable European money demand', *Open Economies Review*, **5**, 249–259.

Artis, M.J. (1999), 'Asymmetric shocks in Europe: measurement and significance', paper presented at the workshop 'Tools for Regional Stabilisation', The Hague.

Artis, M.J. and W. Zhang (1997), 'International business cycles and the ERM: Is there a European business cycle?', *International Journal of Finance and Economics*, **2**, 1–16.

Backus, D.K., P.J. Kehoe and F.E. Kydland (1994), 'Dynamics of the trade balance and the terms of trade: The J-curve?', *American Economic Review*, **84**, (1), 84–103.

Bakker, A.F.P. (1996), *The Liberalization of Capital Movements in Europe: The Monetary Committee and Financial Integration, 1958–1994*, Dordrecht, Boston and London: Kluwer Academic Publishers.

Bakker, A.F.P. (1998), *Met gelijke munt*, Amsterdam and Antwerpen: Uitgeverij Contact, 4th edition.

Bakker, A.F.P. and A.J. Kapteyn (1997), 'De internationale rol van de euro', *Congres, De juridische aspecten van de euro*, Amsterdam: Vrije Universiteit Amsterdam, 95–112.

Balassa, B. (1964), 'The Purchasing Power Parity doctrine: A reappraisal', *Journal of Political Economy*, **72**, 584–596.

Banque de France (1998), 'Opinion of the Monetary Policy Council of the Banque de France' (27 March 1998), Paris: Banque de France.

Bauer, P.W. (1990), 'A re-examination of the relationship between capacity utilization and inflation', *Federal Reserve Bank of Cleveland Economic Review*, **26**, 2–12.

Baxter, M. and M.J. Crucini (1993), 'Explaining saving–investment correlations', *American Economic Review*, **83**, 416–436.

Bayoumi, T. (1990), 'Saving–investment correlations: Immobile capital, government policy, or endogenous behaviour', *International Monetary Fund Staff Papers*, **37**, 360–387.

Bayoumi, T. and B. Eichengreen (1993), 'Shocking aspects of European monetary integration', in F. Torres and F. Giavazzi (eds), *Adjustment and Growth in the European Monetary Union*, Cambridge: Cambridge University Press, 193–229.

Bayoumi, T. and B. Eichengreen (1996), 'Operationalizing the theory of optimum currency areas', CEPR Discussion Paper 1484, London: Centre for Economic Policy Research.

Bayoumi, T. and E. Prasad (1997), 'Currency unions, economic fluctuations and adjustment: Some new empirical evidence', *International Monetary Fund Staff Papers*, **44** (1), 36–58.

Beck, N. (1994), 'An institutional analysis of the proposed European Central Bank with comparison to the US Federal Reserve System', in P.L. Siklos (ed.), *Varieties of Monetary Reforms: Lessons and Experiences on the Road to Monetary Union*, Dordrecht, Boston and London: Kluwer Academic Publishers, 193–218.

Begg, D., P. de Grauwe, F. Giavazzi, H. Uhlig and C. Wyplosz (1998), 'The ECB: Safe at any speed?', *Monitoring the European Central Bank*, **1**, London: Centre of Economic Policy Research.

Bergsten, C.F. (1975), *The Dilemmas of the Dollar*, New York, NY: New York University Press.

Bergsten, C.F. (1997), 'The dollar and the euro', *Foreign Affairs*, **76** (4), 83–95.

Berk, J.M. (1997), 'Trade flows as a channel for the transmission of business cycles', *Banca Nazionale del Lavoro Quarterly Review*, **50**, 187–212.

Berk, J.M. (1998a), 'Monetary transmission: what do we know and how can we use it?', *Banca Nazionale del Lavoro Quarterly Review*, **51**, 145–170.

Berk, J.M. (1998b), 'The information content of the yield curve for monetary policy: A survey', *De Economist*, **146**, 303–320.

Berk, J.M. and J.A. Bikker (1995), 'International interdependence of business cycles in the manufacturing industry: The use of leading indicators for forecasting and analysis', *Journal of Forecasting*, **14**, 1–23.

Berk, J.M. and K.H.W. Knot (1999), 'Comovements in long-term interest rates and the role of PPP-based exchange rate expectations', *DNB Staff Reports* 37, Amsterdam: De Nederlandsche Bank.

Berk, J.M. and P.A.G. van Bergeijk (1999), 'Is the yield curve a useful information variable for the Eurosystem?', MEB Series 1999-09, Amsterdam: De Nederlandsche Bank.

Berman, E., J. Bound and S. Machin (1998), 'Implications of skill-biased technological change: International evidence', *Quarterly Journal of Economics*, **113**, 1245–1279.

Bernanke, B. and I. Mihov (1997), 'What does the Bundesbank target?', *European Economic Review*, **41**, 1025–1053.

Berndsen, J.E., J. de Haan and G.H. Huisman (1998), 'Amsterdam (Ex)changes', *Financiële & Monetaire Studies*, **16** (4).

Berndsen, R.J. (1997), 'The EMU-debt criterion: An interpretation', *Banca Nazionale del Lavoro Quarterly Review*, **50**, 505–533.

Bhattacharya, R. and J. Binner (1998), 'The shocking nature of output fluctuations in some EU countries', *Applied Economics*, **30**, 1101–1125.

Bijsterbosch, M.G. (1998), 'Inflatiemaatstaven voor het monetaire beleid: Aanvullingen op de CPI', MEB series 1998-04, Amsterdam: De Nederlandsche Bank.

Bini Smaghi, L. (1998), 'The democratic accountability of the European Central Bank', *Banca Nazionale del Lavoro Quarterly Review*, **51**, 119–143.

BIS (1999), *Central Bank Survey of Foreign Exchange and Derivatives Market Activity 1998*, Basle: Bank for International Settlements.

Blanchard, O.J. and L.F. Katz (1997), 'What we know and do not know about the natural rate of unemployment', *Journal of Economic Perspectives*, **11**, 51–72.

Blanchard, O.J. and L.H. Summers (1987), 'Hysteresis in unemployment', *European Economic Review*, **31**, 288–295.

Blinder, A.S. (1996), 'The role of the dollar as an international currency', *Eastern Economic Journal*, **22** (2), 127–136.

Blommestein, H.J. (1998), 'The new financial landscape and its impact on corporate governance', in M. Balling, E. Hennesey and R. O'Brien (eds), *Corporate Governance, Financial Markets and Global Convergence*, Dordrecht, Boston and London: Kluwer Academic Publishers, 41–73.

Boeschoten, W.C., G.J. de Bondt and J.A. Bikker (1996), 'EUROMON: A macroeconomic model for the European Union', Research Report 462, Amsterdam: Econometric Research and Special Studies Department, De Nederlandsche Bank.

Bolt, W. (1999), 'Fiscal restraints, ECB credibility, and the Stability Pact: A game-theoretic perspective', Research Report 568, Amsterdam: Econometric Research and Special Studies Department, De Nederlandsche Bank.

Bolt, W. and P.J.A. van Els (1998), 'Output gaps and inflation in the EU', Research Report 550, Amsterdam: Econometric Research and Special Studies Department, De Nederlandsche Bank.

Bosworth, B.P. (1993), *Saving and Investment in a Global Economy*, Washington, DC: Brookings Institution.

Bovenberg, A.L., J.J.M. Kremers and P.R. Masson (1991), 'Economic and Monetary Union in Europe and constraints on national budgetary policies', *International Monetary Fund Staff Papers*, **38** (2), 374–398.

Brandolini, A. (1995), 'In search of a stylised fact: Do real wages exhibit a consistent pattern of cyclical variability?', *Journal of Economic Surveys*, **9**, 103–163.

Broer, D.P. and W.J. Jansen (1998), 'Dynamic portfolio adjustment and capital controls: A Euler equation approach', *Southern Economic Journal*, **64**, 902–921.

Browne, F., G.A. Fagan and J. Henry (1997), 'Money demand in the EU countries: A survey', *European Monetary Institute Staff Papers* 7.

Buiter, W.H. (1999), 'Alice in Euroland', *Journal of Common Market Studies*, forthcoming.

Buiter, W.H., G. Corsetti and N. Roubini (1993), 'Excessive deficits: Sense and nonsense in the Treaty of Maastricht', *Economic Policy*, **16**, 57–100.

Cabrero, A., J.L. Escrivá, E. Muñoz and J. Peñalosa (1998), 'The controllability of a monetary aggregate in EMU', Working Paper 9817, Madrid: Research Department, Banco de España.

Calmfors, L. (1998a), 'Unemployment, labour market reform and monetary union', IIES Seminar Paper 639, Stockholm: Institute for International Economic Studies, Stockholm University.

Calmfors, L. (1998b), 'Monetary union and precautionary labour market reform', Working Paper 174, Munich: Center for Economic Studies, University of Munich.

Canova, F. (1999), 'Does detrending matter for the determination of the reference cycle and the selection of turning points?', *Economic Journal*, **109**, 126–150.

Catte, P., G. Galli, and S. Rebecchini (1994), 'Concerted interventions and the dollar: An analysis of daily data', in P. Kenen, F. Papadia, and F. Saccomanni (eds), *The International Monetary System*, Cambridge: Cambridge University Press.

Cecchetti, S.G (1995), 'Inflation indicators and inflation policy', NBER Working Paper 5161, Cambridge, MA: National Bureau of Economic Research.

Cecchetti, S.G. (1997), 'Measuring short-run inflation for central bankers', *Federal Reserve Bank of St. Louis Review*, **79**, 143–155.

CEPR (1993), 'Making sense of subsidiarity: How much centralization for Europe?', *Monitoring European Integration*, **4**, London: Centre for Economic Policy Research.

CEPR (1995), 'Flexible integration: Towards a more effective and democratic Europe', *Monitoring European Integration*, **6**, London: Centre for Economic Policy Research.

Chamie, N., A. Deserres and R. Lalonde (1994), 'Optimum currency areas and shock asymmetry: A comparison of Europe and the United States', Working Paper 94/1, Ottawa: Bank of Canada.

Christodoulakis, N., S.P. Dimelis and T. Kollintzas (1995), 'Comparisons of business cycles in the EC: Idiosyncrasies and regularities', *Economica*, **62**, 1–27.

Clarida, R., J. Galí and M. Gertler (1998), 'Monetary policy rules in practice. Some international evidence', *European Economic Review*, **42**, 1033–1067.

Clostermann, J. (1996), 'Der Einfluss des Wechselkurses auf die deutsche Handelsbilanz', Discussion Paper 7/96, Frankfurt: Deutsche Bundesbank.

Cohen, B.J. (1971), *The Future of Sterling as an International Currency*, London: Macmillan Press.

Committee of Governors (1990), *Draft Statute of the European System of Central Banks and of the European Central Bank, Europe*, Brussels: Agence Internationale d'Information pour la Presse, Document No 1669/1670, 8 December 1990.

Conference Board Europe (1997), *Perspectives on a Global Economy: Understanding Differences in Economic Performance*, Report 1187-97-RR, Brussels: Conference Board Europe.

Corrado, C. and J. Mattey (1997), 'Capacity utilization', *Journal of Economic Perspectives*, **11**, 151–167.

Cuddington, J.T. (1982), 'The saving–investment approach to the current account', Technical Report 32, Ottawa: Bank of Canada.

De Bandt, O. (1998), 'EMU and the structure of the European banking system', paper presented at the SUERF CFS Conference *The Euro: Challenge and Opportunity for Financial Markets*, Frankfurt, 15–17 October 1998.

De Bondt, G.J., P.A.J. van Els and A.C.J. Stokman (1997), 'EUROMON: A macroeconometric multi-country model for the EU', *DNB Staff Reports* 17, Amsterdam: De Nederlandsche Bank.

De Grauwe, P. (1996a), 'Monetary union and convergence economics', *European Economic Review*, **40**, 1091–1101.

De Grauwe, P. (1996b), 'The economics of convergence: Towards monetary union in Europe', *Weltwirtschaftliches Archiv*, **132**, 1–27.

De Grauwe, P., H. Dewachter and D. Veestraeten (1998), 'Explaining recent European exchange rate stability', mimeo.

De Haan, J. (1997), 'The European Central Bank: Independence, accountability and strategy – A review', *Public Choice*, **93**, 395–426.

Delors Report (1989), Committee for the Study of Economic and Monetary Union, *Report on Economic and Monetary Union in the European Community*.

Den Butter, F.A.G. and F.J. Folmer (1997), 'Endogenizing technical progress in the Netherlands', Beleidsstudie Technologie/Economie, The Hague: Ministry of Economic Affairs.

De Nederlandsche Bank (1998), 'Advice of De Nederlandsche Bank on the start of Stage Three of Economic and Monetary Union', 25 March 1998, Amsterdam: De Nederlandsche Bank.

Deutsche Bundesbank (1998), 'Opinion of the Central Bank Council concerning convergence in the European Union in view of Stage Three of Economic and Monetary Union', 26 March 1998, Frankfurt: Deutsche Bundesbank.

Dickey, D.A. and S.G. Pantula (1987), 'Determining the order of differencing in autoregressive processes', *Journal of Business and Economic Statistics*, **4**, 455–461.

Duchêne, F. (1996), *Jean Monnet: The First Statesman of Interdependence*, New York, NY: Norton.

Duisenberg, W.F. (1999), 'Mr Duisenberg discusses the arrival of the euro', *BIS Review*, **5**, 1–7.

Dykes, S.E. and M.A. Whitehouse (1989), 'The establishment and evolution of the Federal Reserve Board: 1913–1923', *Federal Reserve Bulletin*, **75** (4), 227–243.

ECB (1999a), 'The stability-oriented monetary policy strategy of the Eurosystem', *European Central Bank Monthly Bulletin* (January), 39–50.

ECB (1999b), 'Euro area monetary aggregates and their role in the Eurosystem's monetary policy strategy', *European Central Bank Monthly Bulletin* (February), 29–40.

ECB (1999c), *Possible Effects of EMU on the EU Banking Systems in the Medium to Long Term*, Frankfurt: European Central Bank.

ECB (1999d), *European Central Bank Monthly Bulletin* (February and April).

ECB (1999e), *Annual Report 1998*, Frankfurt: European Central Bank.

ECB (1999f), 'The implementation of the Stability and Growth Pact', *European Central Bank Monthly Bulletin* (May), 45–72.

Economic Report of the President (1999), Washington, DC: United States Government Printing Office.

Economist, The (1998), 'Euro towers or fawlty towers?' *The Economist* (31 October 1998).

ECU Institute (ed.) (1995), *International Currency Competition and the Future Role of the Single European Currency*, The Hague: Kluwer Law International.

Edey, M. (1994), 'Costs and benefits of moving from low inflation to price stability', *OECD Economic Studies*, **23**, 109–130.

Eikelboom, A.J., S.W. Schrijner and G.F.T. Wolswijk (1998), *The International Role of the Euro: Competitor for the Dollar?*, Amsterdam: Economics Department, ING.Bank

Emery, M.E. and C.P. Chang (1997), 'Is there a stable relationship between capacity utilisation and inflation?', *Federal Reserve Bank of Dallas Economic Review* (first quarter), 14–20.

EMI (1996), *Monetary and Exchange Rate Cooperation between Euro and other EU Countries*, Frankfurt: European Monetary Institute.

EMI (1997a), *The Single Monetary Policy in Stage Three: General Documentation on ESCB Monetary Policy Instruments and Procedures*, Frankfurt: European Monetary Institute.

EMI (1997b), *The Single Monetary Policy in Stage Three – Elements of the Monetary Policy Strategy of the ESCB*, Frankfurt: European Monetary Institute.

EMI (1998), *Convergence Report* (March), Frankfurt: European Monetary Institute.

Engel, C.M. (1993), 'Real exchange rates and relative prices: An empirical investigation', *Journal of Monetary Economics*, **32**, 35–50.

European Commission (1995), 'Technical note: The Commission Services' method for the cyclical adjustment of government budget balances', *European Economy*, **60** (November).

European Commission (1996), 'Economic evaluation of the internal market', *European Economy – Reports and Studies*, 1996 (4).

European Commission (1997), 'Economic Policy in EMU', *Economic Papers* 124.

European Commission (1998), *Convergence Report* (March), Brussels: European Commission.

European Commission (1999a*), Economic Forecast 1999–2000*, Brussels: European Commission.

European Commission (1999b), 'The impact of the introduction of the euro on capital markets', Brussels: Directorate General II, European Commission.

Eurostat (1997), *Statistics in Focus: Economy and Finance,* 1997 (4), Luxembourg: Eurostat.

Eurostat and University of Florence (1996), *Improving the Quality of Price Indices: CPI and PPP*, International Seminar Proceedings Florence 1995, Luxembourg: Office for Official Publications of the European Communities.

Faruqee, H. (1995), 'Pricing to market and the real exchange rate', *International Monetary Fund Staff Papers*, **42** (4), 855–881.

Fase, M.M.G., and C.K. Folkertsma (1997), 'Measuring inflation: An attempt to operationalize Carl Menger's concept of inner value of money', *DNB Staff Reports* 8, Amsterdam: De Nederlandsche Bank.

Fase, M.M.G., and P.J.G. Vlaar (1998), 'International convergence of capital market interest rates', *De Economist*, **146** (2), 257–269.

Fase, M.M.G. and C.C.A. Winder (1998), 'Wealth and the demand for money in the European Union', *Empirical Economics*, **23**, 507–524.

Feldstein, M.S. (1997), 'The political economy of the European Economic and Monetary Union: Political sources of an economic liability', *Journal of Economic Perspectives*, **11**, 23–42.

Feldstein, M.S. and C.Y. Horioka (1980), 'Domestic saving and international capital flows', *Economic Journal*, **90**, 314–329.

Franco, D. and T. Munzi (1997), 'Ageing and fiscal policies in the European Union, *European Economy – Reports and Studies*, 1997 (4).

Frankel, J.A. and K. Dominquez (1993), *Does Foreign Exchange Intervention Work?*, Washington, DC: Institute for International Economics.

Frankel, J.A. and A. McArthur (1988), 'Political vs. currency premia in international interest differentials', *European Economic Review*, **32**, 1083–1121.

Frankel, J.A. and A.K. Rose (1997), 'Is EMU more justifiable ex post than ex ante?', *European Economic Review*, **41**, 753–760.

Frankel, J.A. and A.K. Rose (1998), 'The endogeneity of the optimum currency area criteria', *Economic Journal*, **108**, 1009–25.

Franz, W. and R.J. Gordon (1993), 'German and American wage and price dynamics: Differences and common themes', *European Economic Review*, **37**, 719–762.

Frenkel, J.A. and M. Goldstein (1986), 'A guide to target zones', *International Monetary Fund Staff Papers*, **33**, 633–673.

Friedman, M. (1961), 'The lag in the effect of monetary policy', *Journal of Political Economy*, **69**, 447–466.

Friedman, M. (1968), 'The role of monetary policy', *American Economic Review*, **58**, 1–17.

Friedman, M. and A.J. Schwartz (1963), *A Monetary History of the United States (1867–1960)*, Princeton, NJ: Princeton University Press.

Funabashi, Y. (1988), *Managing the Dollar: From the Plaza to the Louvre*, Washington, DC: Institute for International Economics.

Garner, A.C. (1994), 'Capacity utilization and U.S. inflation', *Federal Reserve Bank of Kansas City Economic Review* (fourth quarter), 5–21.

Garner, A.C. (1995), 'How useful are leading indicators of inflation?', *Federal Reserve Bank of Kansas City Economic Review* (second quarter), 5–18.

Gartner, C. and G.D. Wehinger (1998), 'Core inflation in selected European Union countries', Working Paper 33, Vienna: Oesterreichische Nationalbank.

Genberg, H. and A.K. Swoboda (1992), 'Saving, investment and the current account', *Scandinavian Journal of Economics*, **94**, 347–366.

Ghosh, A.R., A.M. Gulde, J.D. Ostry, and H.C. Wolf, (1997), 'Does the nominal exchange rate regime matter?', NBER Working Paper 5874, Cambridge, MA: National Bureau of Economic Research.

Giorno, C., P. Richardson, D. Roseveare and P. van den Noord (1995), 'Potential output, output gaps and structural budget balances', *OECD Economic Studies*, **24**, 167–209.

Golub, S.S. (1990), 'International capital mobility: Net versus gross stocks and flows', *Journal of International Money and Finance*, **9**, 424–439.

Gonzalo, J. (1994), 'Five alternative methods of estimating long-run equilibrium relationships', *Journal of Econometrics*, **60**, 203–233.

Gordon, R.J. (1975), 'Recent developments in the theory of inflation and unemployment', *Journal of Monetary Economics*, **2**, 185–219.

Gordon, R.J. (1997), 'The time-varying NAIRU and its implications for economic policy', *Journal of Economic Perspectives*, **11**, 11–32.

Gordon, R.J. (1998), 'Foundations of the Goldilocks economy: Supply shocks and the time-varying NAIRU', *Brookings Papers on Economic Activity*, 1998:2, 297–346.

Groeneveld, J.M. (1999), 'Forces behind the consolidation trend in the European banking industry', *Kredit und Kapital*, forthcoming.

Group of Ten (1998), *The Macroeconomic and Financial Implications of Ageing Populations*.

Heer, B. and L. Linnemann (1998), 'Procyclical labor productivity: Sources and implications', *Zeitschrift für Wirtschafts und Sozialwissenschaften*, **118**, 221–247.

Heeringa, W.L. (1999), 'Begrotingsbeleid in de EU: De moeizame weg naar evenwicht', MEB series 1999-19, Amsterdam: De Nederlandsche Bank.

Hernández-Catá, E. (1997), 'Liberalization and the behavior of output during the transition from plan to market', *International Monetary Fund Staff Papers*, **44**, 405–429.

Hess, G.D. and C.S. Morris (1996), 'The long-run costs of moderate inflation', *Federal Reserve Bank of Kansas City Economic Review*, **81**, 71–84.

Hess, G.D. and K. Shin (1998), 'Intra-national business cycles in the United States', *Journal of International Economics*, **44**, 289–313.

Higgins, M. (1997), 'Demography, national savings and international capital flows', *Federal Reserve Bank of New York Staff Report* 34.

Hodrick, R.J. and E.C. Prescott (1997), 'Postwar U.S. business cycles: An empirical investigation', *Journal of Money, Credit, and Banking*, **29** (1), 1–16.

Houben, A.C.F.J. (1997), 'Het stabiliteitspact en de begrotingsdiscipline in de EMU', *Economische Statistische Berichten* (5 March), 184–188.

Houben, A.C.F.J. (1999), *The Evolution of Monetary Policy Strategies in Europe*, forthcoming.

IMD (1997), *The World Competitiveness Yearbook*, Lausanne: International Institute for Management Development.

IMF (1983), *International Financial Statistics, Supplement on International Reserves*, No 6, Washington, DC: International Monetary Fund.

IMF (1999), *World Economic Outlook May 1999*, Washington, DC: International Monetary Fund

Issing, O. (1999), 'The Eurosystem: Transparent and accountable or Willem in Euroland', *Journal of Common Market Studies*, forthcoming.

Jacobs, J.P.A.M. (1997), *Econometric Business Cycle Research, with an Application to the Netherlands*, Capelle a/d IJssel: Labyrint Publication.

Jansen, W.J. (1996), 'Estimating saving–investment correlations: Evidence for OECD countries based on an error correction model', *Journal of International Money and Finance*, **15**, 749–781.

Johansen, S. (1991), 'Estimation and hypothesis testing of cointegration vectors in Gaussian Vector Autoregressive Models', *Econometrica*, **59**, 188–202.

Kapteyn, P.J.G., P. Verloren van Themaat and L.W. Gormley (eds) (1998*),* *Introduction to the Law of the European Communities*, London and The Hague: Kluwer Law International, 3rd edition.

Kenen, P.B. (1995), *Economic and Monetary Union in Europe: Moving beyond Maastricht*, Cambridge: Cambridge University Press.

Kettl, D.F. (1986), *Leadership at the Fed*, Boston, MA: Yale University Press, Kluwer International.

Kindleberger, C.P. (1985), 'The dollar yesterday, today and tomorrow', *Banca Nazionale del Lavoro Quarterly Review*, **38**, 295–308.

Klau, M. (1988), 'Exchange rate regimes and inflation and output in Sub-Saharan countries', BIS Working Paper 53, Basle: Bank for International Settlements.

Knight, M. and F. Scacciavillani (1998), 'Current accounts: What is their relevance for economic policy making?', IMF Working Paper WP/98/71, Washington, DC: International Monetary Fund.

Knot, K.H.W. (1996), *Fiscal Policy and Interest Rates in the European Union*, Cheltenham, UK and Brookfield, US: Edward Elgar.

Kotlikoff, L.J. (1998), *Generational Accounting around the World*, Chicago, IL: Chicago University Press.

Krugman, P.R. (1989), *Exchange Rate Instability*, Cambridge, MA: MIT Press.

Krugman, P.R. (1992), 'The international role of the dollar: theory and prospect', in P.R. Krugman (ed.), *Currencies and Crises*, Cambridge, MA: MIT Press; previously published in J.F.O. Bilson and R.C. Marston (eds) (1984), *Exchange Rate Theory and Practice*, Chicago, IL: University of Chicago Press.

Kydland, F.E. and E.C. Prescott (1977), 'Rules rather than discretion: The inconsistency of optimal plans', *Journal of Political Economy*, **85**, 473–492.

Laney, L.O. (1988), 'The reserve role of the dollar and the United States as net debtor'*, Federal Reserve Bank of Dallas Economic Review*, (September), 1–13.

Lannoo, K. 'What role for the ECB?' *Financial Regulator*, **2** (3), 35–40.

Latter, T. (1996), 'The choice of exchange rate regime', *Handbooks in Central Banking*, **2**, London: Bank of England.

Lensink, R. (1996), *Structural Adjustment in Sub-Saharan Africa*, London and New York: Longman.

Lucas, R.E. (1973), 'Some international evidence on output–inflation trade-offs', *American Economic Review,* **63**, 326–334.

Lucas, R.E. (1976), 'Econometric policy evaluation: A critique', reprinted in R.E. Lucas (1985), *Studies In Business Cycle Theory*, Cambridge, MA, MIT Press, 104–131.

Masson, P.R. and M. Knight (1986), 'International transmission of fiscal policies in major industrial countries', *International Monetary Fund Staff Papers*, **33**, 387–438.

Masson, P.R., J.J.M. Kremers and J. Horne (1994), 'Net foreign assets and international adjustment: the United States, Japan and Germany', *Journal of International Money and Finance*, **13**, 27–40.

Masson, P.R. and B.G. Turtelboom (1997), 'Characteristics of the euro, the demand for reserves, and policy coordination under EMU', in P.R. Masson, T.H. Krueger and B.G. Turtelboom (eds), *EMU and the International Monetary System*, Washington, DC: International Monetary Fund, 194–224.

McCauley, R.M. (1997), 'The euro and the dollar', BIS Working Paper 50, Basle: Bank for International Settlements.

McCauley, R.M. and W.R. White (1997), 'The euro and European financial markets', in P.R. Masson, T.H. Krueger and B.G. Turtelboom (eds), *EMU and the International Monetary System*, Washington, DC: International Monetary Fund, 324–388.

McElhattan, R. (1978), 'Estimating a stable-inflation rate of capacity utilization', *Federal Reserve Bank of San Fransisco Economic Review* 78, 20–30.

McElhattan, R. (1985), 'Inflation, supply shocks and the stable-inflation rate of capacity utilization', *Federal Reserve Bank of San Fransisco Economic Review*, **1**, 45–63.

Meade, E.E. (1988), 'Exchange rates, adjustment, and the J-curve', *Federal Reserve Bulletin*, **74** (10), 633–644

Millard, S., A. Scott and M. Sensier (1999), 'Business cycles and the labour market: Can theory fit the facts?', Working Paper 93, London: Bank of England.

Mishkin, F.S. and A.S. Posen (1997), 'Inflation targeting: Lessons from four countries', *Federal Reserve Bank of New York Economic Policy Review*, **3**, 9–110.

Mitchell, B.R. (1980), *European Historical Statistics, 1750–1975*, London: Macmillan Press.

Mundell, R.A. (1983), 'International monetary options', *Cato Journal*, **3** (1), 189–210.

Obstfeld, M. (1986), 'Capital mobility in the world economy: Theory and measurement', *Carnegie-Rochester Conference Series on Public Policy*, **24**, 55–103.

Obstfeld, M. (1994), 'International capital mobility in the 1990s', in P.B. Kenen (ed.), *Understanding Interdependence: The Macroeconomics of the Open Economy*, Princeton, NJ: Princeton University Press, 201–261.

Obstfeld, M. (1997), 'Europe's gamble', *Brookings Papers on Economic Activity*, 241–317.

Obstfeld, M. (1998), 'EMU: Ready or not?', *Essays in International Finance* 209, Princeton, NJ: Princeton University.

Obstfeld, M. and G. Peri (1998), 'Regional non-adjustment and fiscal policy', *Economic Policy*, **26**, 205–259.

OECD (1989), *Employment Outlook*, Paris: Organisation for Economic Cooperation and Development.

OECD (1994a), *The OECD Jobs Study: Facts, Analysis and Strategies*, Paris: Organisation for Economic Cooperation and Development.

OECD (1994b), *Employment Outlook*, Paris: Organisation for Economic Cooperation and Development.

OECD (1995), *Employment Outlook*, Paris: Organisation for Economic Cooperation and Development.

OECD (1997a), *Indicators of Tariff and Non-Tariff Barriers*, Paris: Organisation for Economic Cooperation and Development.

OECD (1997b), *Code of Liberalisation of Capital Movements*, Paris: Organisation for Economic Cooperation and Development.

OECD (1997c), *Implementing the Jobs Strategy: Member Countries' Experience*, Paris: Organisation for Economic Cooperation and Development.

OECD (1997d), *Labour Force Statistics*, Paris: Organisation for Economic Cooperation and Development.

OECD (1999a), *Economic Outlook 65*, Paris: Organisation for Economic Cooperation and Development.

OECD (1999b), *EMU: Facts, Challenges and Policies*, Paris: Organisation for Economic Cooperation and Development.

Oort, R.M. (1998), 'De internationale rol van de euro', *Financiële & Monetaire Studies*, **16** (2).

Oudshoorn, C. (1999), 'EMU, beleidsconcurrentie en marktwerking', in P.A.G. van Bergeijk and C.A. Ullersma (eds), *De betekenis van de EMU voor het nationale beleid*, Rotterdam: OCFEB, Erasmus University Rotterdam.

Papademos, L. and F. Modigliani (1990), 'The supply of money and the control of nominal income', in B.M. Friedman and F.H. Hahn (eds), *Handbook of Monetary Economics*, Amsterdam: North-Holland, 400–494.

Peersman, G. and F. Smets (1998), 'The Taylor rule: A useful monetary policy guide for the ECB?', paper presented at the conference 'Monetary policy of the ESCB: Strategic and implementation issues', Milan, July 1998.

Persaud, A.D. (1997), 'The international role of the euro', in *EMU: A User's Guide*, London: JP Morgan.

Poole, W. (1970), 'Optimal choice of monetary policy instruments in a simple stochastic macromodel', *Quarterly Journal of Economics*, **84**, 197–216.

Portes, R. and H. Rey (1998), 'The emergence of the euro as an international currency', *Economic Policy*, **26**, 305–342.

Prati, A. and G.J. Schinasi (1997), 'EMU and international capital markets: structural implications and risks', in P.R. Masson, T.H. Krueger and B.G. Turtelboom (eds), *EMU and the International Monetary System*, Washington, DC: International Monetary Fund, 263–319.

Prem, R. (1997), 'International currencies and endogenous enforcement: An empirical analysis', IMF Working Paper WP/97/29, Washington, DC: International Monetary Fund.

Quah, D.T. and S.P. Vahey (1995), 'Measuring core inflation', Working Paper 31, London: Bank of England.

Raymond, R. (1990), *Special Report on a Common Framework for the Monitoring of Monetary Policies*, report by the Group of Experts under the chairmanship of Mr Raymond, Committee of Governors of the Central Banks of the Member States of the European Economic Community, Basle.

Røed, K. (1997), 'Hysteresis in unemployment', *Journal of Economic Surveys*, **11**, 389–418.

Rotemberg, J.J. and M. Woodford (1991), 'Markups and the business cycle', in O.J. Blanchard and S. Fischer (eds), *NBER Macroeconomics Annual 1991*, Cambridge, MA: National Bureau of Economic Research, 63–129.

Samuelson, P. (1964), 'Theoretical notes on trade problems', *Review of Economics and Statistics*, **46**, 145–154.

Seater, J.J. (1993), 'Ricardian equivalence', *Journal of Economic Literature*, **31**, 142–190.

Sibert, A.C. and A. Sutherland (1997), 'Monetary regimes and labour market reform', CEPR Discussion Paper 1731, London: Centre for Economic Policy Research.

Sims, C.A. (1980), 'Macroeconomics and reality', *Econometrica*, **48**, 1–48.

Sinn, H.W. (1993), 'How much Europe? Subsidiarity, centralization and fiscal competition', CEPR Discussion Paper 835, London: Centre for Economic Policy Research.

Sleijpen, O.C.H.M. (1999), *Does European Monetary Union Require Fiscal Union? Some Evidence from the United States*, forthcoming.

Smits, R. (1997), *The European Central Bank: Institutional Aspects*, The Hague, London and Boston: Kluwer Academic Publishers.

Staiger, D., J.H. Stock and M.W. Watson (1996), 'How precise are estimates of the natural rate of unemployment?', NBER Working Paper 5477, Cambridge, MA: National Bureau of Economic Research.

Staiger, D., J.H. Stock, and M.W. Watson (1997) 'The NAIRU, unemployment and monetary policy', *Journal of Economic Perspectives*, **11**, 33–49.

Stiglitz, J.E. (1997), 'Reflections on the Natural Rate hypothesis', *Journal of Economic Perspectives*, **11**, 3–10.

Stokman, A.C.J. (1999), 'Wage moderation in the European Union: Some experiments with the multi-country model EUROMON', Research Report 588, Econometric Research and Special Studies Department, Amsterdam: De Nederlandsche Bank.

Szász, A. (1999), *The Road to European Monetary Union*, London: Macmillan Press.

Taylor, J. (1993), 'Discretion versus policy rules in practice', *Carnegie-Rochester Conference Series on Public Policy*, **39**, 195–214.

Taylor, J. (1998), 'The ECB and the Taylor rule', *International Economy* (September/October), 24–25.

Tesar, L.L. (1991), 'Saving, investment and international capital flows', *Journal of International Economics*, **31**, 55–78.

Tinbergen, J. (1956), *Economic Policy: Principles and Design*, Amsterdam: North-Holland.

Tyrväinen, T. (1998), 'What do we know about productivity gaps and convergence in EMU economies?', Discussion Paper 31/98, Helsinki: Bank of Finland.

Van Bergeijk, P.A.G. (1999), 'Systeembreuken: Staat de econoom nu echt met lege handen?', Research Memorandum 9901, Rotterdam: OCFEB, Erasmus University.

Van Bergeijk, P.A.G. and R.C.G. Haffner (1996), *Privatization, Deregulation and the Macroeconomy*, Cheltenham, UK and Brookfield, US: Edward Elgar.

Van Bergeijk P.A.G., R.C.G. Haffner and P.M. Waasdorp (1993), 'Measuring the speed of the invisible hand: The macroeconomic costs of price rigidity', *Kyklos*, **46**, 529–544.

Van Bergeijk, P.A.G., G.H.A. van Hagen, R.A. de Mooij and J. van Sinderen (1997), 'Endogenizing technological progress: The MESEMET model, *Economic Modelling*, **14**, 341–367.

Van Bergeijk, P.A.G. and N.W. Mensink (1997), 'Measuring globalization', *Journal of World Trade*, **31** (3), 159–168.

Van Bergeijk, P.A.G., J. van Sinderen and B.A. Vollaard (eds) (1999), *Structural Reform in Open Economies*, Cheltenham, UK and Northampton, MA, US: Edward Elgar.

Van den Berg, C.C.A. and C.P.M. van Oorschot (1999), 'De functie van Lender of Last Resort in de Derde Fase van de EMU', MEB Series 1999-08, Amsterdam: De Nederlandsche Bank.

Van den Dool, G. and G.A. Frankena (1997), *Het Europees Monetair Instituut: Voorloper van de Europese Centrale Bank*, Amsterdam: De Nederlandsche Bank.

Van Els, P.J.A. (1995), 'Real business cycle models and money: A survey of theories and stylized facts', *Weltwirtschaftliches Archiv*, **131**, 223–264.

Van Gelderen, J. (1913), 'Springvloed: beschouwingen over industrieele ontwikkeling en prijsbeweging', *De Nieuwe Tijd*, **18**, 245–277, 370–387, 445–464.

Vanthoor, W.F.V. (1999), *Chronological History of Economic and Monetary Union in Europe*, Cheltenham, UK and Northampton, MA, US: Edward Elgar.

Vijselaar, F.W. and R.M. Albers (1999), 'Cyclical convergence in Europe', MEB Series 1999-11, Amsterdam: De Nederlandsche Bank.

Vlaar, P.J.G. and H. Schuberth (1999), 'Monetary transmission and controllability of money in Europe: A structural vector error correction approach', *DNB Staff Reports* 36, Amsterdam: De Nederlandsche Bank.

Von Hagen, J. (1997), 'Monetary policy and institutions in EMU', *Swedish Economic Policy Review*, **4**, 51–116.

Von Hagen, J. (1999), 'A fiscal insurance for EMU', paper presented at the workshop 'Tools for Regional Stabilization', The Hague.

Von Hagen, J. and B. Eichengreen (1996), 'Fiscal restraints, federalism and European Monetary Union: Is the excessive deficit procedure counterproductive?', *American Economic Review*, **86**, 134–138.

Weber, A. (1994), 'Foreign exchange intervention and international policy coordination: Comparing the G3 and EMS experience', CEPR Discussion Paper 1038, London: Centre for Economic Policy Research.

Wellink, A.H.E.M. and K.H.W. Knot (1996), 'The role of exchange rates in monetary policy: The European Monetary System', in *Monetary Policy Strategies in Europe: A Symposium at the Deutsche Bundesbank*, Berlin: Vahlen, 77–107.

White, W.R. (1998), 'The coming transformation of continental European banking', BIS Working Paper 54, Basle: Bank for International Settlements.

Winder, C.C.A. (1997a), 'On the construction of European area-wide aggregates: A review of the issues and empirical evidence', *Bulletin of the Irving Fisher Committee on Central Bank Statistics*, **1**, 15–23.

Winder, C.C.A. (1997b), 'Structural time-series modelling of monetary aggregates: A case study for eleven European countries', *Journal of Forecasting*, **16**, 97–123.

Woodford, M. (1994), 'Nonstandard indicators for monetary policy: Can their usefulness be judged from forecasting regressions?', in N.G. Mankiw (ed.), *Monetary Policy, NBER Studies in Business Cycles* 29, Chicago, IL: University of Chicago Press, 95–115.

Wynne, M.A. (1999), 'The European System of Central Banks', *Federal Reserve Bank of Dallas Economic Review* (first quarter), 2–14.

Wyplosz, C. (1997), 'EMU: Why and how it might happen', *Journal of Economic Perspectives*, **11**, 3–21.

Zarnowitz, V. (1992), *Business Cycles: Theory, History, Indicators and Forecasting*, Chicago, IL: University of Chicago Press.

Zellner, A. and F.C. Palm (1974), 'Time series analysis and simultaneous equation econometric models', *Journal of Econometrics*, **2**, 17–54.

Index